Psychoanalysis in Social and Cultural Settings

Psychoanalysis in Social and Cultural Settings examines the theory and practice of psychoanalysis with patients who have experienced deeply traumatic experiences through wars, forced migrations, atrocities and other social and cultural dislocations.

The book is divided into three main sections covering terrorism, refugees and traumatisation, with another two focusing specifically on transcultural issues regarding establishing psychoanalysis in China and on research related to themes outlined in the book. Major key psychoanalytic themes run through the work, focusing on identity and the self, fundamentalism, resilience, dehumanisation, cultural differences and enactment.

Offering key theory and clinical guidance for working with highly traumatised patients, this book will be essential for all psychoanalysts and therapists working with victims of terrorism, war and other deeply traumatic life events.

Sverre Varvin is a training analyst at the Norwegian Psychoanalytic Society and professor emeritus at Oslo Metropolitan University. He has extensive experience in research and clinical work with severely traumatised people. He is a leading person in the development of psychoanalytic therapy in China as chair of the International Psychoanalytical Association (IPA) China Committee.

Relational Perspectives Book Series

Adrienne Harris, Steven Kuchuck & Eyal Rozmarin
Series Editors
Stephen Mitchell
Founding Editor
Lewis Aron
Editor Emeritus

The Relational Perspectives Book Series (RPBS) publishes books that grow out of or contribute to the relational tradition in contemporary psychoanalysis. The term *relational psychoanalysis* was first used by Greenberg and Mitchell[1] to bridge the traditions of interpersonal relations, as developed within interpersonal psychoanalysis and object relations, as developed within contemporary British theory. But, under the seminal work of the late Stephen A. Mitchell, the term *relational psychoanalysis* grew and began to accrue to itself many other influences and developments. Various tributaries – interpersonal psychoanalysis, object relations theory, self psychology, empirical infancy research, feminism, queer theory, sociocultural studies and elements of contemporary Freudian and Kleinian thought – flow into this tradition, which understands relational configurations between self and others, both real and fantasied, as the primary subject of psychoanalytic investigation.

We refer to the relational tradition rather than to a relational school to highlight that we are identifying a trend, a tendency within contemporary psychoanalysis, not a more formally organised or coherent school or system of beliefs. Our use of the term *relational* signifies a dimension of theory and practice that has become salient across the wide spectrum of contemporary psychoanalysis. Now under the editorial supervision of Adrienne Harris, Steven Kuchuck and Eyal Rozmarin, the Relational Perspectives Book Series originated in 1990 under the editorial eye of the late Stephen A. Mitchell. Mitchell was the most prolific and influential of the originators of the relational tradition. Committed to dialogue among psychoanalysts, he abhorred the authoritarianism that dictated adherence to a rigid set of beliefs or technical restrictions. He championed open discussion, comparative and integrative approaches, and promoted new voices across the generations. Mitchell was later joined by the late Lewis Aron, also a visionary and influential writer, teacher and leading thinker in relational psychoanalysis.

Included in the Relational Perspectives Book Series are authors and works that come from within the relational tradition, those that extend and develop that tradition, and works that critique relational approaches or compare and contrast them with alternative points of view. The series includes our most distinguished senior psychoanalysts, along with younger contributors who bring fresh vision. Our aim is to enable a deepening of relational thinking while reaching across disciplinary and social boundaries in order to foster an inclusive and international literature.

A full list of titles in this series is available at https://www.routledge.com/Relational-Perspectives-Book-Series/book-series/LEARPBS.

Note

1 Greenberg, J. & Mitchell, S. (1983). *Object relations in psychoanalytic theory*. Cambridge, MA: Harvard University Press.

Psychoanalysis in Social and Cultural Settings

Upheavals and Resilience

Sverre Varvin

Routledge
Taylor & Francis Group

LONDON AND NEW YORK

First published 2022
by Routledge
2 Park Square, Milton Park, Abingdon, Oxon OX14 4RN

and by Routledge
605 Third Avenue, New York, NY 10158

Routledge is an imprint of the Taylor & Francis Group, an informa business

British Library Cataloguing-in-Publication Data
A catalogue record for this book is available from the British Library

Library of Congress Cataloging-in-Publication Data
A catalog record has been requested for this book

ISBN: 978-1-032-07236-4 (hbk)
ISBN: 978-1-032-07235-7 (pbk)
ISBN: 978-1-003-20605-7 (ebk)

DOI: 10.4324/9781003206057

Typeset in Times New Roman
by MPS Limited, Dehradun

Contents

List of Illustrations

Figure

Tables

Contributors

Stephan Hau, PhD, licensed psychologist, licensed psychotherapist, psychoanalyst (SPAF/DPV, IPA), is a professor for clinical psychology at the Department of Psychology, Stockholm University. As a member of the scientific research staff of the Sigmund-Freud-Institut in Frankfurt/Main, Germany, he has carried out experimental dream research for over 15 years. Since 2005 he lives and works in Sweden. Besides the clinical work, his research interests cover processes and outcome of psychotherapies and supervisions, educational research, experimental research on the perception and processing of affects.

Vladimir Jović, MD, PhD, psychiatrist and psychoanalyst, training analyst of the Belgrade Psychoanalytical Society, lives in Belgrade, where he has a private psychiatric and psychoanalytic practice. For 11 years (2009-2020), he worked as a professor at the Faculty of Philosophy at the University of Priština (Kosovska Mitrovica). He was a founding member, manager and consultant at the Center for Rehabilitation of Torture Victims in IAN, Belgrade, where he was working in various programs for rehabilitation of torture victims as well as projects for the prevention of torture. His main scientific interest is in the field of psychological trauma, post-traumatic states and societal mechanisms of violence, dehumanisation and torture. Currently, he is a Member of the Board of Trustees of the UN Voluntary Fund for Victims of Torture.

Bent Rosenbaum, is an MD specialist in psychiatry and has a degree of DMSci (Doctor of Medical Science). He is an adjunct professor at the University of Copenhagen, Department of Psychology, and a senior researcher at the Clinic for Psychotherapy, Psychiatric Centre of Copenhagen, The Capital Region of Copenhagen.

He is also training as a supervising analyst in the Danish Psychoanalytic Society and has a part time psychoanalytic practice.

Previously, he has been president of the Danish Psychiatric Association, president of the Danish Psychoanalytic Society (2003–2011) and member of the council of the European Psychoanalytic Federation. He was also European co-chair of the IPA committee for New Groups and member of the IPA Board. His primary research areas have been psychodynamic psychotherapy for people with psychosis, traumatised people and people with suicide risk. His main theoretical interest is psychoanalysis, semiotics and qualitative research.

Sverre Varvin, MD. Dr. Phil, is a training analyst at the Norwegian Psychoanalytic Society and professor emeritus at Oslo Metropolitan University. He has worked clinically and has done research on traumatisation and treatment of traumatised patients, especially in the refugee field. He has done process and outcome research on psychoanalytic therapy, reis a training analyst atsearch on traumatic dreams and on psychoanalytic training. He has twice been president of the Norwegian Psychoanalytic Society and he has had several positions in IPA. He is presently chair of IPA China Committee.

Foreword

The chapters in this book span more than 30 years' worth of struggle with problems posed to me primarily by my patients and also of research on traumatisation and refugees' experiences in my work in the human rights field.

What happens when a person is exposed to cruelty in a social and political context that deem such acts as just and defendable? What do these people bring with them when they flee from their country of origin and how do they try to overcome not only the traumatisation and human rights violations they have experienced, but also the disastrous fact of having to leave their homes, manage dangerous escapes and then try to adapt to an often totally new and strange cultural and social context?

I was often shocked listening to the stories of ordinary men, women and children who had been exposed to cruelties and disruptive experiences just because they were who they were: ordinary people with work, family, relationships and networks. How come these ordinary people, with their particular cultural and religious backgrounds and their specific social situations, were attacked for political and ideological reasons?

Several difficult and complex themes and problems came up in my attempt to understand how and why these things happen. The sad fact is that it is ongoing. There are now around 80,000,000 displaced people in the world – the highest number since World War II – and there has been a radical increase in the succeeding years. Losing our homes, networks and cultural resources is unimaginable for most of us and the task of building a new home, establishing new networks, finding work, preserving one's cultural values while at the same time struggling with the effects of traumatisation and persecution is a huge task. I have learned to admire how the refugees I have met struggle to achieve this, often under dire circumstances.

In this process, I have learned that the problems of these multi-traumatised persons cannot be reduced to a PTSD diagnosis (which often is the case in psychiatry). I have learned that human rights violations imply severe attacks on their humanness leading to a devastating experience of dehumanisation with profound effects on the psyche. I have also learned that culture is integral to psychic life and forms how life's hardships are perceived and worked with. Culture is not something you are taught but something you live on all levels of psychic life.

This has shown me that psychoanalysis always works in a cultural and social context. Psychoanalysis has been an important companion in my work in these fields; in my clinical work with traumatised refugee patients, in my research, in my attempts to reflect on how the social and cultural contexts are integral parts of the psyche and the way people relate to themselves and others and in practical human rights work in different places such as The Balkans, Turkey, China and Norway. In human rights work, being able to think psychoanalytically on how groups with traumatised people function and think in tense situations of negotiation and attempts at reconciliation did help, even if my role as a third party often was exhausting.

The first part of the book approaches the question of cruelty against others. How do murderous attacks on others start and prevail? What are the dynamics at the societal and group levels that often make ordinary people participate in atrocities? Wars, persecutions, genocides and terror attacks are merciless. The victim is exposed and made helpless. One cannot argue with a gun, a bomb or a torturer. There is no dialogue. I felt the effects of being made totally helpless when this also happened near me and my family in Oslo back in July of 2011 (see Chapter 1). This most likely made my understanding of traumatisation somewhat better. The chapters in this part of the book attempt to understand the dynamics of violence against people and, to some degree, the perpetrator's mind. In the end, however, the feeling of horror in relation to these attacks on humanity still leaves me with a feeling of profound helplessness.

The second part of the book represents my attempts to understand and to help, through psychoanalytic psychotherapy, people who have been exposed to extreme traumatisation and who live in exile. The main background for the first chapter in this part spans more than ten years of clinical work, starting in the late 1980s with traumatised refugees. Meeting traumatised persons not only led to profound questioning of the basis of our knowledge in the psychoanalytic field but also on the existential basis of life in general. This work resulted in my dissertation for the Degree of Philosophy at the University of Oslo in 2002, revised for publishing one year later named "Mental Survival Strategies after Extreme Traumatisation" (Varvin, 2003a). It became clear to me that extreme traumatisation, like torture, is an attack on basic mental functions and tend to destroy the capacity to trust and to be in a relationship. Dori Laub formulated this as harming or destroying the inner relations to empathic others (Laub, 2005b; Laub & Lee, 2003; Laub & Podell, 1995). This main insight is foundational in attempting to understand the defective capacity of symbolisation and creating meaning from experience that we see in traumatised people. Symbolisation and creating meaning from experience starts in the infant-caregiver dyad. It is the basis for the ability to relate and to be part of a social and cultural community. To comprehend this process, we need insights from different fields: anthropology, sociology and semiotics, in addition to psychoanalysis. Obeyesekere has called the process whereby experience achieves meaning the "work of culture" (Obeyesekere, 1990), demonstrating how culture is in the mind. Conversely, when cultural bonds and social relations are disrupted, the meaning-giving function deteriorates and suffering becomes private and, in the worst case, devoid of meaning, which is the case for many traumatised persons.

I try to show how psychoanalytic treatment can help people regain the ability to relate to themselves and others, to not constantly be haunted by the ghosts of their past and to be able to regain the possibility to live with others and become able to mourn losses. This is often only a partial process, but certainly, from my experience and also shown in our re-search, it may give people a better quality of life (Opaas et al., 2020; Opaas & Varvin, 2015b).

Establishing the capacity for mourning is central in the understanding, treatment and healing of traumatised individuals. It is, however, often a painful process of reconciliation with loss of close ones, culture, social roots and future possibilities. This may be the central concern in any area of psychotherapy with traumatised patients.

My meetings with patients from many different cultures deepened my understanding of how cultural habits, ways of understanding and also ways of seeing possibilities are integral to the mind and how it appears in one's relation to others. How people express psychic suffering differ in important ways; something that is not foreign to psychoanalysis as a profoundly inter-cultural discipline. When a patient says, "all is well", we listen to the subtext; ask what is behind, what is "really" expressed. A Somali man told me that you never burden others with your suffering, hence you say "all is well". He illustrated this with an episode from the war when inspecting his soldiers during battle while bullets flew above their heads. Everybody said "all is well" and continued fighting.

On a more profound level, we see how culturally determined expressions of pain is hindered by consequences of traumatisation where "the body takes over" (Stora, 2007; van der Kolk, 1994). Bodily pain is one of the most frequent ways to express pain for traumatised people (Dahl et al., 2006). I am convinced that psychoanalytic therapy may be the best solution that severely traumatised people can have – and this may be my main aim with the chapters in this part of the book.

Research has been an integral part of my work. In Part 3, I want to show how integration of clinical work and research can inform and hopefully improve the clinician's work. This has been, at least, the case for me. I am certain that psychoanalysis needs diverse research approaches and that qualitative approaches may be the best approach in capturing the essence of what psychoanalysis is all about.

Dreams are central to psychoanalysis. Investigations regarding dreams of traumatised persons, called traumatic dreams, are relatively sparse. In our research (studying traumatised persons in a sleep laboratory), we found that severely traumatised people make ordinary dreamwork processes, wherein they try to restore relations and meaning during dreaming, but they often fail. In their dream narratives, we saw their struggle to restore inner relations to empathic others and re-establish the symbolising function of the mind. At this level, psychoanalytic therapy seems to be the appropriate approach in helping with the restoration of these basic functions of the mind.

With the "Essay Method" (Chapter 11), I try to show how a psycho-analytic-inspired approach to clinical material, where experiences are seen in context, may enrich our understanding of what characterises psychoanalytic therapy and also show in what way the clinicians may succeed or not in creating a psychoanalytic process.

My work in China has, in many ways, brought together my work on traumatisation and my attempts to understand the significance of culture in the mind and how social, historical circumstances mark minds and form relations between people, which is the theme of the fourth part of the book. Profound insights may be achieved from the literary field, very much because writers are able to see what we in other professional fields may overlook or turn a blind eye to due to our theoretical and professional biases and which may take a long time to realise during our research. As we know, poets use a language that may evoke emotions, while a scientific treatise, in contrast, may be devoid of connotations to bodily emotional states in its theoretical parts, even though the subject may be about emotions themselves.

I found such insights from Chinese writer Yu Hua (Chapter 12). Yu Hua describes how individual destinies are deeply interwoven in the grand historical process. China has a history of severe traumatisation on a mass scale caused by invasions, social upheavals (e.g., the cultural revolution), hunger and natural disasters. These experiences are part of most families throughout history and these affect their lives deeply. The growth of psychoanalytic therapy in China has been a welcome possibility for people not only to get help but also to reflect on how history determines destiny. Yu Hua's many books pose questions at the margins of what is politically allowable. This has been a great help to both the individual through psychoanalytic therapy and on a cultural and societal level. My work in China has also allowed me to understand Chinese culture to a somewhat deeper level and to increase my understanding of how social, historical and cultural factors are interwoven in the fabric of the mind and in close relations, especially in the ways parents and grand-parents transmit experiences of hardship to next generations through practices in upbringing and in social family relations. We see how culturally determined practices are highly influenced by how a trau-matising social situation has formed possibilities of bringing up children and maintain emotional ties.

It is my hope that this book may bring some insights on how psycho-analysis not only may work in diverse cultural and social fields but also how the cultural and the social factor dimension actually is integral to and in the minds of people – and most importantly, to show that psycho-analysis may be developed and be a helping profession regardless of cultural and social diversity.

Permissions

Chapter 2: Varvin, S. (2019). Originally published as "Psychoanalysis and the situation of refugees. A Human Rights perspective" in *Psychoanalysis, Law and Society* (2019). Montagna, P & Harris A, eds. London and New York. Routledge. pp. 9–26. It is reproduced here by kind permission of Routledge Publishing House.

Chapter 3: Varvin, S. (1995). Originally published as "Genocide and ethnic cleansing. Psychoanalytic and social-psychological viewpoints" in Scandinavian Psychoanalytic Review, 1995, 18:192–210. A revised version is published here with the kind permission of Taylor & Francis Ltd, http://www.tandfonline.com.

Chapter 4: Varvin, S. (2005). Originally published as "Humiliation and the victim identity in conditions of political and violent conflict" in Scandinavian Psychoanalytic Review, 2005, 28:40–49. A revised version is published here with the kind permission of Taylor & Francis Ltd, http://www.tandfonline.com.

Chapter 5: Varvin, S. (2017). Originally published as "Fundamentalist mindset" in Scandinavian Psychoanalytic Review, 2017, https://doi.org/10.1080/01062301.2017.1386010. A revised version is published here with the kind permission of Taylor & Francis Ltd, http://www.tandfonline.com

Chapter 6: Varvin, S. (2017). Originally published as "Our relations to refugees: between compassion and dehumanization" in *The American Journal of Psychoanalysis* 2017;Volume 77(4) pp. 359–377. It is reproduced here in a revised version with the kind permission of The American Journal of Psychoanalysis.

Chapter 7: Varvin, S. (2000). "The present past. Extreme traumatisation and psychotherapy". Originally published in German as "Die gegenwärtige Vergangenheit. Extreme Traumatisierung und Psychotherapie" in Psyche – Zeitschrift für Psychoanalyse 54 (09/10), 2000. It is reproduced here in an updated English version with the kind permission of Psyche– Zeitschrift für Psychoanalyse.

Chapter 8: Rosenbaum, B. & Varvin S. (2007). Originally published as "The influence of extreme traumatisation on body, mind and social relations" in *Int J Psychoanal.* 88:1527–1542. It is reproduced here by the kind permission Taylor & Francis Ltd, http://www.tandfonline.com *on behalf of Institute of Psychoanalysis.*

Chapter 9: Varvin, S. (2016). Originally published as "Psychoanalysis with the Traumatised Patient: Helping to survive extreme experiences and complicated loss" in *International Forum of Psychoanalysis* 2016; Volume 25.(2) s. 73–80. It is reproduced here with the kind permission of International Forum of Psychoanalysis.

Chapter 11: Varvin, S. (2019). Originally published as "THE ESSAY METHOD"

"A qualitative method for studying therapeutic dialogues" in *Scandinavian Psychoanalytic Review of psychoanalysis,* DOI: 10.1080/ 01062301.2019.1692622. It is reproduced here with the kind permission of Taylor & Francis Ltd, http://www.tandfonline.com

Chapter 13: Varvin, S (2014). Originally published as "West–East differences in habits and ways of thinking: the influence on understanding and teaching psychoanalytic therapy" by Sverre Varvin and Bent Rosenbaum in *Psychoanalysis in China* edited by David E. Scharff and Sverre Varvin, pp. 123–136 (2014, Karnac). It is reproduced here by kind permission of Phoenix Publishing House.

Part I

Social terror

Introduction

In regressive situations of upheaval and social crisis, situations can develop where a need to find a group or another nation who can serve as the cause of problems. In such processes, facts and ideologies mix, and animosity and hate towards others may develop. There are many examples, historic and actual, where this need to define a group to blame and hate has dominated and caused destructive consequences for the population. The recent situation in the United States is an example. A deep split in society has come to the surface during the Trump regime, a divide that has historical roots in societal atrocities done by one part of the population against another (e.g., genocide against original settlers, slavery and racism).

The historical background for the development of hate against groups is complex. It has, however, repeatedly been shown that societies, especially leaders, experience difficulties in addressing this issue or even deny these past atrocities, which is an important aspect (Bohleber, 2002, 2010).

Impediments in working through these past atrocities characterises societies where internal wars, genocides and attacks against other people and groups have happened throughout society. Some examples are the genocide of Jews, the genocide in Rwanda, Apartheid in South Africa and other countries, the wars and genocide in the Balkans, the atrocities during the cultural revolution in China and the recent genocide of Yezidis. There are too many examples, with each situation having its own special characteristics and historical background but also having striking similarities on several levels. A

DOI: 10.4324/9781003206057-101

common feature seems to be the need to find someone, whether a religious group, an ethnic group or a nation, to blame when internal problems arise. A "solution" is proposed, often by deviant leaders, that can activate the masses, which may be turned into a mob with enormous destructive potential. The masses then find something that binds them together; these are not bonds of love and care but of hatred.

A constant work on several levels is thus needed to preserve human decency and avoid human rights violations to counteract the inherently violent tendencies in individuals and groups.

The need to curb aggressive and destructive forces was also central in Einstein and Freud's dialogue on war. Einstein asked Freud whether it is: ".. possible to control man's mental evolution so as to make him proof against the psychoses of hate and destructiveness"? Freud's answer was simple. While affirming, "an instinct for hatred and destruction", he held that the best way to counteract war and violent aggression is supporting "emotional ties between (a group's) members" (Freud, 1933, p. 201).

In this section of the book, I have assembled articles that attempt to approach the problem of societal aggressiveness and destructiveness from different perspectives and in different situations. It is my experience that psychoanalytic reflection and human rights practices based on these reflections can be essential in understanding and relating to situations of destructiveness and atrocity. I am convinced that Freud's simple statement on supporting emotional ties between groups is accurate and salient – but also extremely difficult to achieve.

Chapter 1

Terror and mourning in Norway

The day after the July 22, 2011 terror attack on Norway's governmental buildings and on a labour youth's summer camp outside Oslo by Anders Behring Breivik that took 77 lives, Vamık Volkan wrote to me:

> Dear Sverre,
> I am very, very sorry about the tragedy in your country. It will be a huge task to help people to mourn. I am thinking of you.
> Your friend, Vamık

It was a national tragedy that affected almost everyone in Norway. In the chaos we felt then, Volkan's words warmed our hearts and gave a direction that was difficult to imagine at the time it happened.

The attack came very close to my world.

Ten minutes after the attack, my daughter called in desperation, saying she was safe. She had managed to get out of the building that was targeted by the bomb. What's more, she was in a terrible situation, being pregnant in her last trimester.

The following night, a call came from the national television station asking for a psychiatrist to come and help. As the severity of the catastrophe and the number of deaths slowly became clearer during the evening hours, it was too much for experienced news reporters to handle.

Yes, we know now – it is a huge task to help people mourn. Some losses are not possible to bear. Many who were at the summer camp on the Island of Utøya, where 69 young people were brutally killed and 110 wounded amidst total terror, still suffer and mourn. The

DOI: 10.4324/9781003206057-1

survivors of the bombing in the governmental section of Oslo can never feel the same safety when going to work again.

But they moved on, most of them. Life slowly went back into a daily rhythm for most, but something had changed forever. Grief takes a long time, and we know that for many, the wounds have not healed (Stensland et al., 2018). When death and loss happen brutally close, it is never forgotten.

We have learned about large-group identity from Vamık Volkan. This collective identity is a silent but important part of our personality. On July 22, Norway's large-group identity came shockingly to the surface. First, many almost instinctually thought – rather unpleasantly – that this must be a new Al Qaeda attack, and as a result, started chasing foreign-looking people in the streets. But it was a narcissistic blow upon discovering that the perpetrator of the attack was one of us, even one who claimed to be more Norwegian than most. Thus, we could not project our anger at an alien enemy. Self-blame and guilt came to the fore, as well as justified anger at the perpetrator.

After this blow to our self-esteem, the ceremonies and memorials brought us together on another level, not the level of ostracism and naming enemies, but more in the direction of self-scrutiny. The official and cultural elite took part in the ceremonies and helped the mourning process.

The trial was a shocking confrontation with another large-group identity thriving in right-wing milieus, especially on the Internet. The perpetrator, Breivik, who showed no remorse, was deemed sane and sentenced to life in prison. His thinking and ideology have, however, affected a large group of adherents and is still thriving.

Breivik attacked the social democrats in the government and the youth camp of the Norwegian Labour Party. The social democrats were targeted as the enemy because they had allowed an Islamic "invasion" in Europe and created what Breivik called Eurabia. To him, it was a religious war where traitors had to be executed. An interesting parallel to Breivik's personal history appeared in the aftermath. The reports that were made public regarding his childhood experiences revealed that he lived without a father present and with a mother who treated him as dangerous and evil and tried to control him in every way. Child-care institutions were involved in his upbringing, and the recommendation from the child psychiatric team was unanimous: Breivik must be removed from his mother. His father fought to get custody, but both he and the psychiatric team gave up after court fights (Borchrevink, 2012).

Breivik was then left with the evilness his mother projected on him. This led him to form an ideology where Islam became the evil force, and the social democrats failed to protect against it. They were traitors – as his father was – and deserved to be killed (Varvin, 2013a).

Breivik and those who think like him desire a society that is autocratic and segregated: enemies of this social order should either be deported or killed (Berwick, 2011). One could see this as one man's lunatic fantasies, but the right-wing groups flourishing in parts of Europe today demand it be taken seriously. Violence and persecution of so-called strangers are alarmingly high (Leirvik, 2012).

Volkan's theory on large-group identity is of help here. When threatened, large groups regress. Volkan has 20 characteristics of this regression, including, among others, group members who lose their individuality, and the group is divided into those who "obediently follow the leader" and the bad ones who oppose. The division between "us" and "them" becomes a high priority, and projective and introjective forces are utilised to purify the group. The chosen trauma solidifies identity, and magical thinking dominates (Volkan, 2004).

The "Breivik society", as this lone wolf terrorist described it in his manifesto, is a prescription for a large group to regress and subsequently become even more violent (Berwick, 2011). (Andrew Berwick was the pseudonym the terrorist Anders Behring Breivik used when publishing his manifesto on the Internet).

The terror attack on July 22nd was preparation for what was deemed necessary in order to purify Europe: it was a true "anti-Jihadist" action performed by a so-called "lone wolf" who was based in an Internet community. This community functioned, to a large degree, as a projection screen for the large group's regressive and primitive aspects, and it allows for instant contact with and support for the individual, who, even if alone and othered, may feel supported by the community and feel his identity enhanced by a large-group identity that focused on a common cause.

Understanding large-group phenomena may help counteract this regressive development of creating the division between us (the good) and them (the bad), and it is necessary to maintain some cohesion. Just after the bombing and killings, the belief that this was an act of foreign groups like Al Qaeda spontaneously appeared, and attacks in public against foreign-looking people happened. This instant regression to a paranoid state transitioned into confusion when it was known that the perpetrator was "one of us". In this situation, leadership is of paramount importance.

How the process was managed afterwards proved important. Rather than promote a narrative of revenge, leaders, with the prime minister as the central force, helped the population through mourning rituals and took care that self-scrutiny could take the upper hand, not projection.

There is still a way to go, even ten years after. The task of helping people to mourn is still going on, however, and will have to continue for years to come.

Chapter 2

Psychoanalysis and the situation of refugees

A human rights perspective[1]

Introduction

Millions of people experience Human Rights Violations (HRV) worldwide. Many groups live under conditions that make them vulnerable and being exposed to HRV under such conditions can have devastating consequences. This concerns, among others, those exposed to trafficking, violence in close relations (mostly women), abuse and neglect of children, victims to paramilitary groups and terrorist groups, victims of religious violent groups, state organised violence, victims of civil wars and so forth. Many are forced to flee.

Today, 79,500,000 people are displaced worldwide due to conflict and persecution (this includes refugees and internally displaced people or IDPs (Internally Displaced People)). Of these, more than 34 000 000 are refugees. There are also 10,000,000 stateless people who have been denied nationality and access to basic rights such as education, healthcare, employment and freedom of movement.

The magnitude of the problem is staggering. Approximately 34,000 people were displaced every day in 2015 and 2016 (UNHCR, 2016). One out of every 133 people in the world today is displaced. Over the past five years, 50 families in Syria were displaced daily and we have seen unimaginable suffering due to indiscriminate attacks on civilians. More than half of refugees and displaced persons are children. The suffering due to war and persecution is today enormous and we can expect serious consequences of massive traumatisation in the years ahead, especially for coming generations.

For refugees, flight has become increasingly dangerous and death tolls are rising (UNHCR, 2016). Women are raped and abducted for

DOI: 10.4324/9781003206057-2

prostitution, many are killed or die at sea, children are violated and forced into the sex industry or slavery (there is increasing evidence that human trafficking networks cooperate with organised crime syndicates (Europol, 2016)), and many are maltreated and/or tortured by police, border guards or organised crime syndicates during flight. One study from Serbia testifies to this sad situation: 220 refugees were examined, and it appeared that torture and degrading treatments were more frequent during flight than in their country of origin (Jovanović et al., 2015).

Conditions for refugees upon arrival are getting worse. Stranded in the refugee camps of Greece, Italy, Serbia, Bangladesh and on islands outside Australia, thousands must survive with little or no access to health care, poor sanitation, insufficient food and minimal human concern. In refugee camps near war zones, conditions have worsened since 2015 when UNHCR budgets were cut by more than half (Clayton, 2015). There are further several neglected crises that seldom reach headlines but where atrocities done are frequent and cruel. This concerns, among others, the situation in Kongo, Yemen and South-Sudan, where millions are displaced, and humanitarian aid is insufficient.

Many refugees or asylum seekers describe their conditions after arrival, even in more affluent countries, as the worst part of their refugee journey. On a daily basis, they face long waiting times, bureaucratic red tape, inactivity and the possibility of being forced to return to their homelands. It is described by many as mental torture. There are reports that the mental and physical health of refugees today are deteriorating (Hassan et al., 2016) not only due to traumatisation in their home countries but very much as result of the conditions during flight (violence, torture, rape, slavery and so forth) and due to the conditions offered to the refugees in centres at the border of Europe (Greece, Italy) and outside, for example in Libya.

It has repeatedly been shown that refugees as a group have endured many potentially traumatising experiences before and during flight, such as near-death experiences, seeing close ones be maltreated or killed, torture, rape and so forth. These experiences represent gross HRV. Most research finds higher levels of known post-traumatic conditions in refugee populations like PTSD, anxiety disorders, depressions, somatising disorders and psychotic disorders (see for example Alemi et al., 2013; Apitzsch et al., 1991; Drozdek et al., 2014; Kroll et al., 2011; Opaas & Varvin, 2015a, 2015b; Teodorescu et al.,

2012; Vaage et al., 2010; Vervliet et al., 2013). The complex traumatising experiences of refugees may disturb personality functions, relational functions, affect regulation and somatic regulation (Allen & Fonagy, 2015; Allen et al., 2006; Rosenbaum & Varvin, 2007a; Schore, 2003; Varvin & Rosenbaum, 2011a).

Those who develop mental health problems in exile often suffer from complex conditions with multi-layered aetiology while living in difficult social situations (poverty, poor housing, lack of support, stressful acculturation process), resulting in poor quality of life. Whole families may be affected and there are possibilities for trans-generational transmission of suffering, for example, related to insufficient early care, traumatisation of children and stressful family situations (Blanck-Cereijido & Grynberg Robinson, 2010; Daud et al., 2005; de Mendelssohn, 2008; Krell et al., 2011; Romer, 2012; Ruf-Leuschner et al., 2014; Silke & Möller, 2012; van Ee et al., 2012; Wiegand-Grefe & Möller, 2012).

In spite of the high degree of resilience, the consequences for refugees in the present situation are potentially very serious both for present and coming generations. It is important to place the situation not only in a psychiatric, psychological and medical perspective but see it as consequence of serious violations of basic human rights. What many refugees and displaced persons have experienced and are experiencing should not happen if human rights, as formulated in internationally accepted conventions, are respected. The psychological consequences are moreover marked by the fact that these basic rights have been violated. The mental situation of experiencing violations of basic human rights affect basic systems of attachment and basic trust, resulting in a narcissistic imbalance and give a blow to hope for future development. Understanding these ramifications of the violated patient in the consulting room of therapists and health workers is of paramount importance. Understanding only in terms of mental problems or diagnosis (for example PTSD), which of course may be important, may bring the special circumstances of the context of HRV in the background.

Human rights matter

Violations represent grave problems for public health and also shake the democratic foundations of society. It affects the healthcare system in that a growing part of healthcare seekers in many western countries have been exposed to HRV. More serious is the fact that healthcare workers themselves have participated and still are participating in HRV in, for example, prisons.

In this chapter I will discuss a human rights perspective on mental problems caused by HRV and how attacks on the fundamental right to be a human affect psychological functioning. I will first shortly present the international system of conventions that attempts to regulate and prohibit the violation of basic rights of citizens.

What are human rights

Every human being's uniqueness is a precondition for ethics and human rights. Human rights are situated on three pillars: ethics and moral principles, laws/conventions and declarations on human rights and basic philosophical principles on being human. Emphasising the uniqueness of every human being has important implications in that it distances from conceptions of human beings as a mass and from treating some groups as inferior in a moral and human sense. Thus, there is an ethical and moral imperative in human rights thinking and it implies certain philosophical conceptions of man. The conventions, laws and declarations concerning human rights are built on these principles. Fundamental values involved are: the right to life, the integrity of the body, personal freedom, safety, the right to have property, the right to have family and private life, freedom of thought, freedom of belief, freedom of speech, right to have work and right to health and welfare.

Human rights are thus moral principles or norms that describe certain standards of human behaviour and are regularly protected as natural and legal rights in national and international law. There are several definitions of human rights and all concern rights to which a person is entitled simply because she or he is a human being. One broad definition may be that human rights are inalienable rights and freedoms that aim to secure all human beings' inherent dignity and that which lay the ground for freedom and justice (Stang & Sveaas, 2016). They are applicable everywhere and at every time in the sense of being universal, and they are egalitarian in the sense of being the same for everyone. The basis for modern human rights is the universal declaration formulated after World War II (UN, 1948).

Several conventions followed that specifies these rights. These are, among others:

International Covenant on Civil and Political Rights (1976).

This convention concerns negative rights in that these rights are not dependent on resources. These rights shall apply no matter the resource or circumstance. They concern a state's duty, for example, to provide freedom of speech, freedom of movement, freedom of religion and not to torture. Adherence to these rights is supervised by the UN's committee on human rights.

International Covenant on Economic, Social and Cultural Rights (1976).

This convention concerns positive rights; rights that require resources and concerns, for example: right to work, pensions and a reasonable living standard. The convention recognises a possible lack of resources, but there is a demand to initiate measures to achieve these goals.

Convention Relating to the Status of Refugees (1951) with additional protocol (1967).

This convention defines who has a right to be granted residence as a refugee in another country. It specifies the duties of countries when receiving refugees. It does not, however, mention the right to seek and admit persons asylum. The Universal declaration from 1948, paragraph 14 says, however, that anybody has the right to seek asylum and accept asylum due to persecution.

There are several other conventions of concern for health workers such as the International Convention on the Elimination of All Forms of Racial Discrimination of 21 December 1965 (ICERD), Convention on the Elimination of All Forms of Discrimination against Women of 18 December 1979 and Convention on the Rights of the Child of 20 November 1989 (CRC) (for further reference see https://www.eda.admin.ch/eda/en/home/foreign-policy/international-law/un-human-rights-treaties.html).

Among these conventions, the context of The Convention against Torture and Other Cruel, Inhuman or Degrading Treatment or Punishment from 1984 is of importance (UN, 1984).

This convention concerns protection against torture, the right to remedy and to justice, the right to reparation, compensation and, in particular, the right to rehabilitation. I will return to the question of torture. (It should be mentioned that other conventions also treat torture as a special case, such as in The American Convention on Human Rights, The European Convention for the Prevention of Torture, The African Charter on Human and Peoples' Rights, The Convention for the Protection of Human Rights and Fundamental Freedoms).

These conventions/declarations and their underlying ethical principles function as guidelines for, among others, health workers in situations of conflict and when under pressure, like situations of dual loyalties (e.g., health workers working in prisons) (Baldwin-Ragaven et al., 2002).

Why is human rights important for health workers?

Human rights is a concern for health workers for the following reasons: (a) everyone including health workers and patients' basic rights and dignity are dependent on human rights, (b) health politics/programmes and all interventions based on these can support or break down with basic human rights, (c) violations of human rights may have serious health consequences, (d) endorsement of human rights promotes public health and (e) the importance of preventing health workers from participating in HRV.

The last item has been documented in recent history concerning doctors' involvement in Nazi genocide and euthanasia programs (Lifton, 2004) and is a major problem in other parts of the world. Even in western countries such as the United States, the American Psychological Association's involvement in torture is documented (Patel & Eikin, 2015). The torture and dehumanisation of people who were suspected to be connected with Al Qaeda and other terrorist groups were HRV sanctioned by state authorities. Health personnel failed to hinder or report torture, they gave medical information to torturers and even forged death certificates.

Dehumanisation

Needless to say, but nevertheless important to be reminded of, torture implies great health risk for the affected, their family and for the foundation of society. Torture is the most dehumanising treatment that is known. It happens in general in dehumanising contexts like persecution, ethnic cleansing and genocide. Today's refugees are especially exposed to these both in their country of origin and during flight.

Dehumanisation is a process that is simultaneously socio-political and psychological, in which fundamental human characteristics are disavowed in other people, such that others are perceived as less than human or non-human. Consequently, actions resulting from dehumanisation can threaten the basic rights of these "others" and endanger their lives and safety.

Dehumanisation on a societal scale often go hand-in-hand with xenophobia and lay ground for malicious violations of basic human rights. This was the case in the genocides during the Balkan wars in the nineties, during the genocide in Rwanda, during the genocide against Yazidis, to mention a few – and strong xenophobic political movements in the western world have in the last decade lead to increasingly malignant behaviour towards refugees, asylum seekers and ethnic minorities.

When xenophobia becomes part of a political or religious narrative and is used to foster intergroup conflict, unconscious processes, both at the individual and group levels, are set in motion. These unconscious motivational forces are organised at primitive mental levels (i.e., undifferentiated and not well structured) and involve fantasies that may be shared by many people in a group or community. Such fantasies are often related to common life themes such as sibling rivalry, the struggle between good and evil or separation-individuation (Bohleber, 2007, 2010), but they are magnified in the xenophobic context where libidinal aspects are separated or split from aggression. Relationships and social fields of mutuality are transformed into fields of projections where the other is cast in the role of projected, unwanted parts of the self or of the group-self. As the other is perceived as "not human", not like "us", then inhumane and violent behaviour may be justified (Varvin, 2017) as fight/flight response (Bion, 1952).

There is thus a complex societal process that led to atrocities (for example torture) where the ground is prepared for ignoring and more or less consciously violate of basic human rights as specified in human rights conventions. Dehumanising processes imply that some persons or groups lose their political status and gradually are deprived of their humanity. A man becomes only a man, that is not a person protected by a state/nation. This "naked" status implies a loss of those characteristics that makes it possible for others to treat this person as a fellow human being (Mitmensch) (Arendt, 2017). Studies on processes leading to genocides demonstrate this with horrifying clarity (Crowe, 2013; Varvin, 1995; Yazda, 2017).

Torture

Torture may be defined as any act by which severe pain or suffering, whether physical or mental, is intentionally inflicted on a person for such purposes as obtaining from him or a third person information or a confession, punishing him for an act he or a third person has committed or is suspected of having committed.

The four Geneva Conventions on the law of war establish firm rules. The common Article 3 states:

> . . . the following acts are and shall remain prohibited at any time and in any place whatsoever . . . violence to life and person, in particular murder of all kinds, mutilation, cruel treatment and torture; . . . outrages upon personal dignity, in particular humiliating and degrading (ICRC, 1949)

The prohibition of torture or other ill-treatment could hardly be formulated in more absolute terms. In the words of the official commentary on the text by the International Committee of the Red Cross (ICRC): "no possible loophole is left; there can be no excuse, no attenuating circumstances" (ICRC, 1949).

In spite of this absolute "no", torture is practised in more than half of the world's countries. There are probably innumerable survivors of torture living in the world today who are suffering; them and their families. We don't know how many have been killed from torture.

Torture happens in what Lifton calls, "'atrocity-producing situations' —These are situations: structured, psychologically and militarily, that ordinary people can readily engage in atrocities". And concerning doctors' participations he states: "Even without directly participating in the abuse, doctors may have become socialized to an environment of torture and, by virtue of their medical authority, helped sustain it. In studying various forms of medical abuse, I have found that the participation of doctors can confer an aura of legitimacy and can even create an illusion of therapy and healing" (Lifton, 2004).

Article 14 in The Convention against Torture and Other Cruel, Inhuman or Degrading Treatment or Punishment states that: "Each state party shall ensure in its legal system that the victims of an act of torture obtains redress and has an enforceable right to fair and adequate compensation including the means for as full rehabilitation as possible".

There are a number of definitions of rehabilitation and services which aims at rehabilitation. "The recently adopted General Comment number 3 to article 14 of the Convention Against Torture, argues that rehabilitation 'should be holistic and include medical and psychological care as well as legal and social services'". Furthermore, rehabilitation "refers to the restoration of function or the acquisition of new skills required as a result of the changed circumstances of a victim in the aftermath of torture or ill-treatment. It seeks to enable the maximum possible self-sufficiency and function for the individual concerned and may involve adjustments to the person's physical and social environment. Rehabilitation for victims should aim to restore, as far as possible, their independence, physical, mental, social and vocational ability; and full inclusion and participation in society" (UNCAT, General comment, nr 3, 2012) cited in Sveaass(2013).

This is a strong statement that implies that all who have been tortured should have the right to redress and rehabilitation wherever they are. It is demanded of any state who has signed the convention that the torture survivor should be provided with help and rehabilitation.

Psychological effects of HRV and torture: what role can psychoanalyst have?

Being exposed to gross HRV, especially torture, affects basic systems of security, exposes the self to humiliation and shaming and sets forth a cascade of anxiety-provoking fantasies. More seriously, it gives the person a feeling of being outside and not part of the human community. As Jean Amery wrote:

.. I am certain that with the very first blow that descends on him, he loses something that we will ... call "trust in the world". Trust in the world includes ... the certainty that by reason of ... social contracts the other person will ... respect my physical ... being. The boundaries of my body are also the boundaries of my self. My skin surface shields me against the external world. If I am to have trust, I must feel on it only what I want to feel. At the first blow, however, this trust in the world breaks down .. He is on me and thereby destroys me ... with the first blow... a part of our life ends and it can never again be revived. ... Whoever was tortured, stays tortured. Torture is ineradicably burned into him. (Amery, 1998)

A patient came cautiously into the consulting room. He looked under the sofa, behind pictures and whispered, "He (the dictator) killed all my family". He was shivering, could hardly breathe properly and looked around with wide-open eyes. I gave him tea. I asked about his daily and nightly life. Hesitatingly and with stammering, he said he could hardly sleep, did not eat much and actually had no own place to live and had to be taken care of by friends. He was terrified all the time. He did not feel safe anywhere. I asked about what food he was eating, which he could not remember. When I asked what kind of food his mother had made for him and he started to remember, he started to cry and could relax a bit.

This man felt totally lost. He felt almost no safe anchoring in his internal world and the external reality was totally unsafe. He did not have the experience of being a human being among others and felt totally alienated. His way of being in the world is seen in other persons who have survived gross HRV. It is a psychological situation reinforced by being in exile and, for many, by not having a proper legal status as citizen. The latter talks about flight and about the people who must live for years in bad refugee camps and wait for their asylum application to be evaluated.

A father, stranded in Nauru, outside Australia wrote the following letter to United Nations Secretary-General Ban-Ki-Moon and Peter Thomson, president of the United Nations Summit on Refugees, held in New York on September 19, 2016:

We simply trusted what they told us. Yet over three years later we are still trapped in Nauru, like rare animals living in an Australian-made zoo.

After being brought to Nauru we spent almost 24 months in detention, before we were finally found to be genuine refugees. Since then, I have not slept even one night without having recurring nightmares of those endless months living in a hot, mouldy tent. We became so alienated from our humanity, we were thoroughly transformed into a bunch of animals after years of living in the most appalling conditions possible (Herald, 2016).

What these stories and similar situations illustrate is the profound dehumanising effect of being placed outside common humanity. It is, as Hanna Arendt described after World War II, situations where the people, despite being deprived of basic rights, are not treated in a more human way but, on the contrary, lose characteristics that make others treat them as humans.

Miss A came to Norway as a refugee after having been arrested, spent time in prisons and concentrations camp due to participation in peaceful political movement in her home country. She had a daughter of ten years. She lived in isolation, had few friends but managed to work part-time. She suffered from post-traumatic problems such a bad sleep, nightmares, anxiety and bodily pains. She had attempted treatment several times, but they came to an abrupt end, mostly because she felt humiliated and not respected. She avoided close relationships, especially to men, as she feared being treated with no respect and – as she later said – that it would be revealed that there was something fundamentally wrong with her.

The last concern was a prominent fear when in therapy. She felt she had to defend herself against a therapist whom she imagined could be dangerous and against involving herself in the therapy as she feared during this process, it would irrefutably be proven that she had been damaged for life. As she said: "That I cannot ever be normal human being". The last statement, it was revealed, was what the "torture team" repeatedly had told her.

Her distrust and defensive attitude were present from the beginning of the therapy. She gradually became more depressed and expressed that hope for improvement was diminishing. During a period with suicidal ideation and intense distrust in the transference where the patient literally felt tortured by the therapist, it was revealed that there had been a medical doctor participating in the torture. She had been given medication to make her reveal secrets and the doctor had "supervised" how much torture she could stand. She realised then how much of her distrust had been determined by what she called "mixing up" present with past. This was a breakthrough in the therapy. A long working through followed wherein earlier determinants of her distrust, especially related to a difficult relation to her father, were also focused. It was also obvious that her relation to her father had been coloured by the experiences with the male torturers.

Conclusion

There is huge work providing conditions for refugees, and especially seriously traumatised refugees, that can provide proper re-humanising conditions. The whole refugee system has to be revised internationally. The situation in most countries is geared towards keeping refugees out. Disproportionately more money is used in Europe on surveillance and border control in order to keep refugees out rather than resources used in providing good, protective and preventive conditions. Governments have furthermore for decades given the task of "helping" refugees on their journey to crueller and more exploiting human smuggler organisations. The condition in refugee camps is appalling.

In this context, some psychoanalysts have done important work on a larger scale (Volkan, 1999), and many provide psychological help for refugees both during flight and upon arrival (Lebiger-Vogel et al., 2015; Leuzinger-Bohleber et al., 2016). Psychoanalytic therapy is also provided in many places and there are prominent psychoanalysts that have developed good strategies for the treatment of severely traumatised persons (among others Henry Krystal, Dori Laub and Sylvia Amati Sas (Krystal, 1978; Laub, 2005b; Sas, 1992a). Psychoanalytic therapy is not, however, offered to the extent that is necessary, especially as psychoanalytic psychotherapy is a very promising tool for what article 14 in the Convention on torture demands: redress and rehabilitation.

The last section has to do with the rehumanising character of the psychoanalytic approach. There is increasing evidence that psychoanalytic therapies are helpful for traumatised persons in comprehensive ways in that this approach may help address crucial areas in the clinical presentation of complex traumatisation (complex PTSD) that are not targeted by other currently empirically supported treatments. This has clearly to do with the re-humanising aspect of this approach; psychoanalytic therapy has a historical perspective, and it works with problems related to the self and self-esteem while enhancing the ability to resolve reactions to trauma through improved reflective functioning. Furthermore, it aims for the internalisation of more secure inner working models of relationships. A further focus is working on improving social functioning. Finally, and this is increasingly substantiated in several studies, psychodynamic psychotherapy for traumatised patients tends to result in continued improvement after treatment ends (Schottenbauer, Glass, Arnkoff, & Gray, 2008).

Psychoanalysis, psychoanalytic therapies and also psychoanalytically informed interventions, for example, in refugee camps, has a broad and basically humanistic character in the sense of re-humanising the individual, making him or her not only come in the process of connectedness with other people but also profoundly help re-establishing basic human bonds. Dori Laub showed that a grave consequence of extreme traumatisation is a breach in the bond to an empathic inner other (Laub, 1998, 2005b). This special object relation is the basis for the experience of being connected to others – and for being and feeling like a human. This meaning is embedded in international declarations that concern human rights. Basic rights concern being part of a human community, feel safety, have the right to family and home and to be protected. These basic rights are givens but not stable – they have to be fought for continuously in different arenas. Psychoanalysts also have in this fight their tasks and obligations.

Note

1 Published in: Psychoanalysis, Law and Society (2019). Montagna, p & Harris A, eds. London and New York. Routledge. pp. 9–26

Chapter 3

Genocide and ethnic cleansing

Psychoanalytic and social-psychological viewpoints[1]

Introduction

Is the genocide of the Nazis a unique case? An abominable ab-
normality in history that can be understood as pathology? A defect in
the otherwise normal development of civilisation in modern society?
Does this society have an "accidental" historical lack of ability to
govern or to repress the primitive nature of mankind, such nature
being an archaic layer that has always been there and which we will
always have to subdue, combat and try to rectify? Or is there a
connection between modern societal development and the tendency
which reached its cruel zenith in the Nazi genocide of the Jews and
other "inferior groups of people"? And is there maybe also a connection between the human and psychological aspect which marked
this (and other) genocidal situations and modern society? In other
words, does modern society constitute a human nature that is not
eternal and universal but which expresses itself in genocidal situations? Is it as Zygmunt Bauman claims in his book "Auschwitz and
Modern Society", that "The possibility of the Holocaust was rooted
in certain features of modern civilization: its implementation, on the
other hand, was connected with a specific and not at all universal
relationship between state and society" (Bauman, 1989, p. 82).

In this essay, I want to discuss this problem, which unfortunately
has attained new actuality at several places in the world in recent
times. What can we learn from the experiences relating to the genocide of the Nazis? What can psychoanalysis say about the complex
relation between "human nature" and society which is produced in
such situations?

DOI: 10.4324/9781003206057-3

As a psychoanalyst, one can meet the victims and see their suffering, but one also encounters the perpetrators through the victims because one constantly asks the question: how was it possible for a human being to do this? And further ask: How was it possible for a state to organise such barbarism? Also: how was it possible for so many to just observe it?

Bauman describes his relation to genocide at the start as a relation to a "picture on the wall", a tragic aberration in the course of history where evil got the upper hand, i.e., "a pathological case". His study, resulting from the fact (among others) that his wife, at last, wrote down her experiences from the Warsaw ghetto, ended up with a quite opposite conclusion: genocide was not a result of the breakdown of modern society and civilisation. The preconditions for the genocide were, quite on the contrary, found in modern society itself.

In many places in today's world, we see state-organised violence, extermination and genocide. On an individual, group and societal level, a very special and sinister regression takes place in such situations. We know this from tales of the perpetrators, but most often from the victims because they bear inside them the effects of the violence and because it is they who suffer and seek help. What characterises this regression?

A Khmer woman who survived the horror regime of Pol Pot narrates in a therapy session:

"We had to leave Phnom Penh. Pol Pot wanted us to work in the countryside. When he asked what I did, I had to say that I helped my mother in the kitchen, If I had said that I went to school I would have been killed. In the nights, it was dangerous because Pol Pot could come. Then Pol Pot said that we should swim across the river. I said that I couldn't swim, but he said that I should do it anyway". Pol Pot was everywhere, all the soldiers were like an extension of him, a part of him, and one had to adjust to it. One's human dignity and individuality was wiped out, and the perpetrators acted as if they were one person.

The following story from one of the perpetrators illustrates the side of the tormentor (from the film "Bosna" by Bernard-Henry Levy). This man poses in the film with a "kind of empty face, but not showing any regret" and talks about how he, at gunpoint, had ordered a woman to take her clothes off. He had then raped her. He then raped six others, killed two of them, and after that, he slit their throats, "and then we were three who shot ten in Anatovizi", he ends his macabre story (Bernard-Henri Levy, 1994).

In this article, I want to say something about what these societal situations are all about and how it is possible to relate to atrocities "when it is all history". The last has to be put in quotation marks because we know that these experiences will never be erased and because we know that these experiences remain in the single person, whether he is the victim, perpetrator or a bystander; they remain as collective attitudes, as memories or as hallucinatory re-experiences. The Khmer woman's near-total hydrophobia bears witness to the fright she experienced when she was just saved from her "swim". The victims dream about violence, fighting wars and battles while sleeping. Children develop phobias or become silent, and many become victims of the silent psychosomatic processes, which in the end might ruin or end their lives.

The genocide during Nazism is one example. As a result of meeting many war refugees from Bosnia-Herzegovina, I would also like to say something about this genocidal situation, which in the Western press has euphemistically been called "an ethnic conflict", a concept which in my opinion contributes to important matters being veiled.

The concept implies equality between the parties, which was not there in the beginning, and it veils the fact that the main purpose was to make an area ethnically clean. For that purpose, several means were used, ranging from expulsion (with the help of international society) to genocide. It is also important to distinguish between cleansing and extinction. Extinction, not cleansing of an area, was, as we know, the Nazis' explicit goal concerning the Jews.

Stating some problems

The growth of the nationalist socialist movement can be viewed both as a symptom of national trauma and as a new and severe trauma in its own right for the German people. The national socialist movement was elected to power as a response to poverty and mass unemployment in Germany during the 1930s, originating from their defeat in World War I and the humiliation of the German nation through the Peace of Versailles. The solution to the problems (national socialism) then became a new and even bigger trauma for the nation, which is more difficult to overcome.

In the 1960s, psychoanalysts Alexander and Margaret Mitcherlich analysed the difficulties of the German nation in assimilating and mourning the losses from the great trauma of World War II. This was the dynamic background, they claimed, for the relative inability after the war in Germany to speak about and deal with the Nazi period (Mitscherlich & Mitscherlich, 1967). The problem of how whole nations can cope with the fact of having participated in atrocities and mass murder has, regrettably, assumed new importance in former Yugoslavia. The many civil wars and totalitarian regimes of today with organised violence on a large scale also raise the question of how a nation can or should treat the problem of dealing with the political and psychological after-effects. The discussion on impunity in many Latin-American countries bears witness to the difficulties and conflicts in which participation in atrocities places the nation.

I will focus on a part of this problem, namely the connection between the atrocities' psychological and social reality and the conditions of society which the population has to face after war (physical or internal) has ended. I will reflect on some social-psychological problems that I believe are relevant. I will use the genocide committed by Nazi-Germany as an example. Each example, of course, is special, and the Nazi genocide is a "unique" example of state-institutionalised cruelty. However, to overlook the connection between the organisation of modern society and the possibility for such a thing to happen is, in the words of Zygmunt Bauman, very dangerous.

For psychoanalysis, it actualises the connection between destructivity and society, a theme which Freud treated in several of his works. The theory of psychoanalysis is, however, only one point of view. The analysis of the social and socio-economic levels demands corresponding methods and theories. The use of psychoanalytic theory does not only mean a transposition of experiences gained through work with single individuals onto a societal level. The psychoanalytic way of understanding implies a special way of reading and interpreting the ideological level and a recognition of the fact that the ideological level can no doubt become a very powerful historical force. It is one of the main points in this article in that this applies to the experience of Nazism and that it is necessary to investigate Nazi ideology's unconscious roots in order to get a better understanding of the sociodynamic forces behind organised violence. Bauman writes, concerning the social changes which are necessary for "the tendency to genocide" to emerge, that they (the social changes) "are united by the general effect of the pronounced supremacy of political over economic and social power, of the state over society" (Bauman, 1989, p. 112). This clearly points to the very important instrumental role the ideology has in the state and politics and shows the place psychoanalysis can have as a method of analysing the ideology's psychological and group psychological foundation.

"Die Historikerstreit" and its background

In 1986, a discussion arose in Germany that was to be named Die Historikerstreit ("the battle of historians"). It lasted for two to three years and many distinguished historians, philosophers and politicians participated. Høibraaten (1994) calls it a battle over the uniqueness of Auschwitz (the national socialists' annihilation of the Jews) in relation to the German identity today (Høibraaten, 1994). He also calls attention to some studies on the question of post-war German identity that were published before Die Historikerstreit and that formed a part of its background. (This applies, among others, to the works of Alexander and Margaret Mitcherlich).

Many important questions were discussed in this "battle", some of which are relevant to our issue. Two important positions were represented by Herman Lübbe on the one side and Alexander and Margaret Mitcherlich on the other. (Mitcherlich's position was partly carried on by others (Habermas). They did not participate in the debate themselves).

In 1967, the Mitcherlichs published their important book "Die Unfähigkeit zu trauern" (The inability to mourn). One of the main themes in this book, which also tries to explain the Germans' extraordinary ability after the war to "not look back", was what has been called the "repression thesis". The Germans had loved Hitler narcissistically, which meant offering him their lives and thinking of him as an extension of themselves which they then idealised. This relationship unleashed an enormous amount of energy, which on the one hand, brought Germany out of a situation of crisis and unemployment and, on the other hand, directed a revolt against the imagined enemies of the Third Reich, primarily the Jews.

The Germans had blindly given themselves to this man and his regime, and when he died, they felt as if they had lost a part of themselves. They could not mourn their victims because they were themselves narcissistically mutilated by the fall of the Third Reich.

The Germans participated in this omnipotent adventure as the master race, and this could only lead to extreme melancholia when it all fell apart. This situation was impossible to face afterwards and therefore had to be repressed. Thus, it was not because the Germans did not want to look their victims in the eyes that they could not mourn, but because they had to repress the melancholia of their own victimisation. In other words, the pain of their own victimisation was an important hindrance to the Germans in facing what they themselves had done.

This explanation has an important precondition which is the existence of an unconscious process at a societal level (i.e., there were unconscious forces and structures in a group that governed both the actions and passivity afterwards). Opposing this view is the position taken by the philosopher Herman Lübbe who said in a speech in the Reichstag building in 1983 that silence on the Holocaust after the war was not determined by some unconscious (dynamic) force but was a necessity out of a certain form of tactfulness. A tactfulness towards those who had participated (except the war criminals). "Life must go on" is an attitude that resembles the impunity argument in the debate in Latin America in recent years. This states that we should all forget about these events, and in many countries, this resulted in a general amnesty for torturers and other perpetrators of abuse (e.g., in Argentina). This means building up democracy through (among other means) a kind of tactful silence. Lübbe also argues that there was no possibility of forgetting because everyone knew. (Many Germans after the war were, among other things, forced to look at films from concentration camps).

The positions of the Mitcherlichs and Lübbe are in accordance with the fact that the work of mourning was not done in the years after the war and that there was no working through or integration. In spite of the danger of oversimplifying, I think Lübbe's position can be associated with what I would call a cognitive approach and reflects a kind of voluntaristic humanism: "if you consciously want to, it is possible to gloss over the deep problems of shame and guilt". (I am aware that it is not possible to reduce Lübbe's position to this statement. I am only making use of parts of his arguments to illustrate a position also seen in other countries with similar problems (e.g., Chile and Argentina)).

The position of the Michterlichs implies recognition of the enormous amount of work, both on an individual and a collective level, that has to be done to face and integrate what happened. Germany and the rest of the world have changed radically since (and because of) Auschwitz, and it is even possible to argue that the Gulags of the Stalin era in the 1930s were precursors of the camps of the Third Reich. Auschwitz has shown that it is possible to accomplish systematic murder on a mass scale, of which the Pol Pot regime of Kampuchea is yet another recent sad example. What, however, separates "Auschwitz" from other examples is that the goal was total destruction of the Jews. There was no possibility for exception as, at least theoretically, it was under the terror of Stalin; one could "change one's mind" and then no longer be in the group of "counter-revolutionaries".

The psychology of genocide

The question of what kind of phenomenon the Nazi genocide, in my opinion, will determine what kind of work has to be done afterwards, and consequently, how one should understand the "silence" in post-war Germany. Is there work to be done on the past or is it important to forget and to go on? Further, what kind of work is there to be done?

For the victims, the survivors and their families, there is no doubt. The past lives within those who survived, and they have to constantly struggle with the after-effects. The Holocaust experience is beyond understanding and even description, and it is close to what we would call "pure evil". It is a serious, difficult and, many would say, nearly impossible task to mourn the losses (Moses, 1993).

First, some characteristics of the Nazi genocide (Chasseguet-Smirgel, 1991; Hilberg, 1961):

1. It was directed not only against the Jews of Germany but against all Jews. The Arian race was to be saved through the extinction of the Jews (One should, of course, not forget the murders of gypsies, the mentally handicapped, homosexuals, etc.)

2. No genocide has ever had such an efficient organisation. Everything was organised like a factory, and very little was left for improvisation. And everything was used, even the bodies, after the killing. Never has a genocide been carried out with such good coordination between the political, military and some spiritual leaders. Science has never contributed so much and been "enriched" so much as by the Nazi genocide

3. The genocide had legal support, from the first anti-Jewish laws in 1933 via the Nuremberg laws in 1935 to "Die Endlösung" (the final solution) agreed upon at Wansee in 1942

4. No other genocide has been so influenced by ideological arguments and by such a type of ideology. (Tendencies to similar ideological elements have been seen in earlier Yugoslavia. An analysis of this level in that conflict remains, however, to be carried out)

5. A result of this was a dehumanising of the victims on a scale never seen before. The cruellest sadism was carried out. Extermination was a goal, in itself, superior to any other goal. Even the goals of the war were subordinated to the task of eliminating the Jews. It was more important to kill the Jews than to get them to work in the factories producing weapons. It was more important that trains with Jews were sent to the extermination camps than the trains with war material were to be sent to the front

I have mentioned the German defeat in World War I and mass unemployment as important preconditions for Hitler's victory in the election of 1932. It is, however, a complicated question of how the German people could be seduced into not seeing what was happening, at least as far as the majority were concerned. It is said that Germany was initially one of the countries in Central Europe where anti-Semitism was least expressed. This makes it important to analyse the problem from several points of view. It is claimed that the Jews in Germany were more progressive and successful in society and most assimilated among the Jews in Europe. In this situation, there seemed to be a struggle on the basis of the "narcissism of the small differences" (Diatkine, 1993; Freud, 1930 (1929)), and this might shed light on how there was at least a social-psychological disposition present for silently accepting that people disappeared. The German intelligentsia's constant cooperation with the regime in power is another frightening example of the fact that education is no guarantee against ideological lunacy. (Many German scientists put the goals of science highest and were satisfied as long as they and their colleagues (except, of course, those who disappeared) got good working conditions, which they, in fact, were given. We know that there were important exceptions, but also that it was extremely difficult to oppose the government).

One key to the understanding of this seems to be the character of the Nazi ideology and propaganda. It managed to glorify the majority of the German people. It was a propaganda system that expanded far beyond the borders of Germany and playing on anti-Semitism in countries like Estonia and Lithuania, which made the situation very dangerous for Jews in a large part of Europe even before the war. This was also a preparation for collaboration during the war by many countries in the endeavour to exterminate the Jews.

My point is that political and socio-economic conditions are not sufficient to explain the grip of the Nazi movement on such a large part of the population of Europe. It is a well-known fact that groups regress under stress and that finding a scapegoat is often seen as a solution in the group process. One member or a part of the group is seen as the cause of the group's or the organisation's problem, and the majority will have the illusion that the elimination of that member will solve the problem (Bion, 1961). This presupposes a special kind of thinking, which is characterised by a certain concreteness and inability to differentiate. In other words, a thinking strongly characterised by primary processes. The members of the group act together in accordance with a thinking that at least is partially unconscious. It is often more correct to say that it is this thinking or this logic that governs the group rather than the other way around. A certain kind of mindless logic governs the functioning of the group. In "Mass Psychology and the Ego", Freud describes how the members give up their superego control and delegate it to the leader (Freud, 1921). Thinking and control are abandoned, and one is guided by the "master" or the charismatic leader. This is a common tendency in groups and accordingly common to human beings. The study of the authoritarian personality (Adorno et al., 1982 (1950)) and the Milgram experiment show what consequences this can have on an individual level (Milgram, 1974). In the Milgram experiment, the participants were ordered by the scientific leader to inflict electric shocks on a person (not knowing that they were fake). This unethical experiment demonstrated that "ordinary" man is indeed able to act cruelly when internal moral control has been abolished and delegated to a leader.

Bauman states the following regarding the coercive means of extermination:

> "Their formidable effectiveness relied mostly on the subjection of their use to purely bureaucratic, technical considerations, which made their use all but totally immune to the countervailing pressures, such as they might have been submitted to if the means of violence were controlled by dispersed and uncoordinated agents and employed in a diffuse way" (Bauman, 1989, p. 98).
> The violence was a technique and as such deprived of feelings and apparently totally rational. It was, in other words, a situation where the inner moral judgment was suspended.

In "The destruction of the European Jews", the historian Hilberg describes how the Nazi machine of destruction functioned like an aggregate composed of parts. Things happened as if they were led by a common understanding, a kind of synchronising (Hilberg, 1961). According to the French psychoanalyst Janine Chasseguet-Smirgel, this is nothing less than a historian's description of unconscious group processes and is in accordance with the way of thinking described above (Chasseguet-Smirgel, 1991). Nobody thinks. The group (or the leader) "thinks" for the individual. In the Nazi movement, one could see how the moral function was suspended and the more primitive ego-ideal projected onto the "Führer". This narcissistic identification with the Führer was accompanied by the regressive group process described above, where concrete thinking dominates. One important characteristic of this is that the phenomenon which should be symbolised and the symbol itself were seen as one. In other words, there was a collapse in the symbolising function at the societal level. This collapse led to action instead of thinking and working with problems and conflicts on a mental level. What has been defined as the problem needs to be removed.

This is commonly observed in clinical practice, especially with more regressed patients. At a group level, and especially when a society functions in this way, it can have devastating consequences. The biological fundamentalism in Nazi ideology is well-known, with its ideas on purity of race and blood, the fusion between mother and earth, society as an organism that must be purified and "liberated" from all unwanted elements, etc. In Nazi ideology and theory, the gardening metaphor is often used. Society is looked upon as a garden where weed by necessity must be removed so that "good" plants shall flourish. It is self-evident that such an ideology in the regressed group situation described above could be extremely dangerous. It hardly seems sufficient, however, to explain the enormous destruction that was carried out by the Nazis.

Chasseguet-Smirgel described in her clinical research a psychic structure, which is possibly a kind of common stage in psychosexual development, called the "archaic matrix of the Oedipus complex". The characteristic of this complex is the desire to eliminate all hindrances on the way into and within the body of the mother (Chasseguet-Smirgel, 1990). In other words, it is a structure where the fantasy of returning into and fusing with the mother's body is central. Further, there is enormous hatred and aggression towards hindrances, both external ones represented by the father and the imagined ones inside the mother's body (i.e., other babies). When this structure with fantasies belonging to it dominates, a "shortcut" is chosen instead of trying to work with the Oedipal problems. This means that there is no grief over lost omnipotence and hence no possibility for maturation and human growth. There is no proper identification with the father and the integrative process is damaged, with the consequence that there will be a tendency towards splitting, denial, primitive projection and projective identification as defences against mental pain. The wish to avoid the work of thinking and the demands of conscience dominates. In fact, Herman Rauschning, a defector from the Nazi movement known for his critical writings on Nazism, said Hitler accused the Jews of having invented both conscience and reason (Rauschning, 1983 (1939)).

Thus, many elements in Nazi propaganda and ideology resemble a primitive level of fantasising, seen most clearly in regressed patients and regressed group situations. Consider the following statement: "The systematic concentration of pure blood, together with the expulsion of all that is foreign or undesirable, is the only way to succeed in eliminating impurities in the body of the nation" (Darré, 1930, in Chasseguet-Smirgel, 1990). Many other examples could be cited.

It is possible then, at least as a reasonable hypothesis, to state that this could represent the psychological foundation for cruel acts on a mass scale? And can it be verified that in situations of crisis, a traumatised anxiety-ridden people see a leader who promises to solve all problems and also to think for them? Individuals can then identify with this grandiose, omnipotent leader and see him as a part of themselves and regress to a state where there is no difference between what one wants and what is possible.

According to Chasseguet-Smirgel, it is the biological foundation (I would prefer the term fundamentalism) of the German Nazi movement that distinguishes it from, say, the Italian Fascist movement, and that can explain why there was not the same degree of cruelty in the latter. The Germans were predisposed by their cultural tradition (according to some by the special version of nationalism and romanticism which prevailed in Germany) and by their traumas to be seduced by Nazi ideology. This historical-psychological explanation evokes scepticism among political scientists, and it is contradicted at least partly by the fact that anti-semitism was not very strong in Germany before the Nazi era. But it is an attempt to explain the special historical circumstances in Germany, which made it possible that the destructive potential of modern civilisation could make headway there. In other words, what laid the ground for the genocidal situation was the special relation between the state and society in Germany in that period.

After the war

Germany was in ruins. The horrible truth about the extermination of the Jews, the gypsies, the mentally handicapped, etc., was revealed to the world. The Nazi ideology was condemned and devalued, and the leaders were either dead, had fled or had been sentenced to death or to long terms of imprisonment. Many soldiers and civilians had been killed. The Germans were in a state of complete shock. The rebuilding of the country seemed to be the solution, and the enormous enthusiasm when a new building or bridge was finished has been described. But the losses, and especially the loss of the "Führer" and what he represented, were consigned to silence. Hitler was the narcissistic love object of the Germans – a highly idealised, omnipotent figure which one could see oneself a part of, and him as a part of oneself. When such an object is totally devalued, it is impossible to mourn. Mourning requires that the lost object is not totally deprived of value and meaning. It requires a certain degree of re-experiencing the relation to the object on a psychic level. This becomes extremely difficult in a climate with total devaluation (a climate which logically leads to the growth of new supporters or to the maintenance of old ones more-or-less hidden).

Appy speaks of the "splitting off" of the Nazi ideals because one could cling to other ideals (e.g., the ideal of humanism) (Appy, 1993). In this "split off" condition, the loss of the Nazi ideals (and by that, the omnipotence) could not be mourned. He points to the forgetting of the illusion of omnipotence, which in his opinion had been at the root of the events of the Holocaust. In fact, mourning would mean taking responsibility for the war crimes of the Nazi regime instead of displaying only isolated regret (Mitscherlich & Mitscherlich, 1967). The Germans were highly traumatised and victimised and were not able either to take responsibility or to mourn. As Vamik Volkan, a psychoanalyst who has written widely on historical and political issues points out, it has serious implications if the inability to mourn becomes a group process.

"A group that has been persecuted transmits its grievance from one generation to the next, ..., and the latest generation is psychologically motivated to repeat in one way or another symbolic or realistic derivatives of the traumatic event in order to change passivity into activity, and to correct wrongs done to the forebearers. At the same time, a victimised group may tend, throughout the generations, to deny responsibility for ever having inflicted mass injury on others. ... I suggest that when the group is unable to mourn its own losses, it may be more likely to cling to the egotism of victimisation" (Volkan, 1993, p. 103).

This means staying in a position of deadlock between the feeling of being hurt and the desire for revenge.

Genocide and modern society

This essay has focussed on the mourning process as a prerequisite for overcoming trauma and victimisation. The Nazi experience can, in this connection, be seen as an avoidance of mourning and a re-experiencing and re-enactment on a more and more primitive level of the desire to overcome the victimisation. Because of its total goal and its well-organised, industrialised form, the Nazi genocide stands out as an extraordinary example. Many will claim that Auschwitz marks a historic watershed, and the Nazi genocide is possibly the only one that has had total destruction as a goal.

We have, however, in our time seen mass extermination in Kampuchea, once more in Europe, in Bosnia Herzegovina and now in Rwanda (Block, 1994). Furthermore, in many former Communist countries, there are ethnic conflicts that could develop into very dangerous situations. The historical background to these problems and conflicts is complex and lies outside the scope of this article. It seems, however, that the ideological climate in the Communist era was not conducive either to doing the necessary work on past atrocities of the Stalin era or victimisation or to doing the work of mourning. When peace eventually comes in former Yugoslavia,[2] difficult work remains to be done, and it will then show if it is possible to lay the ground for the prevention of a new terror/victim situation. The need for the sentencing of war criminals is one aspect of this.

It is, however, an extremely complicated task for peoples and nations to try to overcome being both perpetrators and victims. One of the lessons of the Nazi experience is that a perpetrator can also be seen as a traumatised victim who tries to solve his own victimisation in an omnipotent way by selecting scapegoats and by trying to exterminate them. We then have the possibility that the inherent primitive logic of the regressed group is reactivated and that derivatives of traumatic situations will be repeated to change passivity into active revenge or to restore earlier violations and losses. There would seem to be abundant opportunities for this in the aftermath of the war in former Yugoslavia, and many observers seem to look at the present conflict/war from this perspective. In other words, it is this ethnic conflict that has developed through the centuries that puts into action repeated vicious circles.

A too historical reading of this conflict can, however, lead to the most dangerous thing of all: ethnic stereotypes. In the Western media, the conflict is regarded as ethnic and one could ask, in whose interest? There are more and more reports on the multi-cultural situation in Bosnia-Herzegovina and in my experience, after having interviewed and treated a number of Bosnian refugees (Lavik et al., 1996), the clear ethnic separation does not exist in their everyday life and in their self-understanding. Nevertheless, there is more and more evidence that this has been a well-planned "ethnic cleansing" in the region where I have my informants (Priedor), there is, according to the UN's Expert Commission, probable evidence of planned and systematic genocide. And this is also in accordance with the experiences of the victims. They tell us that it happened suddenly. They were totally unprepared and had no opportunity to understand what happened and why. Even now, it seems not possible to understand for many. The soldiers came from the outside. They acted as if they had a plan. In a very short time, there were clear separation lines in the local society. Many had horrible experiences where comrades at school, colleagues and friends, shot at them; it was a systematic tendency that was not possible to overlook. In the beginning, the terror and the murders were carried out by paramilitary groups. It seemed, however, that these groups did not work on their own. In all probability, this was an action that was planned from the top of the hierarchy. During a short period in 1992, more than 200,000 people were killed, and more than 2,000,000 people were forced to flee. This was, then, a genocide planned from the top of the bureaucracy, carried out by paramilitary groups and, by and by, organised by the local bureaucracy and the military. In all probability, these operations were supported by the Serbs from Serbia, with Milosevic at the top. A primitive group process was set in action where cultural and friendly links were destroyed, friend and enemy were identified according to the logic of the primitive group, pathological splitting, selection of scapegoats, devaluation and destruction of the selected scapegoats without any consideration for earlier ties and loyalties in the different local communities. To look upon this as an ethnic conflict obscures the facts. Bosnia-Herzegovina was a multi-cultural society with different religions, but there was a marked degree of integration between those who now are called ethnic groups. Zygmunt Bauman warns strongly against treating the Holocaust just as an abnormal phenomenon. This is dangerous, he claims and is bordering on the suicidal because we then do not see those conditions in the society where these phenomena have their roots. He mentions three aspects in modern society: modern technology, the scientific and rational organisation of the world and the vision of a utopic society.

He points not only to the utopian character of the Nazis' vision of society but also to the fact that, at least in the earlier period of modern society, there existed visions of a healthy and clean society. In addition, one could add the rationalistic character of modern society as has been described by Max Weber. This rationality implies goal-oriented thinking where ethical considerations tend to be separated from the implementation of society's tasks. The splitting of functions in sectors in the system has a consequence; the results disappear from view and that the implementation of part projects becomes an object in itself. This seems, according to Bauman, to be one explanation of the fact that the German bureaucracy could function as effectively as it did in the implementation of the destruction of the Jews without the necessity of any individual, working in the bureaucracy, being especially hostile to Jews.[3] Nazism was, as we have seen, an example of this type of society, and we have seen how the Utopia of the perfect society has its roots in "the normal psychology", as, for instance, has been conceptualised in the theory of the archaic matrix of the Oedipus complex. We have seen how the dream of a greater Serbia has played a central role in former Yugoslavia and has given rise to a manipulatory enemy picture of the Muslims. The parallels with the Nazi propaganda against the Jews are very close indeed.

With the conception of the unclean society, there unavoidably follows the identification of unclean elements. Together with a "rational" ideology, there are also primitive group processes. The bureaucratic compartementalisation of functions in society, where one office don't know what the others do, can have, as a consequence, that identification and extermination of unwanted, unclean elements, disappears from view (also where the bloodshed is going on, e.g., in the camps, the rational organisation/compartmentalisation of work can function in the service of denial).

A more complicated version of such destructiveness is posed by Hans Magnus Enzenberger in his book "Civil war" (Enzenberger, 1994). He describes our time as the era of civil wars, where everyone's fight against each other dominates. The ideological fundament, which is put forward as regards Nazism, no longer exists or is present only as a thin veneer. Man as a species, Enzenberger claims, has entered into a new phase where we have begun to kill and exterminate each other without any pretext or cause. Violence and destruction are present everywhere. Not only in the civil wars in Angola, Afghanistan, Bosnia and Rwanda but also in the metropoles of Western society. The senseless violence can change every subway train into a miniature Bosnia, he claims. Civil war, or more correctly, war against others, is the prototype. Enzenberger seems to point to the growing atomisation, powerlessness and cultural impoverishment in post-modern society as a background. In other words, he gives a description of a situation where the primitive group processes are spreading and encompassing constantly greater areas in society.

It is beyond the scope of this article to analyse this argumentation in-depth, but I find it worth noting that Enzenberger is pointing to Sisyphus as an everyday hero, as the one who gives hope. He is the one who again and again starts to rebuild.

"They wanted to make Sisyphus an existential hero, an outsider and a rebel of tragic proportions, larger-than-life, and crowned in diabolic glory. Perhaps that is wrong. Perhaps he was something much more important, an everyday figure. The Greeks interpreted his name as the grammatical superlative of sophos, clever: Homer even called him the cleverest of men. He wasn't a philosopher; he was a trickster. The story goes that he caught Death and bound him hand and foot. And Death remained defeated until Ares, the god of war, freed him and handed Sisyphus over to him. But Sisyphus overcame Death a second time and managed to return to earth. They say he reached a ripe old age. Later, as a punishment for his human un-derstanding, he was condemned to push a heavy boulder up the side of a hill for the rest of time. The name of this stone is peace' (Enzenberger, 1994, p. 71).

Does Enzenberger here give a description of the destruction produced by the society of our time, a destruction where the ideological supras-tructure is no longer necessary? Is it "the archaic matrix of the Oedipus complex" in its muteness as we perhaps can see it in our times' dom-inating clinical condotions characterised by different forms of symbo-lisation defects (inability to transform bodily experiences to mental content) seen in different variants of the psychosomatic illnesses?

An answer cannot be given here, but there seems less reason than ever to view this form of destructivity as an isolated pathological case, a failure of civilisation's taming of the "eternal destructive forces" in the human mind, in other words, as a "picture on the wall".

Conclusion

Auschwitz, the genocide in Bosnia and other genocides are each unique, but they also have something in common. They represent, of course, a fault in our civilisation's usual way of functioning. However, there seems to be continuity or a connection between the organisation and way of functioning of modern society and the possibility for genocide. And it is people and groups of people who are the executors. As psychoanalysts, we have a privileged vantage point for the study of the destructive processes. However, a focus on pathology and personality can lead to an isolation of the problem and a projection limited to special personalities or characters. This critique can be directed against the Adorno et al. (1950) famous study of the authoritarian personality. The experiences from the Nazi genocide have shown, as well as experiences from the genocides in Bosnia (when its history is documented), that there are acts that can be performed by ordinary people when there are conditions of a "specific and not-universal relation between state and society" (again to cite Bauman, 1989, p. 82). It is not always the case, as we usually suppose that cruelty arises when reason and rationality disappear. The genocides have shown that it can be the other way around. Genocide has happened under the reign of a certain kind of rationality. Of course, cruelties happen where irrationality and uncontrollability reign, but in this case, they are often sporadic and of short duration. Many of the genocides were logically and rationally planned, and the executors each acted in a rational way in accordance with this (of course mad) logic. It remains for psychoanalysis and other disciplines, in my opinion, to draw the necessary conclusions from this both practically and theoretically. "Society-determined cruel acts" are, therefore, phenomena that need further analysis. A study of primitive group processes together with knowledge of archaic destructive aspects of the personality (Kernberg, 1992) will provide a basis, but it is also desirable to gain more empirical knowledge of the dynamics in such situations. Psychoanalytic knowledge about the unconscious processes is, therefore, a privileged point of departure for the understanding of what happens in what Bauman calls "genocidal situations".

Notes

1 Published in Scandinavian Psychoanalytic Review, 1995, 18:192–210. A revised version is published here with the kind permission of Scandinavian Psychoanalytic Review.
2 This essay was written during the war in former Yugoslavia.
3 Implied here is a critique of modern society's universalisation of man; man as an abstract object, divorced from the concentration on the single concrete individual. Even if this in its extreme consequence can enforce cruelties and absurdities, it is also a precondition for the fact that we can talk about general, equal rights for everybody, including human rights. It is an ethic that is based on the ability, at the same time, to take into consideration the distinct and the common, which is the democratic society's defence against inhumanity.

Chapter 4

Humiliation and the victim identity in conditions of political and violent conflict[1]

The battle between good and evil

Osama bin Laden perceives the war against America, the Jews and the influence of Western imperialism as a cosmic war between the forces of good and evil. Terrorist acts are justified through a special interpretation of Islam and a paranoid analysis of the current situation. According to Islamic fundamentalist theoreticians, Islam is being threatened by the decadent civilisation of the West, which desecrates Islam and makes it impossible to establish an authentic Islamic society (Hübsch, 2001). After the USA stationed troops on holy ground in Saudi Arabia, the violence and terror were intensified. Bin Laden issued a fatwa requiring all Muslims to murder Americans wherever they could be found and to steal their money and valuables. This is the will of Allah, it was claimed, and those who carry out such deeds will be rewarded. This is a cosmic war, a battle between good and evil. A pretext of this sort makes it possible to demonise the adversary, dehumanise everyone who is not one of "us", and justify committing atrocities against innocent people. Everyone is equally guilty.

An extremist, violent, religious fundamentalism of this sort is nothing new, nor is it unique in this day and age. It can be found among Christian fundamentalists, among Jewish fundamentalists in Israel, and among Sikhs and Hindus in Asia and has characterised extremist religious movements throughout history. The Crusades, for example, are still very much present in the historical consciousness of many Muslims. Ideologically and fundamentalistically inspired violence and terror have, however, seldom been expressed as powerfully.

DOI: 10.4324/9781003206057-4

It also, perhaps, never had as highly organised global support. Lastly, if Western intelligence is to be believed, it never had such destructive potentials as they have today. The fact that the opposing side (US) has also used nearly the same sort of language, describing the situation as a battle between good and evil, a war against an evil empire, etc., and has also pursued a consistently confrontational strategy, has led to an escalation of violence and a weakening of the middle-ground approach and has made it more difficult to practise humane strategies.

The situation has also developed into a battle for the moral high ground that could be characterised as a double standard when one considers the recent history of the implicated parties. It is as though the ideological and psychological dimensions have become predominant, whereas previously, the struggle concerned land, wealth and political power.

Terror is fascinating

Terror and terrorism are fascinating – and this is the significant driving force behind many forms of terrorism. Mark Juergensmeyer, a well-known researcher in this field, regards religiously inspired terrorism more as a "public performance" than a political strategy. The strategies of al-Qaeda and other religious terrorist groups are obviously not especially productive when it comes to acquiring actual political power and influence. As Mark Juergensmeyer points out, these strategies are more an expression of the attempts of desperate groups to attain a feeling of restoration and power (Juergensmeyer, 2000).

Terror exists and has existed in many different contexts, with different rationales and very different ideological contents. What these different kinds of terror have in common, however, is that they are used to dominate and oppress and to gain psychological influence. Terror is a strategy for occupying the soul, not territory. It is not primarily a strategy for achieving economic dominance or other kinds of such dominance (Varvin, 2003c). Terror has had many facets and often tremendous potential for violence. State-sponsored terror has many similarities with the current terrorist threats with regard to both its motivation and its justification, but the difference is that in this case, the perpetrators are desperate groups who are in control of a government's power structure. Nazism represented an ideological-

political excuse for mass murder that has clear similarities with today's religiously-based violence. Both Stalin's terrorist regime and
Mao's China carried out mass murders, and in both places, these
actions were supported on ideological grounds. The dictatorial regimes in Latin America also took systematic steps to remove undesirable elements. The political- ideological-religious justifications in
all these contexts represented a mental instrument that could validate
dehumanising the chosen enemy, justify subjecting this enemy to
atrocities, and give "meaning" to the apparent necessity of exterminating undesirable, dangerous or harmful "elements" as part of
a greater struggle – a cosmic battle: a battle between good and evil, or
a battle to re-establish the ideal realm on earth (Bohleber, 2002;
Hoffman, 1998; Lifton, 2000; Vedantam, 2003).

It may be necessary to mention that destructive state-subsidised
terror, and for that matter, the aggressive imperialistic and domination-
motivated warfare that occurred in Vietnam, has held the greater
potential for violence and destruction than has been within reach of
Al-Qaeda and similar terrorist organisations.

What makes people participate in atrocities?

What is the reason for all of this violence? What is it that makes
groups and individuals initiate, participate in and commit atrocities that is justified on political, ideological or religious grounds?
More specifically, how does a person develop what is called a
terrorist mentality: a mental condition in which "the other" is
diminished or dehumanised? A condition in which others become
the carriers or representatives of something evil, something ob-
jectionable that must be exterminated, or in which others are
considered valueless, and can be killed and merely regarded as
"collateral damage"?[2]

This question has been asked from many different perspectives,
and the premises for discussion have been determined by researchers
from various disciplines. The insights that psychoanalysis provides
into aggression and destructiveness are central but have not been
taken into account to any great extent by other groups of professionals and are not widely discussed in the public debate. The question is, to what extent is it justified and fruitful to place terrorism and
terrorists on the "psycho-analyst's couch"?

According to the precepts of social psychology, a psychoanalytical process directed towards the individual that aims at reducing socially destructive acts to basic conflicts of drives and/or personality disturbances will not be particularly fruitful, entailing a reductionism in that findings from studies of individuals are generalised to groups. This narrow view of psychoanalysis overlooks, among other things, the fact that Freud regarded group psychology and the group mentality as primary elements in the historic development of individuality and the ability to think independently. According to this point of view, when individual differences are dissolved in mass movements, the result will be a regression to levels where individuals relinquish their individuality, regress to "group mentality functioning", and project those aspects of their personality that involve morals and ethical judgements onto a leader who can make the group act "as though it were one person". Thus, regression occurs at both the individual and the group level to a fundamental mentality that is characterised by a lack of differentiation and the relinquishment of personal responsibility (Freud, 1921).

Empirical research and experiments in social psychology confirm this assumption and have demonstrated that practically everyone is capable of committing atrocities given the appropriate conditions and circumstances. Both Browning's study of members of an ordinary German police battalion who willingly participated in the genocide of Jews in Poland and Russia (Browning, 1998) and the Milgram experiment, which demonstrated how "ordinary" people could commit atrocities under the guidance of an authority figure (Milgram, 1974), have shown how so-called ordinary people not only follow orders, but can also murder other people "of their own free will" (under the influence of the group pressure inherent in these situations, or rather in a situation in which the group mentality is activated), as long as a leader gives them a justification for doing so. Freud showed how individuals in such situations projected both the superego and the ego ideal onto the leader, thus relinquishing their own individuality, with a subsequent regression that resulted in their following the leader (Freud, 1921).

Social psychology, however, loses its focus on the individual and cannot explain how the group mentality reduces the individual to being merely a member of the group who, with an individualised but group-based justification, can follow the orders of the leader. Social psychology is thus unable to analyse the processes in the individual that lead to committing atrocities.

In this context, it is important to analyse the individual terrorist's mentality precisely because it is vital to an understanding of the impact of the group mentality on the individual, or, as Freud says, how the group mentality of the individual is "awakened". In his farewell letter, Mohammed Atta, the terrorist leader of the attack on the Twin Towers in New York, explained the process that had led him to the attack the September 11 and described what would happen to him afterwards and how his body was to be handled after his death. Why did he insist that no woman was to touch his corpse? Another example is that of Palestinian and other suicide bombers, who make video films in which they express their conviction that the action they are about to carry out is right, that it is the will of Allah, and that it will ensure them a place beside God: "and they shall be provided with goods", as it says in the Qur'an. This involves complex individual processes in a group context that must be analysed as such. I will return to this topic and Atta's farewell letter later.

However, it has been difficult for psychoanalysis to answer the question of how large groups of people can jointly agree to define others as enemies and how this conception has been able to develop into collective atrocities and genocide situations. It is a basic tenet of psychoanalysis that social and collective values and judgements are represented in the individual, largely by the superego and the ego ideal (Freud, 1967; Freud, 1917, 1923). Bion, among others, has analysed how small groups function and how primitive group processes may destabilise superego functions in the individual (Bion, 1961). However, psychoanalysis has had difficulties explaining how social groups can be caught up in political-ideological-religious insanity and commit genocide or how entire cultures can be disposed towards terrorist acts. Vamik Volkan has analysed this problem thoroughly, and I will return to his findings later (Akhtar, 2003; Volkan, 1996, 1997, 1999). In this context, I will also question how social psychology can explain the process by which individuals can be seized by mass phenomena of a regressive nature and how they can internalise the schism between good and evil. Social learning theories are hardly sufficient to explain the intensity with which actions based on this schism are carried out.

Rather than entering into a metatheoretical discussion, I will present some rudiments for understanding collective aggression using the following themes as a starting point.

1. Demonisation of the other
2. Establishment of humiliation as a motif
3. Religion and the function of ideologies

Traumatisation of the group and society

Demonisation of the other

The Function of Dehumanisation: Juergensmeyer's comprehensive studies of religiously-based terrorism shows that the demonisation of others is a recurring feature of practically all terrorist movements (Hindu, Sikh, Christian, Muslim, Jewish) (Juergensmeyer, 2000). Virtually all of these terrorist movements have arisen from fundamentalist movements, and demonisation follows psychoanalytic schemas for various types of anxieties that are connected with psychosexual stages: dirt, impurities (anal), poison (oral), lack of intelligence and strength (phallic), etc. The Christian Identity movement, for example, calls its enemies "mud people" (ibid, p. 172). Often one can see a combination of these themes, and the connections between the dehumanising and demonising rhetoric and key unconscious fantasies become apparent.

Akhtar claims that the dehumanisation of others is an expression of a strategy (Akhtar, 2003). It is a defensive manoeuvre that protects the terrorist from "the dread of empathy" and against regret and guilt feelings (p. 139). The murder of innocents is justified through religious rhetoric that is surprisingly similar in different religions. Projection and projective identification are key elements. One's own undesired characteristics are ascribed to others, often to the extent that one actively tries to make them assume these characteristics (such as degradation of inmates in concentration camps, where in some situations people had to act inhumanely in order to survive).

The function of dehumanisation is to protect against "normal" feelings and regrets. Moreover, it is a means of getting rid of undesired and devalued aspects of oneself.

Establishment of humiliation as a motif

Most fundamentalist movements are based on a victim identity. "We have had to endure humiliation. Others have taken our country from us, they have murdered our children, and they are responsible for starving and terrorising us". There is often a kernel of truth in thought systems that are characterised by paranoia, and terrorist movements often arise in environments and cultures that actually have been the victims of massive traumatisation that may have occurred more recently or generations ago. However, the historical reality is also exploited ideologically by groups and individuals who have not been subjected to such humiliation. The rhetoric surrounding vulnerable and abused people is used by fundamentalist groups and terrorist organisations, for example, when actively recruiting members among young and marginalised European Muslim men (Moussaoui, 2003). This type of rhetoric has been seen in such different connections as in Hitler's Germany, Palestine, Israel, Ireland and in the USA in connection with September 11. Being or having been a victim justifies revenge, actions designed to "protect" the group's integrity, etc. We can see here how the dynamics of narcissism apply at both individual and group levels. The role of the victim is cultivated as though it were a badge of honour, the group's identity is marked by narratives of victimisation, and individuals identify themselves with the victim and obey leaders who say that the only way they can rise above "the others" is by taking on the identity of the victim. A feeling of being special, of entitlement, accompanies the role of the victim. The leaders exploit this situation, often far beyond reasonable limits.

The ideological narratives are often characterised by the type of vengeful rhetoric found in the Old Testament. The "other" must be humiliated, and this applies not only to the individuals who have themselves been responsible for inflicting the original humiliations but also to their descendants or to anybody who can be identified as their supporters or helpers. "An eye for an eye, a tooth for a tooth". The humiliation of the "other" implies a need to exterminate or remove that which is undesired, or one's own projected undesired aspects, often through the use of violence.

We have seen that the dehumanisation of the "other" can function as protection against "normal feelings", as Akhtar expressed it

(Akhtar, 2003). In violent situations, this often fails. The cries of the victim may be too persistent. The victim of one's violent attacks becomes a living indictment; a representative of primitive superego elements whose accusations are inexorable. This can lead to additional violence. This is one of the key dynamics behind the escalation of violence that has occurred in primitive genocide and genocide-like situations such as in Bosnia and Rwanda.

The dynamic of violence in these connections have two dimensions according to this line of argument:

A. A dimension of shame-narcissism. The effect of groups and individuals having been traumatised and humiliated is the internalisation of a victim-victimiser dynamic that may have an impact on the identity of the group and the individuals within it. The attempt to shift the passive position to active may result in identification with the violator or aggressor, which in turn may serve to justify the need to find scapegoats. In such situations, humiliation and shame can become the motivating force behind the desire for revenge, and humiliating others can, in a magical sense, be seen as a way of dealing with one's own shame. This can lead to a violent dynamic resulting in the ultimate humiliation with violent means
B. A dimension of paranoid persecution. When violence has been committed, the existence of the victim can weaken the defence of dehumanisation. The perpetrators have had the illusion that his projected aspects could be destroyed and disappear, but the victim, or the victimised family or group, is still there, like a living accusation. The victim "sticks" to the perpetrator as if glued and further dehumanisation can aggravate the situation. In the end, murder is the "only possibility" remaining in a regressive group situation. Thus, a malign dynamic arises that leads to further murders

An individual case

At the individual level, I have observed a dynamic that, at the level of fantasy, is similar to the above in highly traumatised individuals, but which has not resulted in concrete action.

A man in his forties described his life as a refugee as an uninterrupted downward spiral. In his homeland, he had been humiliated and tortured, and in exile, he had lost everything he owned. He had a broken home, no place to live, no education and no job. He suffered incessantly from his post-traumatic problems, which had increasingly affected his personality to the point where he was sceptical of and suspicious towards practically everybody. He described how his misery as a refugee was due to "refugee policy", the lack of benefits from the social welfare office, the humiliation inflicted on him by the employment office, etc. He spoke in a very insistent manner. In my role as his psychoanalyst, I was not the actual address for his complaint, and, in addition, I was barely able to get a word in edgewise. "The oppression has been endless", he said. "Nobody can understand it". He had been confronted with obstacles everywhere, and nobody had understood his situation. "I can blow up the Parliament-that's no problem. That's where all the hypocrites are, the ones who say that they wish us well but work against us all the time". He then elaborated on how this would be accomplished and assured me that he had the necessary knowledge and could get hold of everything he needed.

When he was confronted with the possibility that people other than the objects of his hatred (MPs) could also be killed, he thought for a moment and said, "You don't understand. This is all about getting rid of it - getting rid of the hypocrisy".

For him, exploding a bomb represented a catharsis that would, with one stroke, rectify the injustices he had experienced, boost his self-image, and send a message to those who had humiliated him. He "solved" his dilemma through what we call identification with the aggressor; he projected the humble, feminised (hypocritical) aspects of his personality onto those responsible for determining policy, and by a magical act, his own weaknesses would be eliminated. There is a psychological parallel to the relationship September 11 terrorist Atta had to his own weaknesses and those of others, especially his relationship to the "feminine", which he perceived as inferior and weak (Bohleber, 2002; Stein, 2003b).

This individual case illustrates aspects of a type of mental functioning that I have called "terrorist mentality" (Varvin, 2003b, 2003c). This man had experienced extreme trauma and had been subjected to a dehumanising and destructive form of aggression that had led to great losses and destroyed a secure and predictable social situation. The humiliation he had experienced in his native country continued when he was in exile, and a process was instigated in which he defined himself more and more as a victim – thus justifying "random violence".

Religion and the function of ideologies

Religion and other cultural narratives and belief systems can function as a means of constructing an identity at both individual and group levels. Under normal circumstances, it is an expression of the role culture plays in helping individuals and groups to imbue the burdens and transitions of life with meaning. Individual suffering can be expressed in accepted collective forms and can thus be experienced as something that is not exclusively private but shared with others. This is what Obeyesekere calls "the work of culture" (Obeyesekere, 1990). Fundamentalist religious and ideological movements have a tendency to arise in situations marked by desperation and little opportunity to develop beliefs freely. In these circumstances, they offer a kind of meaning to the group in its desperate condition, a meaning that is potentially violent: they can list reasons, identify the "guilty" parties, and justify violent acts. At the individual level, such fundamentalist religious-political ideologies help to form mentalities that can build bridges between unconscious fantasies and consciousness, thereby presenting solutions for individual and collective problems (Bohleber, 2002). The fundamentalist ideologies appeal to collective fantasies. These fantasies are primitive in the sense that they offer clear solutions, are paranoid in their structure, relieve guilt and encourage violence. They incorporate a dehumanising dynamic that functions in connection with organised violence and terror, whether these are state-sponsored or organised along political, religious or ideological lines. This may include terror and violence committed by terrorist organisations, paramilitary groups or ordinary military units that are in a state of more-or-less moral disintegration. (The film Apocalypse Now illustrated how this dynamic emerged in Vietnam within an army that was in a state of organisational and moral disintegration).

The fundamentalist political-religious ideology offers a "higher" purpose or principle. Violence is thus not necessarily based on a personal desire to kill or injure people (a recognisable and human type of hatred) and desire for revenge, although this may play a role

(Juergensmeyer, 2000). Correspondingly, those who commit evil actions, who represent what we call the quality of evilness (and here I refer to the undifferentiated dehumanising treatment of others), seldom perceive their actions as evil (Stein, 2003a).

Thus, the type of evil we are talking about here does not refer to intentional, evil acts but to something that may be characterised as objective evil. People who are involved in such acts may appear idealistic and dispassionate while they are carrying out their destructive deeds. These acts may be committed after meticulous planning and careful, dispassionate calculations. Support from a God, an omnipotent leader or a higher religious principle is often cited. I previously mentioned the farewell letter left by the terrorist Atta. The following quotation from his letter expresses this frame of mind or mentality quite clearly:

"... everywhere you go say that prayer [this refers to a special prayer used for occasions of martyrdom] and smile and be calm, for God is with the believers. And the angels protect you without you feeling anything", and "You should feel complete tranquillity, because the time between you and your marriage ... is very short". ["Marriage" refers to the act of sacrificing oneself through the "suicidal" terrorist act and the following union with God in heaven.] (cited in Stein, 2003a).

The Japanese sect Aum Shinrikyo formulated the principle that it was proper to kill people when their karma was at its peak in order to protect them from the suffering they would endure if their karma declined. "It was for their own good". Even the Nazis did not go this far (Lifton, 2000).

Violence that is based on ideological grounds seems to have become increasingly dehumanised in recent decades in the sense that who the victims are is of little importance in many contexts (although when studying the history of bestiality, it is difficult and perhaps meaningless to determine who was the worst, unless one feels the need to present one's own particular enemy as the absolute worst in history). From an ideological point of view, the attack on the Twin Towers on September 11 marked the USA's entrance into history as the victim of the aggression of a foreign power (although Pearl Harbour was actually the first such episode), making it possible to exploit the event in a political-ideological sense in various ways. And there is no doubt that September 11th has been exploited politically.

Although it is difficult to classify terrorism as more or less humane, it does seem reasonable to refer to an escalation of evil. Terrorism might have been more "humane" in the past. The first "recognised" terrorists of modern times, the Russian members of the movement "Will of the People" (in Russian "Narodnaya Volya") in the 19th century, for example, would call off a planned attack if their prospective victims were together with their families, and were otherwise satisfied with attacking key figures in positions of power (Varvin, 2003a). In contrast, the Aum Shinrikyo movement released the lethal gas Sarin in Tokyo's underground railway system in the 1990s with the aim of killing anyone who happened to be there. This movement represents an entirely different destructive potential. Its members decided that they had to kill everyone in order to "save the world" and had manufactured gas enough to murder millions of people (Lifton, 2000).

The religiously inspired ideologies of violence have their roots in religion but present a distorted version of them. According to Meddeb, a well-known researcher in the field of Islam who is himself a Muslim, the concept of the martyr is mentioned only once in the Qur'an (Meddeb, 2003): "Above all do not believe that those who were killed on the path of God are dead; they are living next to their Lord, provided with goods" (Qur'an, :169, quoted in Meddeb 2003, p. 156). Those who die in Jihad, holy war, "[will be] living next to the Lord in the same place as that of the angels, [which gives] the bliss of angels during the celestial stay in the divine dwelling" (Meddeb, p. 156). According to Meddeb, this constitutes the only textual background in the Qur'an for claiming that because Islam is threatened, it is permissible to kill all Americans in the name of Allah, as Osama bin Laden announced in his fatwa.

Fundamentalist religious ideology, whether Islamic, Christian or connected with other denominations, can play a vital role for groups in a crisis or during periods of radical change where there is a high degree of individual and collective frustration and suffering. Group fantasies or collective fantasies that arise from group and individual suffering and frustration can be expressed in religious-political ideologies that, in turn, have mainly been designed to define the frustration of the group. This is borne out by the fact that victim discourses occupy such a large place in fundamentalist thinking For individuals, such religious-political ideologies can function as an intermediary between individual and collective frustrations and traumas, thus serving as a perverted version of "the work of culture".

Fundamentalism does not become a cultural discourse that can convey, express and help work through individual suffering, as Obeyesekere has described it, but instead represents a means of reinforcing its most regressive elements. Within fundamentalist ideology, individuals and groups can find a collectively accepted way of expressing suffering and humiliation. Hatred can be given a focus and an objective, and a pretended reparation of traumas and humiliations, whether real or imaginary, can take place.

According to Bohleber, a number of common features can be identified in the ideological justifications for the kind of modern terrorist violence that we see in, for example, the so-called Islamic fundamentalist movements and in other totalitarian connections (Bohleber, 2002). The following elements are essential (Varvin, 2003b):

- The myth of an ideal past (original Communism, society at the time of Mohammed, etc.)[3]
- A utopian dream of the perfect society in which "paradise lost" will be re-established. Therefore, all that is "unclean" or regarded as "contaminated" must be removed. An example of this is the murder of intellectuals that took place in Cambodia during the Pol Pot regime
- Aggressive defence against external influences. This is the consequence of the utopian ideology. Certain factors that "come from the outside", from other groups or societies, must be opposed by violence if necessary (for fundamentalist Muslim groups, this includes influences from the decadent West or "threats" from the Jews)
- Death cult. Dying for the cause is often glorified, as in the case of suicide bombers. Martyrdom was glorified during the Iran-Iraq war, during which the Iranians sent thousands of young men out to "clear minefields" by walking through them. Killing can also be justified in a quasi-religious sense as "helping" a person, as was the case with the Aum sect in Japan
- Preoccupation with purity of blood. Nazism was a clear example of this, but it also exists elsewhere. One must not mix one's blood

with other "races" or groups to maintain its "purity", and in some cases, eradicate that which is impure (e.g., through ethnic cleansing). In such connections, there is often a common sense of entitlement (we have a right to this land, etc.) and a glorification of the role of victim (being a victim confers enhanced status and implies entitlement to special compensation). These elements can be present to varying degrees, but as Bohleber points out, they are characteristics of Nazi ideology as well as of certain newer terrorist groups and several totalitarian states. The common denominator of these ideological elements is their powerful dehumanising potential since there must be, by necessity, a large number of people who fall outside the definition, do not fit in, are not pure, etc., and who may thus be subjected to oppression, exile and even murder. Societies in which this type of ideology dominates have, therefore, a tendency to produce large numbers of victims

Societies or groups that have been traumatised may attempt to shift their situation from a passive to an active one by themselves, subjecting others to humiliations. Specific groups (ethnic groups, for example) and local communities may be victimised as a result of this process. This type of development can occur in what Volkan calls traumatised societies (Volkan, 2003).

Traumatisation of the group and society

We have seen that a religious-fundamentalist ideology can unite individual frustration and misery with a common sense of understanding, which is often described as collective fantasies. According to Volkan, collective misery can be represented as the development of a common identity centred around a "chosen trauma" (Volkan, 1997, 2003). A chosen trauma is a shared representation of a group's or society's victimisation. The following situation can arise:

A catastrophic change, such as increased social poverty or war, can threaten the group's identity. Collective regression can follow. A common history that includes the traumas experienced by previous generations may be activated and can serve as a means of clarifying the current crisis. This type of explanatory narrative can exist as an undercurrent in the psyche of a people, and thus be passed down from generation to generation more-or-less unconsciously. In a crisis, a kind of collapsing of time can occur, making the traumas of the past as topical as the current traumas (a situation that is typical of individual traumatic states). Old conflicts and traumas fan the flames of the current ones, and through narratives connected to these more or less verifiable historic events, ideologies are constructed that offer simple solutions in the form of revenge, murders, etc., as can be seen in ethnic cleansing. This was typical of Milosevic's ideological justification for murder in the Balkans, and has been seen in similar conflicts elsewhere, for example in India (Kakar, 1996; Volkan, 2003).

The structure of this type of response is similar to the transfer of traumas from generation to generation in families. When the children of traumatised parents can identify themselves with, or be identified with, their humiliated and traumatised parents, the next generation may be able to grieve for the losses occurred or take revenge. They can perceive it as a task to correct and repair the damage that has been done. The next and subsequent generations are thus "assigned" a damaged self-image to which they must relate in one way or another.

At the collective level, such reactions can, according to Volkan, "accumulate" and create shared mental images of previous traumas and violations. Volkan calls this image the "chosen trauma", and at a conscious ideological level, it can serve as a means of officially glorifying the role of victim while maintaining an underlying less conscious awareness of being degraded and victimised.

Kakar, for example, has described how Muslims in Hyderabad, India, during an ethnic conflict with Hindus, viewed their own expulsion in terms of the expulsion of Muslims from Andalucía centuries earlier (their "chosen trauma"). This "Andalucía syndrome" added extra fuel to the ongoing ethnic war in the area (Kakar, 1996).

In these situations, the dynamic force of the conflict is the unconscious representation at group level of the traumatised and devastated self, both as an individual phenomenon and as the group self. It is important to emphasise that this concerns mental representations. Often these are not commensurate with actual historical facts, but they nevertheless serve as psychological justifications and a social force in a specific political context. This was the case when Milosevic cited the supposed Serbian defeat at the hands of the Ottomans in 1389 as a psychological/ideological justification for whipping up sentiments against the Bosnian Muslims. Historical research indicates that if earlier massive traumatisation played any part at all in this horrific war, it was most likely the horrors of World War II that were the active component. In addition to the massive traumatisation inflicted by the German occupying forces, there were practically no groups that avoided involvement either as victimisers or as victims in conflicts within former Yugoslavia (Glenney, 1999).

Conclusion

Who is recruited to the ranks of terrorists and other violent groups? What is it that makes such groups choose a violent and dehumanising strategy? Islamic terrorism started in connection with the war in Afghanistan, especially after its end. The victory over the Communists was the first victory achieved by Islam for centuries. This illustrates a phenomenon that many people have pointed out: active resistance, including terrorism, does not necessarily arise in situations of oppression and hopelessness, but perhaps more often when there are signs that the situation is in the process of being overcome.

When the war ended, thousands of Mujahedin warriors from many Muslim countries were suddenly "unemployed". They returned to their native countries to find no jobs available, they had no education other than fighting, and their prospects for the future were poor. They joined the masses of unemployed people in Muslim countries. Heinsohn estimates that there were around ten million unemployed young men in Muslim countries (Herzinger et al., 2002). Few opportunities are open to men with this background in traditional cultures. With neither money nor work, no prospect of marriage, no family nor sexual life, many of these men joined radical and fundamentalist Muslim groups. A similar trend can be seen in the Palestinian areas and Europe, where young, marginalised men are recruited to fundamentalist groups.

Segregation, marginalisation and rejection of a group are key prerequisites for them to become more radical and develop in a fundamentalist and violent direction. The processes that form such isolated, radicalised groups seem to be especially well suited for promotion of the development of primitive mental processes in individuals, which in turn prepare individuals to participate in atrocities. A key element is the dehumanisation of others, the process by which the other gradually loses human characteristics and can become an anonymous victim. According to the Polish sociologist Bauman, this process of making others anonymous (and thereby enabling the perpetrator to ignore their suffering) is characteristic of developments in modern society; in areas where the democratic foundation is not sufficiently secure (Bauman, 1989). These factors, among others, have made the presence of a humanistic ideology and human rights important in preventing aggression. When groups gradually develop their own existence outside the surrounding society, it seems as though primitive processes at group level promote mental processes (group mentality) that we in other contexts (e.g., clinical) would call pathological. This, in turn, can result in the development of a terrorist mentality. This can occur among so-called "ordinary", non-traumatised people, but there is little doubt that having experienced traumatisation fertilises this development. And it is quite probable that learning how to become a terrorist in such a group, and participating in terrorist activities, can in themselves be traumatic experiences. The knowledge we have gleaned from terrorist training camps confirms that the recruits are subjected to extreme traumatisation (Volkan, 1997) Thus, yesterday's victims become tomorrow's victimisers in this context.

Humiliation is a central concept in understanding the development of terrorism – and in combating it. It is also vital to exercise restraint in using the expressions "terrorism" and "terrorist"; these words have been used indiscriminately by those in power to describe resistance movements and protests in war and occupation situations. Many of the leaders of influential countries today (such as Brazil at the beginning of 21st century) were called terrorists not long ago.

The knowledge that psychoanalysis has acquired throughout the years on man's aggressive tendencies and drives has relatively seldom been used in analyses of current social conflicts, wars, genocide and terrorism. However, Sigmund Freud's thinking was heavily influenced by such phenomena, especially by how they manifest themselves in groups and mass movements. He argued that historically, individual psychology developed from group psychology and that the group mentality of human beings formed the foundation of the individualised mentality, as previously noted.

Thus, psychoanalysis has a good starting point for studying the psychology of violent group processes. Psychoanalytic studies of this type of aggression and destructiveness can therefore make a significant contribution to the understanding of organised violence, whether it is carried out under governmental or "private" auspices. However, these are complex phenomena that need interdisciplinary study. The most fruitful contribution that can be made by psychoanalysis is perhaps in answering questions such as: "Why does violence breed violence?" and "Why can yesterday's victim become tomorrow's victimiser?" In other words, studying the dynamics that lead to the escalation of violence and the obstacles that lie in the path of non-violent processes in traumatised societies.

Notes

1 Based on an article published in: Scandinavian Psychoanalytic Review, 2005, 28:40–49 and is used here with the kind permission of Scandinavian Psychoanalytic Review.
2 I believe that in this connection, it may be reasonable to regard violent terror as a continuum that ranges from individual acts of terror to attacks on large groups of people, including genocide.
3 The myth of peaceful coexistence at the time of Mohammed is refuted by historical research demonstrating that, on the contrary, the societies of that era were riddled by violence and civil war (Inamdar, 2001).

Chapter 5

Fundamentalist mindset[1]

Introduction

Fundamentalism has increasingly become a part of the political discourse in western countries and is, to a large, degree associated with Islamic Jihadism. Fundamentalism has, however, been a concern in all religions, especially in Christianity, where the term had its origin more than 100 years ago. Then, the concern is how not to lose hold of the fundaments, the concepts that, with a lack of which, there could not be a proper belief system.

The idea that the adherence to fundaments may develop into fundamentalism understood as rigid adherence to basic principles has seldom been on the agenda in professional and scientific contexts. Therefore, it is of interest when this was set on the agenda in a psychoanalytic congress, The Nordic Psychoanalytic Congress, in 2016. A certain worry must have been present when the congress committee invited to reflect on fundaments and, in connection with this, fundamentalism. Fundaments are, according to Oxford Thesaurus, synonymous with Basic and describe as "principles, understanding, research and rights. Something described as basic is seen as a necessary minimum, to which further elaboration may or may not be added. Something that is fundamental to something else is essential to it" (OUP, 2017).

Every profession and science consider what may be the fundamentals characterising their approach and this has been an ongoing discussion in psychoanalysis as well.

Concern with fundamentals has appeared several times in the history of psychoanalysis:

DOI: 10.4324/9781003206057-5

Franz Alexander's "Fundamentals of Psychoanalysis" (Alexander, 1963 (1948)), Lacan's seminar on the four fundamental concepts of psychoanalysis (Lacan, 2004) and several works on the fundamentals of psychoanalytic technique, and, among others, Etchegoyen's seminal book on technique (Etchegoyen, 2006). In these works, fundamentals are discussed and understood as more or less evident, even if controversies appear on which concepts or technique should be chosen. However, from clinical practice and supervision one learns that tendencies toward a more absolute understanding of this or that school's recommendations appear from time to time "to"; imply a certain resistance against change and flexible adaptation and cling to what has once been taught as the true or correct way. It is interesting that this dilemma between sticking to tradition, fundamentals and renewal was formulated already in 1941 by the then president of the American Psychological Association in a presidential address with the evocative title "Fundamentals and Fundamentalism in the Preparation of Applied Psychologists". He gave a tentative, but in our context quite precise definition of fundamentalism or the fundamentalist attitude, namely as…: "the attitude, namely, that the tried is the true, that the old is the established, and the traditional is of superior worth just because it is old. It is essentially an emotion of horror when doubt is expressed of the ancient and sanctified—and an emotion of anger towards the doubter. If you want to be called a sound man, you must never call in question the fundamentals". (English, 1941, p. 4)

The belief that that the tried is true and that the traditional is of superior worth is still, more or less, being used in psychoanalytic institutes and their training programs. What English formulated is anxiety for change that is common for all professions, and when this anxiety is not faced and worked through, fundamentalistic tendencies can develop as a defensive mechanism.

Reflection on the relation between fundaments and fundamentalism may thus give insight into possible basic problems within psychoanalysis as a scientific and clinical profession. Such reflections may, however, also open general considerations on the relation between fundaments and fundamentalism.

In the following, I will first discuss the problem of a fundamentalist mindset, a psychological attitude that works as a defence against

change. Then I will discuss the problems of fundaments and fundamentalistic tendencies within psychoanalysis. I will then reflect on the
developments of fundamentalism in religion and politics and look at
some historical roots of fundamentalism in Europe and the Orient as
a defence against modernisation. I will argue that psychoanalytic
understanding of collective fantasies may help comprehend "collective" fundamentalism that may lay ground for developing strategies
for counteracting malignant fundamentalism.

Basic is the relation to change. In the philosophy of science, this type
of change is formulated by Thomas Kuhn as a fundamental change in
the basic *concepts* and *experimental* practices of a *scientific discipline*
(Kuhn, 1962). Kuhn contrasts paradigm shifts, which characterise a
scientific revolution, to the activity of *normal science*, which he describes
as scientific work done within a prevailing framework or *paradigm*.
Paradigm shifts arise when the dominant paradigm under which
normal science operates is rendered incompatible with new phenomena,
facilitating the adoption of a new theory or paradigm. Kuhn's work
related to natural sciences has been applied to other disciplines as well.
What is common, however, is the resistance and critique when paradigm shifts are on the agenda. In psychoanalysis, we have several examples of what seemingly represent proposals of paradigm shifts (e.g.,
self-psychology, relational psychoanalysis). The climate for reflection
and possible integration of insights from these different schools has,
however, been difficult. Change in the basics (i.e., change in paradigms)
naturally evokes anxiety and defence mechanisms – and sometimes
fundamentalistic tendencies, even in psychoanalysis. The group processes involved is well-described by Bion (1961).

Fundamentalism and fundamentalist mindset

Fundamentalism as a discourse represents rigid adherence to basic
principles in line with the origin of the fundamentalism among British
and American Protestants in the late 19th and early 20th centuries.
This Protestant movement was peaceful and was based on fears of
deleterious changes within the Christian community (Strozier
et al., 2010).

Fundamentalism is now, however, mostly connected with a special
interpretation of Islam and the relation to religious-inspired violence
is often highlighted.

This mindset denotes a set of assumptions held by individuals and groups that create a powerful incentive for choices and behaviours. Mindsets are changing slowly and are bound up with identities and subject to a kind of mental inertia. The mindset is first and foremost related to group thinking which is shared thinking and can be aligned with a "Weltanschauung" or worldview. Fundamentalist mindset is characterised by dualistic thinking, paranoia and rage in a group context; an apocalyptic orientation that implies a distinct view on time, death and violence. As a rule, in fundamentalist groups, there is dependence on charismatic leaders and often accompanied by an idea that a totalised conversion is necessary (Strozier & Boyd, 2010).

Fundamentalism is understood as rigid adherence to basic principles. It exists in all religions, in political movements, in institutions of different kinds and is possible to discern in scientific and professional debates. Fundamentalist mindset is something that usually develops within the context of a fundamentalist movement, political, religious or otherwise, where the ideological aspect may be underdeveloped, and the psychological side have become more dominant.

When Strozier and Boyd associate fundamentalist mindset with paranoia, rage and an apocalyptic orientation, they underline the inherent or latent danger of violence in fundamentalism. Fundamentalism does not, however, necessarily imply violence. In fact, most people we call fundamentalists today are not violent and try to pursue their goals by peaceful means, be it the wish to create a state ruled by Sharia or a Christian community. The Muslim Brotherhood in Egypt is another such example.

In discussing Islam, one must differentiate between Islamic fundamentalists who pursue goals by persuasion and preaching from what is called "Jihadists" who believe that violence is the most important way to change matters. Among Jihadists, one must again distinguish between nationalist or patriotic jihadists and what may be called global or transnational Jihadists. The former appears in local contexts with the aim of liberating their group from oppression. Some Palestinian and Chechen groups belong here, as well as several other groups in the Middle East and Asian region (Khosrokhavar, 2010). The latter are organised more or less as transnational organisations that are extremely violent, are totally occupied by a purist version of their belief and are indiscriminate in their violent attacks against people they deem as nonbelievers and outsiders.

There are thus a variety of groups and types of organisations with different motives and means to achieve their aims, and that is connected with what we call fundamentalism. Fundamentalism is thus not something bad in itself. Many have found peace in a fundamentalist conviction or belief, salvage from their inner torments and conflicts, which made it possible for them to lead a more harmonious life. The question is, however, whether adherence to fundaments and what we see today as fundamentalism has any necessary or logical connection.

To put it in another way: does fundamentalism basically concerns the fundaments of a religion, a political ideology or a scientific discourse? And in connection with this, is there a logical connection between fundamentalism and Jihadism or other extremely violent and mass-killing politico-religious movements? Is fundamentalism the problem, or do we need to contextualise this and look at multiple determinants such as the study of the influence of historical, societal and unconscious processes in groups and individuals?

First, it may be appropriate to look at our own profession: psychoanalysis. It would be unconvincing to use psychoanalysis to analyse and understand present-day fundamentalist attitudes and movements without having analysed our own backyard and hopefully understand that we as professional subjects and psychoanalysis as a scientific organisation are not very different from others and equally susceptible to influences from the external world and its tensions, conflicts and problems.

Fundamentalism in psychoanalysis

In the last century, Psychoanalysis developed into a diverse field with several schools and traditions, all with their own languages or dialects and often with quite diverse and, at times, idiosyncratic understandings of central concepts. In conceptual research on two psychoanalytic concepts, enactment and unconscious phantasy, it was, at times, difficult to discern similarities and common ground across these different schools (Bohleber et al., 2013, 2015). It was also amazing to observe to what degree different schools did not cite each other, confirming an impression of tribalism, a core mark of fundamentalism.

Controversies have sometimes led to the splitting of psychoanalytic groups. These splits have certainly been multi-determined where personal animosity, institutional rivalry, ideological forces and societal conditions have played a role alongside theoretical controversies. Having observed some of them close up has increased my respect for unconscious forces that develop on a group level. Primitive defences like splitting and projective identifications, idealisation and mere denial have prevailed in spite of the protagonist's presumably solid psychoanalytic training and thorough personal analysis.

In the heat of battle, the ability for rational argument and mentalisation tend to get lost – and this condition may prevail for such a long time that the history of the original conflict and split might nearly become forgotten.

Heated debates and severe antagonisms are, of course, not particular for psychoanalysis and can be seen in any profession. During my time in psychoanalysis and in my work for IPA, there has been a marked improvement of the intellectual debate, but still, arguments flourish that deem other positions as dangerous or damaging to psychoanalysis; a "we-them" discourse typical for fundamentalist movements.

Research is a case of matter here. There has, as is known, been a long struggle to get acceptance for formal research in psychoanalysis and, among others, there are regional differences regarding the value or even the potential damage ascribed to research.

I will present a rather simple example: there is quite solid research showing that transference interpretations are important and useful for patients with severe personality pathologies but less important for neurotic disturbances. Interpretations should be used with caution also for personality disturbances and some researchers came up with the advice that not more than 1–4 interpretations per session are to be recommended (Høglend, 2014). Clinicians may dismiss this finding as it is expressed in a mechanistic, formal scientific language that certainly will not fit with psychoanalytic approaches focusing on the here-and-now and the indeterminism of the analysand-analyst relationship. The clinician's difficulties with empirical research, in addition to troubles inherent in understanding the logic of arguments in other disciplines, are, however, related to a problem of language or rather a dialect; clinical psychoanalysis and empirical research are expressed in quite different languages even if they concern similar clinical problems. There are also reciprocal difficulties and even unwillingness to learn the other group's language. Shahar makes in this connection a heuristic distinction calling the language of psychoanalysis the language of poetics and holds that research represents a schematic language (Shahar, 2010). Either language or dialect is useful in relation to their respective domains and valid in relations to their objects of study. They do not, however, communicate very well. Concrete reception of such research findings ("this is senseless"), expressed in the other's language (e.g., counting of interpretations in sessions), may easily lead to stricter adherence to "psychoanalytic fundamentals" and has, as a consequence, an impediment to reciprocal understanding and also to the development in each discipline's field of inquiry.

This example represents a shielding of oneself from being influenced by "the other" or from something outside, one of the salient figures in fundamentalism to which I will return later.

The question in the background may then be to what degree psychoanalytic societies and institutions, as well as their members, are prone to be caught in the lures of such fundamentalist attitudes (it may be better to refer to these as fundamentalist states of mind or fundamentalist mindsets). These are states of mind that avoid ambiguity, deplores diversity with a more or less prominent tendency to manichaeistic thinking (dualistic cosmology describing the struggle between a good, spiritual world of light, and an evil, material world of darkness).

It can be argued that such states of mind tend to develop within basic-assumption groups (Bion, 1961) and, as such, are a danger in every group formation and group process. Fundamentalism, then, becomes a symptom of underlying anxiety for the group's cohesion and functions as a defence against change. If psychoanalysis develops an ideology that advocates adherence to fundamentals, this will then represent an illusory way to safeguard the group's cohesion.

In general, this may count for all kinds of fundamentalist tendencies in groups.

Fundamentalism, understood in this way, is a question of degrees and may be related to certain critical phases or crisis in a group's developmental process, and the group may when this has been worked through, return to more normal business of rational argumentation.

I will argue, however, that there are situations that we may call the fundamentalist trap.

This is not always easy to identify and may have devastating influences on a group or an organisation's development. Such a trap may develop in any group – also psychoanalytic. In other words, when keeping the fundamentals in mind, the danger is that this may develop into a belief in fundamentals, and as with any belief, an atmosphere may develop where fundamentals should not be questioned.

When fundamentalist traps become a characteristic of a group, a conviction may develop that someone has deviated from the essentials, that they are absolutely wrong, that the influences from them will shake the fundaments and harm the cohesion of the group accompanied by a predominance of dualistic thinking and lack of rational argumentation.

Having thus stated that fundamentalism is an inherent possibility also on the psychoanalytic scene, I will, in the following statements, discuss fundamentalism on a quite different scene: a scene where the basic problems of fundamentalism may be seen through a magnifying glass. This concerns fundamentalism as it appears in political and religious movements, especially in present Islamist movements. On this basis, one may get a clearer view of the relation between fundaments and fundamentalism.

Islamism and xenophobia; suitable partners?

Fundamentalism is not only seen in religious movements and fundamentalism leading to violence has a long history. Nazism and Stalinism being prime examples in the last century. The genocides of the last century were much more violent and deadly than today's Jihadism: the Armenian genocide, the Jewish and Roma genocide, the Kampuchean genocide, the Maya Indians genocide in Guatemala, the Rwandan genocide and the Bosnian genocide, to mention the most important. It is interesting that present Jihadist violence has created more public attention, more analysis and political concerns in the west than most of the genocides in the last century, with the exception of the Holocaust. This is certainly connected with the global aspiration of one fraction of the Jihadist movement, a global ambition quite similar to the Nazis' dream of the Third Reich.

The meaning of Jihad as it appears in the west is also worth noticing. In Islam, Jihad has several meanings, the most important being the internal fight to free oneself from bad thoughts/feelings, a sort of inner purification (Vogt, 1993). There has been a kind of coproduction between western anti-Islamism and the radicalisation in Islam that resulted in designating the outward, violent Jihad as practically the only known meaning of Jihad in the west. The concept of inner religious struggle, quite similar to the same in Christianity and other religions, has come in the background in the western reception of Jihad.

The radical version of Jihad may serve purposes on both sides. It inspires maximisation of differences, dualistic thinking that makes the other the bad other and lay ground for a reciprocal need to demonise the other. This has a historical background in western relation to the orient, to which I will return. One part of this picture is the fright-inspired movement in Europe that is stirring group anxieties of being invaded by something bad.

Different consequences follow from the extreme dehumanising practices relating to refugees that we can observe at Europe's borders and also in the growing xenophobia in Europe.

Xenophobia refers to a phobic attitude towards strangers or the unknown, that is, psychological attitudes, often embedded in a more loosely organised network of ideas, about groups of persons that are constructed as alien and representing something that may be dangerous for the cohesion of one's group. It arises especially when people feel that other groups, for example, foreigners/refugees, may threaten their entitlement to benefits they feel are exclusive for them.

Islamism or Islamic fundamentalism, on the other hand, refers to a more structured set of political ideologies based on religious fundamentalist Islam. It represents a religious-ideological view of the world and how one should live and organise society and entails clear ideation of "them and us". One of the most virulent forms was recently seen in the so-called Islamic State's genocide on the Yezidies, a religious minority in the Middle East (Varvin & Lægreid, 2020).

Common to both phenomena is a hostile attitude towards those who are outside, the strangers, and a concomitant fear of being negatively influenced. Both are organised as social movements that can result in hostility and also violence against those defined as "others", "strangers" and in the case of Islamism, "non-believers". Both are fundamentalist, but xenophobia often has a lesser defined structure of their ideation.

The Jihadist version of Islamic fundamentalism includes an expansionistic view; the different other should change or else be driven away, extinguished or cleansed. It is noteworthy that similar ideas also appear in the European xenophobic context (Borchrevink, 2012).

These are typically group ideologies and when they appear and dominate the group's ideation, strong underlying large-group processes seem to be at work and, when strong enough, a potential for violence appears. The underlying large-group processes are characterised by collective fantasies that have deep roots in the way groups function.

These "them-us" ideologies connected with Islamic fundamentalism and xenophobia seem thus to appeal to primitive fantasy levels shared by members of a group. These fantasy constructions are often related to certain developmental phases, especially adolescence (Bohleber, 2010), to which I will return.

The mental functioning involved is characterised by primitive and undifferentiated explanations of relations between self, group and the other, as formulated in the theory of mindset (Strozier et al., 2010). The ideologies and the underlying collective fantasies imply solutions to, or modifications of, an individual's or group's frustrations and material problems, thus their appeal.

Xenophobic and Islamist ideologies function as containers for these fantasies that are mainly formulated on a private, primitive level, and the ideologies give them shape and a place in the social order. The implicit and often explicit content of these extreme ideologies have moreover a fantasy-like form that is appealing exactly because they "touch" the individual's and group's feelings (e.g., longings, aggressions, etc.) contained in the shared fantasies. The promise of ideal solutions in these ideologies, such as the ideal future society, meets the regressive pull in these fantasies and makes it easier for disenfranchised individuals to join.

Fantasies are collective in the sense that many individuals in the same group share them.

Political narratives, exegeses of religious myths or other ideological myths contain narratives that appeal to and are congruent with such collective fantasies. When they are implicit, they function as a nonconscious force that, to a lesser degree, is available for reflection and change and may appear as given truths.

The relational scenarios embedded in these fantasies are often related to the group's historical experiences, especially centred around the present and past traumatisation, and may give meaning to actual and recent problematic experiences for the group and their members. An example was the myth of the battle of Kosovo Polje in 1392, where the Ottomans supposedly killed King Lazar and conquered Balkan territories, which was used by Milosevic as justifications for attacks on Bosnian Muslims (Volkan, 1997). In certain Islamic fundamentalist theory, the fall of the Caliphate plays a similar role.

The versions of history given need not cohere with the facts and there are often displacements of affectionate cathexis from other historical times. The effects of massive intergroup violence and traumatisation during World War II in the Balkans probably found expression in the ancient historical myth on Kosovo Polje as it was, in that context, possible to identify Muslims as a suitable enemy. One may then see a mixture of myths and historical facts in such situations where the lack of working through on a societal level of these groups' traumatisation has laid the ground for the later emergence of tensions and conflict between groups.

In conflicts with high tensions on both sides, interpersonal and inter-group processes may emerge that are determined by unconscious motivation and are expressed as strong interpersonal and inter-group psychological forces. The parties in a conflict may, as a consequence, act irrationally and against conscious intentions. By being demonised by the other party, members of the group may act in the image of the projected demons and behave in ways alien to their own ethical and political standards. In conflicts, opponents are thus cast in roles and positions that are not necessarily part of their own worldview or maybe only partly so. They feel and often act in terms of the others view of them and the other's agenda. The opponents may, in such situations, be highly dependent on each other in order to have their worldview confirmed. The religious-inspired dialogue between President Bush and Osama bin Laden after 9/11 was an example where both cast the other in the position as representing evil forces, thus confirming each other's religious position: "this is a conflict between the bad and the good". This again paved the way for the escalation of conflict and violence.

The development of fundamentalist mindset in its violent form is thus also a result of inter-group processes, a co-creation, rather than only a disposition of one or the other group and its members.

Psychoanalysis and groups

Conflicts involving groups are arenas for primitive mental forces; reciprocal projections and massive projective identifications; that is, the party who projects applies pressure (interpersonal, inter-group) to get the other to act in accordance with a fantasised scenario, which often involves distribution of roles as the good or the bad, victim or perpetrator (Klein, 1946).

The following picture emerges:

1. Political, religious and other intergroup conflicts with violent tendencies are, to a large extent, determined by underlying unconscious mental forces acting both on an individual and a group level
2. The unconscious motivational forces are organised on primitive mental levels (undifferentiated and not well-structured) and involve fantasies that may be shared by many people in a group or community
3. The content of these fantasies is often related to common life themes such as sibling rivalry, struggle to distinguish between what is good and bad or themes related to separation and individuation. That is, life themes that, under normal circumstances, are worked through and more or less possible to overcome may be magnified and made part of the group's collective consciousness (Bohleber, 2010). Related to sibling rivalry, one may see different themes becoming a preconscious or unconscious part of a group's mentality: "the other got more than I, he was treated favourably, or he even cheated in order to get advantages". When these common fantasy themes are organised by a religious-political ideology, they can develop into an emotional force supporting these ideologies. An example is xenophobic ideation on how the foreigners "steal our jobs and fuck our women"
4. The collective memory of groups and nations of past traumatisation and humiliations may also determine fantasies of a more violent kind, concerned with revenge and rectification of wrong-doings. This may add a more severe and destructive character to these fantasies
5. Cultural, political and religious ideologies and discourses may inspire individual and collective fantasies by giving form and

content to pain and frustration, for example, in defining the guilty, the enemy etc. The ideologies and political rhetoric may, however, also be projection screens for the individual's and the group's fantasies which then, in turn, take on a more violent character marked by primitive mechanisms such as splitting and projections, scapegoating, dehumanisation of the others and so forth. Such ideologies may thus organise a group's identity and supply identity themes for the individual in regressed mass-psychological situations

6. The collective fantasies represent in themselves strong emotional/psychological forces. When they are organised within a context of religious-political ideologies, they may become social forces determining the way conflicts are solved or not solved and have an influence on whether the crisis escalates or not

I will relate these propositions shortly to Islamic fundamentalism and xenophobia in the European context.

Europe and Islam

Islam, has for centuries, been part of the European religious and cultural context. The specific xenophobic characteristic of European's relation to Islam, Islamophobia, is, to a large degree, a matter of relations within the European community. The tension between western culture and Islam or Islamism does not, according to this line of argument, represent a clash between civilisations but rather social and historical conflicts in Europe as well as internal conflicts and contradictions within Islam (also in Europe).

Meddeb, an Arabic intellectual and Muslim, describes the present Islamic fundamentalism, as a result of "The malady of Islam", that is; an overall intellectual deterioration within Islam, where ideologies alien to the intentions within the Quran and the corpus of texts that represents these intentions are used for political purposes that has more to do with the cohesion of the group, the Umma, than with developmental possibilities within Islam (Meddeb, 2003). According to this view, we are dealing with tensions, not between them and us, Islam and the west, but the basic question concerns rather a contradiction between modernism and traditionalism. This has been a theme that has been important in the west, especially in relation to

National Socialism and earlier in relation to "anti-enlightenment" and anti-modernistic movements (Burama & Margolit, 2004).

Europe's relation to Islam has a long history of scepticism and fear, reaching back to medieval times. There has been an attitude towards Islam marked by projections of aggression and mysticism. "For a very long time the Christian West perceived the Muslims as a danger before they became a problem", remarked the historian Maxine Rodinson (cited in Geisser, 2004, p. 38). In mediaeval times, Europe needed, according to this line of reasoning, a common enemy in the process of achieving its religious and ideological unity. An image of this medieval enemy was reinvented and achieved special political force during the ethnic cleansing and genocide in the Balkan war in the '90s (Glenny, 1999).

After a period of enlightened interest in Islam in the 17th and 18th century where the picture of Islam emerged as exemplary of tolerance, moderation and open-mindedness, a fearful image of Islam again emerged in the 19th century that involved danger and threat to western values. The traditional theological consideration (Jihad vs Crusaders) and the need to protect and unify Christian identity prevailed as a trend through the centuries. In the last century, a more "modern" and maybe stronger form of Islamophobia emerged in different parts of Europe, especially with the increase of Muslim communities in Europe. According to the European Monitoring Centre on Racism and Xenophobia, this new Islamophobia is characterised by an increase in physical violence and of anxiety and hostility with some right-wing parties using the fear of Islam for populist purposes (Crickley & Winkler, 2006).

There is an obvious confusion regarding differences and nuances in Islam and vulnerable refugee groups easily become prey to prejudices and unnecessary restrictions in this context.[2]

European Islamophobia has gained strength from the development of Islamic fundamentalism. In its extreme forms, as for example advocated in the writings of Qutb of The Muslim Brotherhood, the west, especially the city-culture, is portrayed as a sinful place with corrupt people only hungering for wealth and pleasure (Heine, 2002; Laqueur, 2001; Serauky, 2000). The Islamic state governed by Sharia is, on the other hand, portrayed as the ideal way of organising society, a place where all needs are satisfied. Based on a fundamentalist reading of the Qur'an, this rhetoric claims that Islamic law shall "triumph on the scale of all humanity for such law is considered the ultimate expression of divine truth" (Meddeb, 2003, p. 157). Taken in its extreme, which some Islamist groups do (especially IS), this implies the horrifying possibility of wiping out all those who will not accept this "divine truth".

Anti-modernism and Europe

The present conflict with Islam in the European context masks a conflict or tension between modernism and anti-modernism or traditionalism. Bohleber argues that anti-modernism has long roots in European culture and he describes similarities between basic ideological claims and fantasies in the Nazi ideology and Jihadist ideology: a myth of an ideal past, a utopian dream of the perfect society, defence against threats from the "other" (from modernism and western influence) and a death cult (Bohleber, 2002). Further in both ideologies, there is a preoccupation with purity and blood: the development of a sense of entitlement and a concomitant glorification of victimhood and martyrdom (Buruma & Margalit, 2004; Volkan, 2003).

For Islamic fundamentalism as well as for the Nazi ideology, although in a different shape, one could add the subordination of women (and the distaste for women liberation) and the total rejection of homosexuality (Varvin, 2003a).

Burma and Margalit further argue that the image of Islam in Europe is heavily coloured by anti-modernism as it appeared historically in the European context. One may say that the European image of Islam is coloured by Europe's "repressed" anti-modernism. This is then taken over by fundamentalist Islam and finds its representation there.[3],[4] The anti-modernism in Islamist movements has inspiration and roots in ideologies of European origin and this "Islamic antimodernism" may, from the European perspective, be seen as the uncanny return of the collectively repressed.

Embedded in the ideological claims of fundamentalist Islam and National Socialism are collective fantasies concerned with the cohesion of the group, with purification and cleansing of the unwanted and dirty, of sacrifice and identification of scapegoats. Women in fundamentalist Islam are seen as both sexually provocative and dirty and must accordingly be controlled. In Nazi ideology, women were to a certain degree idealised but nonetheless controlled, which is the other side of the same coin. Furthermore, there are fantasies of melting together with the almighty as an aim for the whole group and, in the case of sacrifice and martyrdom, unification with God in paradise. Ruth Stein, in her analysis of Atta, one of the terrorists of 9/11, called this vertical desire for God a homoerotic bond to the almighty (Stein, 2003b).

Adolescence and fundamentalism

Bohleber claimed that these fundamentalist fantasies are concordant with mental processes in late adolescence (Bohleber, 2002). Identity-seeking and identity problems, together with a tendency to regressively adhere to group norms, are characteristic of this period in life. The need to find representatives for ego ideals other than those of the parents, together with the need to split off unwanted, shameful aspects of the self, may ease adherence to totalitarian groups with charismatic leaders.

In traditional Islamic societies, the group, clan or family play a more important role than in western culture. Man belongs to the Umma, comprising all Muslim or rather all "humanity". The late adolescence process may therefore be different in this context in that belonging to the greater family of Muslims, rather than a drive towards individualism, may become the aim of becoming a grown-up. The main task for boys or young men in the Islamic context is the transition from being a son in the family to being head of one's own family. For women, this often means transition from subordination under father to the same under the husband. For this transition to happen, certain societal conditions must be present; first and foremost, the ability to bring income to the family.

The very high unemployment rate in Muslim countries and among Muslims in the European context makes the transition to manhood/womanhood difficult and sometimes filled with impossible dilemmas for young Muslims (Herzinger et al., 2002). The material conditions to fulfil the cultural tasks are not available and one can see a prolonged late adolescence stage full of material and instinctual frustrations. In addition, there are wars with atrocities towards the civilian population, injustice and persecution, which affects many and also represent possibilities for identification with the oppressed for those not directly affected.

This situation represents fertile ground for ideologies that have "secure" explanations and promise solutions to frustrations. At present, fundamentalist ideologies, with their tendency to place the guilt on others and thus support a passive-aggressive attitude, seem to be a tempting alternative for many young Muslims and maybe especially for the more disenfranchised who have been living on the margins with no secure identity as has been the case with many IS-terrorists in Europe.

There are striking similarities between ideologies of Islamist groups and right-wing vigilante groups and it is also significant that Islamophobia and xenophobia are highly represented in the younger generations in Europe and markedly in groups marginal to the labour markets. A study of German youth during the nineties showed furthermore that xenophobic attitudes in these marginalised groups were often established in early adolescence and did not change significantly in the next ten years or so (Boehnke, 1998).

How to become a killer?

Religious-political ideologies offer solutions to frustrations on individual and group level. They not only organise the group's way of thinking, but they also organise the inner mental space of the individual and influence unconscious processes on a group level. That is, they contribute to the formation of the group's and the individual's identity and give motivation for action and also long-term strategies. Collective fantasies and ideologies are structured as relational scenarios; there are antagonists and protagonists in a drama involving projective processes. At this primitive level, an important aim is to avoid unwanted aspects of self, get rid of guilt and a need to portray the other as dirty, sinful and so forth.

The development of a jihadist or terrorist fundamentalist mindset where one is prepared to kill for the sake of the "good" goes somewhat beyond these theorisations. There are certain processes that make the ordinary man a killer that happens outside the ideological level and even beyond most known mental processes. Browning's study of the ordinary men of the Hamburg police battalion who willingly engaged in the savage murdering of Jews in the eastern part of Europe during Nazi occupation testifies to this (Browning, 1998). Most of them were not active politically, but they had learned, of course, that Jews were bad through year-long propaganda. In Rwanda, the Tutsis were called cockroaches, an effective way of dehumanising them in a "milk-drinking country where everyone knew that cockroaches in the milk made it undrinkable.

The Norwegian mass murderer Breivik's testimony on the difficulties he had with the first murder and how it became "easier" afterwards testifies to an inherent primitive process in the mere act of killing (Varvin, 2013a). Reports from killings in concentrations camps during the Balkan war revealed how killing could be an escape from remorse and guilt in that the suffering victim became the representative of primitive guilt, which thus, magically, could be removed by exterminating him or her (Varvin, 2001). The willingness to kill or the act of killing contains complex dynamics that cannot be subsumed only under a theory of the fundamentalist mindset. Space does not allow discussing this further.

Conclusion

I started with some questions: does fundamentalism basically concern the fundaments of a religion, a political ideology, a scientific discourse? And is there a logical connection between fundamentalism and Jihadism or other extremely violent and mass killing religious-political movements?

A question discussed in this paper was whether fundamentalism, in its more malignant form, necessarily has something to do with adherence to the fundamentals or basics and whether fundamentalism, in itself, prepared for extremism and violence. It became obvious that it was necessary to look at societal and historical contexts and seek multiple determinants and also study unconscious processes in individuals and groups.

The analysis has brought indications that fundamentalism is more of a symptom than a cause or reason for the highly dichotomous tendencies one can see in groups and societies in times of crisis. There is a complicated reciprocal relation between real-life frustrations and problems on individual and group levels, unconscious forces, and the fundamentalist religious-political ideologies that flourish in regressive group processes.

The forces at all of these levels seem to reinforce each other. The experienced suffering and frustrations are in many ways real, based on historical and societal processes where atrocities on a grand scale have happened, where large groups have been molested or killed and where underprivileged have been subjected to structural violence, a sort of violence where the societal organisation and political processes give the poor and underprivileged even worse conditions (Galtung, 1969).

In this line of reasoning, fundamentalist movements are not only an answer to but also a symptom of socio-political conditions that have a long history and that have produced, and is producing, wars and inhuman conditions that mostly affect the underprivileged. Even if Europe is seen as the source of modern humanism, the practices, both historical and actual, against the others on the margins of Europe or in countries close by (Middle-East, Maghreb etc.) are, to a large degree, characterised by Social Darwinism (survivor of the fittest and the idea that bad things happen to bad people). How refugees are treated today testifies to this.

There seems to be a deep need in every society to define the stranger and to select others or groups as scapegoats or as the roots of societies problems. It may be that what binds people together is what they agree to hate. If so, humanity implies constant work to counteract this inherently violent tendency in individuals and groups. The need to curb these aggressive and destructive forces was also central in Einstein and Freud's dialogue on war. Einstein asked Freud whether it is: ".. possible to control man's mental evolution so as to make him proof against the psychoses of hate and destructiveness"?

Freud's answer was simple. While affirming "a drive for hatred and destruction", he held that the best way to counteract war and violent aggression is supporting "emotional ties between (a group of people's) members" (Freud, 1933, p. 201).

We live in a time where fundamentalism and thereby antagonism between groups is growing. This is especially evident in the precarious balance in Europe today regarding relations to Muslim groups. While the vast majority of Muslims live a peaceful and adjusted life, the general public's image of Muslims is more and more characterised by solid prejudices (Islam cannot adapt, Muslims support terror, Islam is a violent political ideology etc.). Restrictions and increasingly harsh conditions for refugees (often identified as potentially violent Muslims) prevail. Under cover of the war against terrorism, refugees and immigrants are rejected at borders and surveillance and other law-enforcement measures are directed against these aliens.

In short – fright of the alien and thus xenophobia is increasing and resulting in what Liz Fekete calls xeno-racism; a hostile and discriminating attitude towards foreigners (Fekete, 2009). This, again, support fundamentalism on all sides in what can be called a spiral of reciprocal interdependent fundamentalisms. "Emotional ties", then, weakens.

The arguments presented in this paper call for work on many levels to counteract this development and underline the need to take into consideration unconscious processes in their societal and historical contexts.

Notes

1 Based on an article published in: Scandinavian Psychoanalytic Review, 2017, https://doi.org/10.1080/01062301.2017.1386010. A revised version is published here with the kind permission of Scandinavian Psychoanalytic Review.
2 Concomitantly there is also desire for dialogue. The European Monitoring Centre notice marked differences regarding manifest xenophobia, violence against minorities in different countries. The Netherlands and Denmark are earmarked as countries where the conditions have deteriorated in the last years. It is interesting to note that more radical violent versions of Islam are present in Denmark but not too any significant extent in Norway, possibly as a result of longstanding, officially sponsored dialogues between Muslim and Christian organisations.
3 The influence was also direct. In Qutb, one of the founders of fundamentalist Islam was much influenced by the French Nobel Prize winner in medicine Alexis Carrel who wrote notoriously on racism and euthanasia. Qutb cited Carrel frequently and his ideas on modern barbarism (Jaahiliyyah) was similar to Carrel's conception of the barbarism of modern Europe (Walther, 2003).
4 Historically, antimodernism was represented in German romanticism in opposition to French cultural and political dominance, which defined modernism at the time. These views were accepted by antimodernist movements in Russia and in Slavic countries and were later embraced by central fundamentalist Muslim ideologists (Buruma & Margalit, 2004).

Part II

The situation of refugees

The enigma of traumatisation

Introduction

Refugees' destinies have, to a large degree, become associated with traumatisation. In discourses and research on refugees, one may see refugee's problems reduced to the problem of PTSD (Posttraumatic Stress disorder), often with multiple additional diagnoses. After many years working with refugees and in the Human Rights field, what has become evident to me is that refugees' and displaced peoples' problem are much more complex and that an understanding of these goes far beyond psychiatric conceptions and categories. Refugees have experienced severe losses; loss of close ones, loss of culture, loss of future possibilities, loss of home and refugees have in the last decades been treated in an increasingly inhuman way. This has not only happened because of persecution, warlords, bombings and other war acts, imprisonment and malignant human smugglers, but also as victims of increasing structural violence instigated and organised by societies and the international community. The prime task for western countries is now to find ways to hinder refugees from reaching a haven of safety in the western world. Border controls are prioritised leading to suffering and deaths on a mass scale where drowning in the Mediterranean is but one example. Refugees are placed in camps and detentions around the world with no security or hope for any stability and future hopes and where basic needs are not met. Children are separated from parents, women and girls are forced into prostitution and many suffer under slavery. Dehumanisation on a mass scale happens before the eyes of the richer part of the world in a situation of what may be called a grand humanistic and moral failure of the world community, especially western countries.

DOI: 10.4324/9781003206057-102

Chapter 6

Our relations to refugees

Between compassion and dehumanisation[1]

Introduction

Europe is now in the throes of a wave of xenophobia fomented by a noisy right-wing movement. When the pendulum swings back, what will stand out most in its aftermath, however, will be the passivity and denial of responsible people who were unable to face their own powerlessness over it. They will be remembered as bystanders and witnesses who failed to help and who allowed refugees to suffer under dehumanising conditions while the raucous right carried out its xenophobic practices.

This failure of the bystander/witness is central to the post-traumatic condition as it confirms the experience of helpless abandonment during traumatisation.

Refugees/asylum seekers have become the chosen strangers of the European political scene. They embody danger. They are perceived as carriers of "trauma" which, intrinsically and naively, is associated with a simplistic trope about violence: "yesterday's victim may become tomorrow's perpetrator". The mere possibility of being destroyed and the nameless anxieties connected with the atrocities that many refugees have experienced contribute to making the traumatised into frightening aliens ready to be cast in narratives about fundamentalist, fascinating and frightening Islam.

This essay will discuss how this state of affairs has come to be; how these suffering people, all of whom have lost their homes and who seek peace and new possibilities, have come to represent such a medieval image of a frightening and disruptive other. Maybe they arrived at a convenient time when rising socio-economic and psycho-

DOI: 10.4324/9781003206057-102

social insecurities caused anxiety and created the need for an external object, an alien force, to encompass this anxiety and the violence connected with it.

On a grand scale, refugees now seem to represent an encounter with the "Uncanny" – an unfamiliar but nevertheless known entity whose human characteristics are diminished or completely denied.

Refugees

We now turn to a refugee family from Iran, stranded on the Island Nauru in the Pacific after trying to enter Australia. Below is part of a letter the father wrote to United Nations Secretary-General Ban-Ki-Moon and Peter Thomson, president of the United Nations Summit on Refugees, held in New York on September 19, 2016:

> We simply trusted what they told us. Yet over three years later we are still trapped in Nauru, like rare animals living in an Australian-made zoo.

> After being brought to Nauru we spent almost 24 months in detention, before we were finally found to be genuine refugees. Since then, I have not slept even one night without having recurring nightmares of those endless months living in a hot, moldy tent. We became so alienated from our humanity, we were thoroughly transformed into a bunch of animals after years of living in the most appalling conditions possible (Herald, 2016).

Here is a letter from a mother stranded in a refugee detention centre in Greece:

1. I used to live in Damascus with a small family
2. We left because of the war unforgiving
3. and I had a good home and work
4. and we have not and will not give up because we draw our strength from the children's innocence and for the future
5. Although my dreams lost" (Kingsley, 2016)

Another newly arrived refugee told me, "The worst part of our flight was when my wife and child, 1.5 years, did not get out of train

somewhere in Europe. Suddenly the train left, and they disappeared".
This Syrian man was head of a family with children, a grandmother
and siblings. They had managed to get out of Syria and had lived in a
refugee camp for a time before they ventured by boat across the
Mediterranean. They tried three times before they succeeded in
passing the coast guard. The boat got lost and what should have been
a half-day journey lasted 12 days. This was less terrifying than the
extreme fear he experienced when trying to find his wife and child.
She could neither speak English nor any foreign language. When the
family, at last, was reunited, they continued, and by chance, ended in
Norway. "Then the worst was to come", he told us. Endless waiting,
inactivity, moving from one asylum centre to another. Everybody in
the family suffered, had anxiety and slept badly. The grandmother
was on the brink of breaking down. They didn't dare tell her that her
sister recently had been killed.

These are just a few of many refugee experiences. Although different, all are marked by experiences in their home country, by the
dangers during flight, and especially by how they were received when
they finally reached a supposedly safe country.

Having to endure extreme dangers during flight and then receiving
years of poor treatment in many European and other host countries
in the West can be illness-producing experiences for refugees. This
can result from long-term exposure to attitudes of fear and exclusion,
based on politically motivated xenophobia, and can best be described
as structural violence – a violence harmful to underprivileged groups
through intolerable living conditions (Galtung, 1969).

In Europe, 2015 was a year of profound change regarding "strangers" or "foreigners", especially refugees and asylum seekers. The
prevailing narrative became that European culture and cohesion were
suddenly being threatened by exposure to a massive influx of refugees
who were flooding the continent by boat, on the Mediterranean, and
on foot through the Balkans.

While it is true that many refugees arrived in Europe in 2015 and
2016, the magnitude is not exceptional, historically. After WWII, for
example, Germany took in roughly 14 million refugees. Several
hundred thousand refugees fled into Europe during the Balkan Wars
during the 1990s. What distinguishes 2015 and 2016 is the marked
change in attitude towards refugees and the intensity of actions taken
to prevent them from entering Europe.

This is a multi-faceted and complicated issue. Some countries have been extremely generous, accepting many who are fleeing their homelands (e.g., Germany and Sweden) while others, because of their location at the borders of Europe, have managed to find compassionate and effective ways of caring for almost all who have come, by boat, by foot or other ways (e.g., Greece, Italy, Serbia).

Strong political and ideological forces have surfaced in almost all European countries characterised by tremendous anti-refugee sentiment in the form of enormous suspicion, conspiracy theories and an outlook that devalues strangers. These expressions of traditional xenophobia led to attitudes and practices that are blatantly dehumanising.

On the other hand, many grassroots movements welcome refugees and represent an opposing compassionate trend. It should also be underscored that when refugees are granted asylum, they often meet with enthusiastic, effective and empathetic employers and NGOs whose well-run community integration programs offer them local employment. In spite of xenophobic propaganda, such integration methods work very well in many local contexts.

On the whole, however, refugees now encounter even greater difficulties during flight and upon arrival. They face malignant xenophobia, on a massive scale, by citizens whose governments increasingly condone or justify inhumane treatment of foreigners. And, they face severe deficiencies in health care, both physical and mental.

In my opinion, the treatment strategies for refugees, which have mainly been developed outside psychoanalysis, do so with an insufficient understanding of the plight of refugees and are, therefore, inadequate and problematic. Professionals, and to a large degree the public, identify the refugee's psychological suffering as problems that are "trauma-related". But their concepts of "trauma" and traumatisation are far too simplified and insufficient to fully comprehend or treat the problems that refugees face (Lesley & Varvin, 2016). As illustrated by the vignettes cited at the beginning, the refugee experience is complex and comprises much more than "trauma". "Trauma", in these contexts, tends to become less of a theoretical concept and more of an object containing the deepest of human fears and images of the most terrifying violence. "Trauma", thus, tends to become an uncanny object not only in political discourse but also, to a certain degree, in clinical discourse. I will return to this later.

Compassion and dehumanisation

The word "compassion" is Latin and means "co-suffering". More than simple empathy, compassion commonly gives rise to an active desire to alleviate another's suffering. It is a concept developed mainly in religious contexts and seldom used in psychoanalysis, except in self-psychology and by some relational psychoanalysts (see Orange, 2006).

Dehumanisation is a process that is simultaneously socio-political and psychological, in which fundamental human characteristics are disavowed in other people, such that others are perceived as less than human or non-human. Consequently, actions resulting from dehumanisation can threaten the basic rights of these "others" and endanger their lives and safety.

Dehumanisation on a societal scale, goes hand-in-hand with xenophobia (Kogan, 2017). When xenophobia becomes part of a political or religious narrative and is used to foster intergroup conflict, unconscious processes, both at individual and group levels, are set in motion. These unconscious motivational forces are organised at primitive mental levels (i.e., undifferentiated and not well structured) and involve fantasies that may be shared by many people in a group or community. Such fantasies are often related to common life themes such as sibling rivalry, the struggle between good and evil, or separation-individuation (Bohleber, 2007, 2010), but they are magnified in the xenophobic context where libidinal aspects are separated or split from aggression. Relationships and social fields of mutuality are transformed into fields of projections where the other is cast in the role of projected, unwanted parts of the self or of the group-self. As the other is perceived as "not human", not like "us", then inhumane and violent behaviour may be justified (Hott, 1974, p. 308) as fight/flight response (Bion, 1952).

When groups or nations have a collective memory of past traumatisation and humiliation, the nature of these fantasies can become even more violent, severe and destructive precipitating revenge or rectification of wrong-doings (Volkan, 2003). A demand for sameness and purity may dominate in order to free oneself and the group from "elements" that endanger its cohesiveness and unity. In response to, or as a defence against, individual or collective pain and frustration, for example, cultural, political and religious discourses may use paranoid rhetoric or tacit support for perverse behaviour to stimulate fantasies against a defined enemy or guilty party.

There is little evidence to support the claim that socio-economic inequality or protests against the elite are primary factors underlying our current rejection of refugees. Ideological narratives that use and provoke existing anxiety and also incite aggressive impulses play a more significant role (Turner, 2015).

Current situation of refugees

In May 2017, more than 65 million people were displaced worldwide due to conflict and persecution (this includes refugees and internally displaced people or IDPs. In December 2020, the number is approximately 80 million people). Of these, 21.3 million are refugees, over half of whom are under the age of 18. There are also 10 million stateless people who have been denied nationality and access to basic rights such as education, healthcare, employment and freedom of movement. Approximately 34,000 are displaced every day (UNHCR, 2016). One out of every 133 people in the world today is displaced. Numbers have since increased. In June 2020, there were 79.5 million forced migrants. 45.7 million people are internally displaced, and 34.1 million have been forced to emigrate (UNHCR, 2020). In the years 2012 to 2017, 50 families in Syria were displaced daily and we are now seeing unimaginable suffering due to indiscriminate attacks on civilians. The suffering due to war and persecution is enormous and we can expect serious consequences of this massive traumatisation in the years ahead, especially for coming generations.

For refugees, flight has become increasingly dangerous and death tolls are rising (UNHCR, 2016). Women are raped and abducted for prostitution, men are killed, children are violated and forced into the sex industry or slavery (there is increasing evidence that human trafficking networks cooperate with organised crime (Europol, 2016)), and many victims are maltreated and/or tortured by police, border guards or organised crime during flight (Jovanović et al., 2015).

Conditions for refugees upon arrival are growing worse. Stranded in the refugee camps of Greece, Italy, Serbia and Australia, thousands must survive with little or no access to health care, poor sanitation, insufficient food and minimal human concern. In refugee camps near war zones, conditions have worsened since 2015 when UNHCR budgets were cut by more than half (Clayton, 2015). Many describe their conditions after arrival, even in more affluent countries, as the worst part of their refugee journey, as we can see in the stories described earlier in this paper. On a daily basis, they face long waiting times, bureaucratic red tape, inactivity, and the possibility of being forced to return to their homelands. It is described by many as mental torture.

Refugees who arrived in Europe in 2015 represented less than 0.1% of the total European population, underscoring the fact that images showing waves of refugees or foreigners flooding the continent are grossly exaggerated.

I could go on describing the situation by listing statistics or quoting refugees my research team has interviewed, but I think this gives a fairly accurate picture of the humanitarian catastrophe in Europe is and with which it is clearly unable to cope. It represents a moral collapse of European humanitarian values and adherence to human rights. This situation did not, however, emerge overnight. Its political roots have developed over decades.

Short note on the history of refugees

Refugees or stateless people, as they were called after World War I, had few rights and no international laws or conventions were regulating their treatment and care. They were also then by many seen as a danger and fears were similar to what we see today, but mostly directed toward Jewish refugees. It was said that if one opened the door to Jewish refugees from Nazism, floodgates would open and cause an influx of hundreds of thousands more Jews from Eastern Europe (Loescher, 1993). As we now know, putting those ideas into practice had deadly consequences.

Ambivalence and scepticism have always characterised some individual and national attitudes towards refugees. However, at different times these characteristics may have been tempered or even dominated by more protective and welcoming positions and practices.

With the founding of the League of Nations in 1920, the Commission for Refugees was established on 27 June 1921. Among other forms of assistance, the "Nansen-Passport" was created to give the stateless some official recognition (Britannica, 2016). Even after the establishment of the United Nations Convention on Refugees in 1951, ambivalence continued. In general, attitudes and practices regarding refugees are highly dependent on current ideological and political priorities. Hungarian refugees were basically welcomed in 1956, while later groups, for example, those coming from Afghanistan, are now met with closed doors.

For decades, fleeing one's country and organising entry into another has been the sole responsibility of the refugees themselves (except those under the United Nations quota system). Over time, this has caused the creation of a huge, well-oiled human trafficking machine, now a significant profit centre for organised crime (Europol, 2016). It is fair to say that attitudes in the West fostered the development of these horrific human smuggling practices, which is now so vociferously decries and condemns.

For a long time, right-wing propaganda has identified refugees or migrants with Islam. Flourishing conspiracy theories warn of the dangers of Islam taking over Europe and instituting Sharia Law, and refugees are often pictured flooding European borders on masse. Less extreme versions of this narrative have gradually become mainstream and even political parties that claim to be social-democratic now practice what they call "strict and just" policies towards refugees, with closed borders and massive rejection.

A fearful narrative about Islam is increasingly dominating the political scene. These narratives of fear and the ideation and collective fantasies moulded on their themes have roots in European History.

Europe and Islam

Islamism or Islamic fundamentalism, as we know it both in Europe and elsewhere, does not signify a "clash between civilizations" but instead represents internal conflicts and contradictions within Islam, determined by historical, cultural and social contexts also rooted in Western history. Meddeb, an Arabic intellectual and Muslim, analysed present-day fundamentalism as the result of a "malady" within Islam: namely, a generalised intellectual deterioration, such that ideologies alien to the intentions of the Qur'an are used for political purposes having more to do with the cohesion of the group, than with the spread of Islam (Meddeb, 2003). According to this view, we are not dealing with tensions between them and us, Islam and the West, but more between modernism and traditionalism. This is a theme that has been important in the West, especially in relation to National

Socialism and the rise of Nazi Germany and earlier in relation to the reactionary "anti-enlightenment" and anti-modernistic trends, which incorporate themes from 18th century Romanticism.

Europe's relationship to Islam is steeped in a long history of scepticism and fear, marked by projections of aggression and mysticism as far back as medieval times (Geisser, 2004). Back then, Europe needed a common enemy to achieve religious and ideological unity. The image of this medieval enemy re-emerges from time to time. In the 19th century, a fearful picture that involved danger and threat to Western values emerged once more, and later, in the ethnic cleansing and genocide of the Balkan wars, malignant anti-Islamic activities developed in tandem with an ultra-nationalistic ideology (Volkan, 1996).

The traditional theological contest between Islam and Christianity (Jihad vs Crusade) and the need to protect and unify a European Christian identity have prevailed for centuries. According to the European Monitoring Center on Racism and Xenophobia, as the number of Muslim communities in Europe has increased in the last 50–60 years, so has xenophobic fear and violence.

European Islamophobia has gained strength as a result of the recent development of more radical forms of Islamic fundamentalism, which portray the West, especially its urban culture, as sinful. In these ideologies, large cities are believed to be filled with corrupt people hungering only for wealth and pleasure (Heine, 2001, 2002; Laqueur, 2001; Serauky, 2000). On the other hand, the Islamic State, governed by Sharia Law, is seen as the ideal way of organising society—one portrayed as a place where all needs are satisfied. Islamists claim that Islamic law shall "triumph on the scale of all humanity for such law is considered the ultimate expression of divine truth" (Meddeb 2003, p. 157). Taken to its extreme, as exemplified now by the so-called Islamic State (ISIS), this implies the horrifying possibility of either converting or killing anyone who does not accept this "divine truth". Central parts of this type of ideology are found in Europe as well.

Anti-modernism and Europe

Bohleber described similarities between basic beliefs and fantasies in Nazi ideology and those found in religious/political fundamentalist ideology (Bohleber, 2002). Common among them is a myth of an ideal past, a dream of the perfect utopian society, a need to defend against external threats (e.g., modernism and Western influence) and a death cult. Additionally, both are preoccupied with purity and blood, a sense of entitlement and a concomitant glorification of victimhood and martyrdom (Volkan, 2003), and also the subordination of women and rejection of homosexuality.

Burma and Margalit claim that antagonism against modernism was deeply rooted in European culture, well before the Nazi cult. As a parallel to "Orientalism" (the study of the West's representations of the East – in art, etc. – as culturally inferior), they developed Occidentalism (the study of the East's representations of the West) and claimed that anti-modernism in Islamic fundamentalism borrowed from discourses that aroused European opposition to the enlightenment (Burama & Margolit, 2004).

Embedded in these ideological beliefs are collective fantasies of group cohesion of purification and cleansing (of the unwanted or dirty), of sacrifice and of scapegoats. Women are seen as both sexually provocative and dirty and have to be controlled. Furthermore, there are fantasies of becoming one with the group through a holy quest and, in the case of sacrifice and martyrdom, unification with God in paradise.

It follows from this that Islamism and Islamophobic and xenophobic fantasies have similar or parallel roots in ideologies that oppose modernism (and now globalisation) and that this has historical Western roots in anti-enlightenment movements.

The growing xenophobia in Europe parallels similar trends in the orient, especially in Islamic extreme fundamentalism's fearful image of the modern West. Victims of this "ideological clash" are, among others, the refugees who now find themselves in painful conditions in camps or detention centres in southern Europe and elsewhere.

This anti-modernistic image of foreigners influences how refugees are perceived in Europe. Are there echoes of this fearful imagery in clinical practice, as well? In the following section, I will discuss this question but limit myself to a few aspects of the care and treatment that refugees receive and what may be relevant for psychoanalysis and the psychoanalytic response to the present crisis.

Posttraumatic processes

As a rule, refugees live under circumstances that are unsuitable for healthy development and, more often than not, conditions that cause illness. Preventive measures and treatment that could be implemented upon arrival are often unavailable. For example, identifying the most vulnerable groups might be helpful but seldom occurs, so mothers with small children, pregnant women, torture survivors, elderly, who could be helped by such measures, seldom get it (NRC & Oxfam, 2017; Turner, 2015; UNHCR, 2017).

Clinicians often identify refugees as persons who have experienced "trauma" or as persons with "trauma". Furthermore, in psychoanalysis, using the word "trauma", is in and of itself, highly problematic because the word implies something static and reified, like a "thing" in the mind, and this usage tends to divert attention from the dynamic and reorganising processes in the traumatised person's mind, body and relationships with others that occur after having been exposed to atrocities (Oliner, 2014) and it coheres with mechanistic models of the mind (van der Hart et al., 2006). Post-traumatic processes depend on the level of personality organisation, on earlier traumatising experiences, on the circumstances during the atrocities, themselves, and, most importantly, on how the survivor is responded to afterwards (Classen et al., 2006; Keles et al., 2016; Opaas et al., 2015; Opaas & Varvin, 2015b; Varvin & Rosenbaum, 2003a; Vervliet et al., 2013). It is the individual's responses to the atrocity, as well as the responses of others and society as a whole, which will, to a large degree, determine the fate of the traumatised person or group. Convincing research has confirmed the importance of responses to the traumatised afterwards, beginning with Hans Keilson's seminal work on Jewish children survivors after the World War II and continuing with later research (Gagnon & Stewart, 2013; Keilson & Sarpathie, 1979; Simich & Andermann, 2014; Ungar, 2012).

Traumatisation and its responses: a short exposition

Traumatised people struggle with mental and physical pain, which is often difficult for them to understand or put into words. Their pain may be expressed as a dissociated state of mind, as physical pain or other somatic experiences and dysfunctions, as overwhelming thoughts and feelings, as behavioural tendencies and relational styles, and as ways of living. The effects of both early and later traumatisation may show up in the symptoms of many diagnostic categories, of which PTSD is just one. Other manifestations of traumatisation psychiatric illness may include depression, addiction, eating disorders, personality dysfunctions and anxiety states (Leuzinger-Bohleber, 2012; Purnell, 2010a; Taft et al., 2007a; Vaage et al., 2010; Vitriol et al., 2009).

Common to these manifestations are deficiencies in the representational system related to the traumatic experiences. These experiences are painfully felt and make their impressions on the body and the mind without, however, being inscribed in the mind's life narratives. They are either not symbolised at all or deficiently symbolised, in the sense that they cannot be expressed in narratives in such a way that meaning can emerge and be reflected upon. The traumatic experiences remain in mind as dissociated or encapsulated fragments that have a disturbing effect on mood and mental stability (Rosenbaum & Varvin, 2007).

As a rule, extreme traumatisation (like rape and torture) eludes meaning when it happens, and it also precludes the formation of an internal third position where the person can create a reflecting distance to what is happening and what has happened. This inner witness, so vital for making meaning of experiences, is attacked during such extreme experiences and when an external witness who could contain and confirm the pain also fails, the traumatised person is left alone (Viñar, 2017).

The traumatised person will try to organise experiences in unconscious templates or scenarios that are expressed in different, more or less disguised, ways in relation to others and the self. When working psychoanalytically with traumatised patients, the analyst will inevitably become involved, through projective identification, with these un-symbolised, fragmentary and usually strongly affective scenarios related to the patient's traumatising experiences. This happens from the first encounter with the patient and is mostly expressed in non-verbal interaction with the patient. It may take a long time before these manifestations can be woven into a meaningful narrative with a historical context that relates to both traumatic and pre-traumatic experiences (Varvin, 2016a).

There is increasing evidence that psychoanalytic therapies are helpful for people who have been traumatised in comprehensive ways. This approach may help address crucial areas in the clinical presentation of complex traumatisation (Herman, 1992) that are not targeted by other so-called empirically supported treatments. Psychoanalytic therapy has a historical perspective and works with problems related to the self and self-esteem, enhancing the person's ability to resolve reactions to trauma through improved refiective functioning. It aims at internalisation of more secure inner working models of relationships. A further focus is work and on improving social functioning. Finally, as substantiated in several studies, psychoanalytic psychotherapy tends to result in continued improvement after treatment ends (Schottenbauer et al., 2008).

Trauma and the social context

For these un-named, insufficiently or never symbolised experiences to approach some kind of integration and be given some meaningful place in the individual's mind, they need to be actualised and given form in a holding and containing therapeutic relationship. This means that the analyst must accept living with the patient in areas of self-experience and memory that are painfully absent of meaning and at times filled with horror (Varvin, 2015, 2016b).

As a rule, however, this is not enough. Without societal, cultural and political acknowledgement of the traumatic events, working on them may be extremely difficult for an individual or a group, and feelings of unreality and fragmentation related to these disturbing experiences may continue.

One of the most difficult contributors to personal suffering in massive social traumatisation, (such as the Cultural Revolution, the genocides of Rwanda, the Balkans, or Kampuchea and now the Syrian disaster) is the feeling of complete helplessness when observing close family members, especially children, being mistreated, or killed, and not being able to help or protect them. This underscores the importance of Niederland's seminal insights on survival guilt (Niederland, 1968a, 1981), a theme very much marginalised in the trauma literature for years.

In summary: how extreme experiences will affect individuals and/ or groups will depend on the severity, complexity and duration of the traumatising events, as well as on context, developmental stage and internal object relations. Furthermore, it will depend upon the extent to which earlier traumatic associations are activated (Opaas & Varvin, 2015), as well as the support and the treatment offered after the event and society's responses to it in general.

Our alienated discourse of the traumatised

The extreme experiences bestowed upon today's refugees have repercussions on individuals, but also on group functioning and on the cultural anchoring of life in exile.

Extreme traumatisation is profoundly identity changing. Both children and adults experience it as something unexpected that should not have happened. It leaves them with a sense of deep helplessness and the experience of being abandoned by all good and helping objects. These profound feelings of helplessness and of being abandoned may continue during the post-traumatic phase, wherein the survivor – to a greater or lesser degree, depending on the circumstances – may develop a deep-seated fear of being alone in an impending catastrophe with no one to help or care. An inner feeling of desperation, and fear of psychosomatic breakdown, with a fear of annihilation, may ensue and much of post-traumatic pathology may be seen as a defence against this impending catastrophe.

According to Winnicott, extreme traumatisation, experienced as catastrophic, evokes primordial anxieties related to earliest fears of breakdown and doom, and life will be more or less impregnated by impending catastrophe afterwards (Winnicott, 1974).

As we see in Syria today, extreme experiences affect the totality of life experiences and the trauma concept is insufficient to capture, or even remotely describe, this situation, but may, however, give some relief to clinicians (and others) from the intolerable feelings evoked by extreme experiences. The term "trauma" becomes a place where alien and intolerable elements may be placed so that some meaning may be assigned to the uncanny experience evoked in the countertransference.

This kind of reductionism is also found in psychoanalytic discourse and very likely has to do with longstanding conflicts about trauma theory within psychoanalysis. At present, it probably also reflects the limited exposure of most psychoanalysts to such extreme phenomena. On the clinical level, a restricted and reductionist concept of "trauma" may reflect the fact that "trauma" has become an object (not a concept) of projection of uncanny fantasies. "Trauma" has come to denote an area for extreme anxiety, destructiveness and perverted Eros, something utterly alien but nevertheless known among others from the "fear of breakdown". There is, as Freud showed, a close connection with what is "Unheimlich" and what is "Heimlich" (Freud, 1919a; Rosenbaum, 2006).

Conclusion

Our encounter with refugees today implies confrontation with the alien and uncanny on several levels. On a societal level, we see chaos-like anxieties being stirred up and exploited by strong ideological forces that evoke a fantasy of salvation through purity and rejection of the alien. On group and individual levels, the anxieties dramatically evoke the conflict between compassion and rejection and, at the same time, undermine reparation and integration.

There is a strong desire for unity and purity behind these projective forces. The ideological climate that emerges, as described briefly, is rooted in European history. The conflict between traditionalism and modernity evokes anxieties, especially when confronted with the alien, represented in narratives on Muslims or Islam. At a deeper level, it concerns the eruption of the Uncanny (das Unheimliche) (Freud, 1919a).

Traumatisation implies an extreme meeting with primordial anxieties, and our relation to the traumatised person tends to provoke similar anxieties. Our attempts to theorise about the experiences of the traumatised may suffer in this meeting with the extreme alien and uncanny and may lead to reductionism on a conceptual level or to avoidance in clinical and other practices.

We are now seeing alienating processes on a large scale in Europe and the West, resulting in immense suffering. It is important that we be aware of similar repercussions affecting the clinical field.

Note

1 Published in *The American journal of psychoanalysis* 2017; Volume 77 (4), pp. 359–377 and reprinted here in revised version with the kind permission of The American Journal of Psychoanalysis.

Chapter 7

The present past

Extreme traumatisation and psychotherapy[1]

Introduction

Disruption and loss characterise the life of many refugees living in exile; disruption of the bond to family and culture of origin, the violent death of friends and relatives, disruption of culture-bound identity and, in the case of trauma, loss of the earlier healthy self and often loss of trust and hope including loss of hope for the future (Lavik et al., 1996). Those refugees who have undergone extreme traumatisation such as torture may, in addition, experience impairment of the minds integrative function. This has potentially far-reaching consequences regarding integrating traumatic experiences, mourning losses and organising their lives in a new context. In addition, many live with a second dissociated or split-off internal reality concerned with their experiences of massive traumatisation.

The traumatised refugee must adapt to an external reality, which is strange, and often confusing and an internal reality that is frightening because of intrusive memories and overwhelming affects. What we describe as posttraumatic conditions may be seen as survival strategies and adaptive solutions to continuing stressful internal and external situations. Many succumb under chronic post-traumatic conditions, but one also observes creative adaptation and accommodation. In spite of unfavourable conditions, few resources and powerful psychological hindrances, many manage their life in exile, learn the language and new skills at the same time as they support an extended family. They become survivors in exile as they were during their persecution (Varvin & Hauff, 1998).

It is a matter of dispute whether the word "victim" or "survivor" should be applied to those who have experienced atrocities and survived.

DOI: 10.4324/9781003206057-7

Both terms have strong emotional connotations and are moreover burdened with associations to adaptive or potentially pathological mental strategies. Seen as a polarity, however, these two terms express some of the dilemmas of the traumatised patient. The encounter with memories of traumatising experiences by, for example, entering psychotherapy threatens to bring forward the experience of oneself as a victim, thus threatening the image of oneself as a survivor. On another level, trying to symbolise and work through aspects of the traumatic experience may give relief but may at the same time provoke the unpleasant re-experiencing of meetings with the perpetrator (Varvin, 1998). Increased ability to symbolise and integrate is nevertheless seen as helpful not only for coming to terms with a difficult past but also for the process of working for a better future. In this article, I will develop some thoughts on the symbolising process and on the possibilities for psychoanalytic therapy with traumatised patients who are in exile.

Mohammed

The following example of emerging mentalisation may illustrate some of the processes involved. A man in his forties from an African country, whom I will call Mohammed, came to treatment shortly after he had been released from nine years of stay in prison under very harsh conditions in his home country. In this part of an early session, he has just tried to talk about his prison experiences (the therapy was conducted in English)[2]:

Vignette I.

Mohammed: Sometimes when I am feeling these pains
I don't feel any problem in my head,
but now I am sitting here I am feeling, I am feeling
eh this pain here on my head - this place. I don't
feel always..
Now I am feeling just on my part,
on this part of my head
I am feeling itching, something like itching,
some sort of unordinary feeling.
(....)[3]

Mohammed:	Its' really in the back of the head, and this his time I feel /// some sort of tension, some sort
Therapist:	yes, you feel some sort of tension now?
Mohammed:	Yes.
Therapist:	can you describe that more specific or
Mohammed:	(breaths heavily for 15 seconds) I don't know, it just came //. (breathes heavily) (one minute pause), please can I /
Therapist:	You want to lay down
Mohammed:	yes, (breaths)
	(.....)
Mohammed:	It's not a pain, it's some sort of feeling, then I feel pain in all my body, I am like a shocked personand eh something is running in my body, something electronic, some sort of feeling, I don't know why I am weeping, I don't know (breaths heavily, cries). I am not / I don't know what will happen I don't know
Therapist:	It's difficult to find what, I think emotionally many things is happening inside you, so eh which will take time to put into words and to find out what it is, and of course it is.. (Patient interrupts)
Mohammed:	it is a sort of feeling which come to me more and more, this kind of eh feeling eh eh, and it's / something coming more and more, the first time when I felt this pain in my hand and my neck it was some sort of a fear and I don't know when I feel this, when I feel like / I am worried and very tensioned and become very emotioned I am feeling <u>cold,</u> very cold (..) [Mohammed is now calmer and more coherent].

> *Mohammed:*   and then I don't know how I will be, what will
> happen and (sniffs),
> I don't know whether I will be treated or not,
> I don't know what sort of illnesses is inside,
> I don't know about my future.

In this sequence, he started by describing different sensations in his body. He was in pain, hyperventilated, felt dizzy and had to lie down. Gradually his experience got a bit more organised. He was crying and then started slowly to talk about his experience in the here and now. He then tried to describe his experience in a time-dimension; "the first time I felt this pain..." and in the last utterance, "I don't know about my future". From an almost pure bodily experience, the patient was gradually able to organise some aspects of his experience. It was not only the memories of his prison experience which was difficult to narrate but also what this meant to him in the "here and now" in the relations to the therapist. Further, he started to think in the context of his life, what would happen with him when being ill in exile, not knowing what "sort of illness is inside".

In this demonstration of the complexities involved in making extreme experiences mental, the following seemed to be involved:

1. Translating bodily sensations into mental categories
2. Organise experience in relation to the present reality; the relation to the therapist and his present situation in exile
3. Organise experience in time; what is past, what is present and how to think about the future

The relation to the therapist was organised differently on these levels. First, the therapist was present for the patient as a person who, by non-verbal means, supported the fact that he was in pain. At the second and third level, the therapist was "an other" for the patient, a person who could recognise him and think about him.

This sequence was from the early part of this therapy and the basic problems concerned with the emerging of traumatic experiences were central throughout the therapy. I see these three levels as an integral part of symbolisation and mentalisation of experience and will use this as a starting point for a discussion of these concepts. I believe they are of importance both for understanding the consequences of severe traumatisation and also for understanding what might be helpful in psychotherapy.

Symbolisation and mentalisation, a psychosemiotic model

There have been several attempts in psychoanalysis to give a more comprehensive understanding of the process from "raw" experience to mental representation. Freud's first attempts resulted in the concept of "representation" (Representanz) which referred to the representation of the drive, or the psychic expression of the endosomatic impulses (Erregungen), which specify the drive as a border-concept between the somatic and the psychic. The "Representanz" has in this conception preserved it's colloquial meaning (of being a representative), namely that the mental representative is representing the somatic in the psyche (Freud, 1915a, 1915b). This conceptualisation was broadened and developed towards a general theory of mental representation and symbolisation.

In the work "The Unconscious" (1915), Freud distinguished between the thing-representation (Sachvorstellungen/Dingvorstellungen) of the unconscious, the word-representation (Wortvorstellungen) of the preconscious and object-representations (Objecktvorstellungen) of the conscious. He struggled with the body-mind problem; how are affective-somatic experiences transformed into psychic experiences. The model of the mind to be presented here portrays how binding is a basic process whereby drive excitation, being a source of (automatic) anxiety, is bound to mental representation. In this way, automatic (overwhelming) anxiety may be transformed into anxiety that may function as a signal (see later) for the ego. Defensive measures may then be taken to avoid catastrophic or automatic anxiety. Implied in this is that the anxiety-provoking situation is interpreted and understood in some way which makes possible a differentiated action.

The question is how this binding process occurs. What characterises excitation (Erregungen) and the different mental representations (Dingvorstellung, etc.)? One might also ask where the significance and meaning of representations originates. As was seen in the above passage, the patient had little capacity to bind the (automatic) anxiety evoked by memories of his prison experience. Gradually, in the interaction with the therapist, a certain orientation was achieved where the excitation was to some degree bound to social meaningful expressions, such as crying (even though he didn't "know" why he cried), and certain anchoring in space and thoughts about present, past and future (what in semiotics would be called deixis).

The "binding of excitation" in the above example implied the mental as the interface between culture and body and the therapist participating as mediator in this process. In this example, the therapist mediated with words but also with symbolic acts (providing a couch for him to lay down). The concept of mentalisation has recently been evoked to describe this process.

Lecours and Bouchard (1997) refers to mentalisation as a linking function, "consisting of a connecting of bodily excitations with endopsychic representations" (Lecours & Bouchard, 1997, p. 855), and thus to a process of psychic transformation whereby "unmentalised" experiences are changed into "mental contents within a human interpersonal and intersubjective matrix" (p. 857). This is a precondition for these experiences to play any endopsychic role. Lecours and Bouchard develop levels of mentalisation and claim that all psychic contents may be placed on a continuum of "increasing 'mental' quality between the poles of somatisation and insight" (p. 857). They see this as an ongoing process where somatic excitation and thus psychic contents are constantly reorganised on different levels of mentalisation, for example, bodily excitation, acting, dreaming and higher levels of abstraction.

Creating mental representations thus means linking basic somatic experiences with images and words. In this process, the mental image of a thing comes to stand for the thing itself (thing-representation and word-representation (Freud, 1915a)).

What concerns us here is this ongoing process of binding excitation and reorganising experience, bodily and psychic. What we may learn from the study of traumatised patients in therapy is how these are processes goes both ways. In the above example, there seemed to be a progressive reorganisation process, even though it was very rudimentary at that stage. The question is what brings this process about.

The mute suffering of the body has been a central concern for psychoanalysis since its beginning. The body becomes the scene for the wordless drama of the traumatising experience. Matthis has developed a semiotic model for this deformation of the symbolising process (Matthis, 1997). The bodily pain, which she calls proto-symbol, is disconnected and the "word" as it may be spoken by the psychoanalyst, the doctor, by the patient herself or someone else may set in motion a symbolic working reaching a fullness which is a part of the chatartic representational work.

The basic confrontation in her theory is between psychoanalysis and the semiotics of Charles Sanders Peirce (Peirce, 1955). She uses Peirce's basically interpersonal model for the ongoing symbolising process to design a model for communication in the analyst-patient relationship. A sign stands in a symbolic relationship to the object only insofar as there is someone who interprets it as such. The same applies to the symptom. The smell of burnt pudding had a relation to a conflict of loyalty for Miss Lucy (Breuer & Freud, 1895), and when, during the cure, the symptom changed to «the smell of a cigar», the reference to sexuality became clearer. This could only happen by a change in the interpreter (interpretans) through the intervention of the analyst, whereby the latter symptom acquired a higher degree of symbolisation and then could be related more directly to Miss Lucy's basic conflicts concerning sexual matters. The model thus accounts for levels of symbolisation and some basic characteristic of the mechanism of the cure.

This may be developed further in relation to trauma. According to Peirce, semiosis is the ongoing process of signing where the interpretant of one sign is a sign that evokes a new interpretant. The interpretant may be a thought, a word, but also an action or affect. Muller claims that this ongoing process of signing is .. "almost instantaneous, and seems to lie at the heart of the 'talking-cure' and of all dialogue" (Muller, 1996, p. 35).

Peirce distinguished three types of interpretants; emotional, energetic (action) and logical (ideas etc.). Repetition compulsion is based on a coerced, enactive and iconic mirroring structured by signs, including the affect states of the other whose logical interpretants are not available to the subject's consciousness. This would, in other words, imply a dependence on the other by subordination (like in the slave-master dialectic) and no way to escape by understanding the others motives and ways of thinking, what Peirce calls access to the logical interpretants, that is a higher-order symbolism. This subordination seemed to be the case in the above example where the patient did not, or only gradually and rudimentary, gained access to language and could orient himself in time and space.

The ongoing process of binding amounts here to a process of linking, which in this context is related to semiosis. It represents the process whereby the individual is connected to culture and where experience is mediated by cultural symbols or signs. Coerced mirroring is a process where this link to culture and the social is cut off.

Traumatised people act as if they are partly outside the cultural realm of common symbols. Their experiences are often short-circuited by the process of cutting off the cultural mediation by signs; in Peirce's thinking, the interpretants of "logic" are eclipsed.

According to this understanding, trauma is pathological just because of this damage to the cultural and social link given by the signifying mediation, damage which curtails the process of transformation of bodily excitation to mental content and also the further reorganisation of levels of mental representation. The importance of the culturally mediated symbols for transforming what may be called bodily memories of trauma becomes more acute for a person in exile estranged from his cultural roots (I will return to this aspect).

Cultural symbolic expressions, including language, is the protection against the "raw experience", and is the medium where we construct our reality. The traumatised have experiences that are "beyond the imaginable" and not signified, badly signified (for example, only as images or bodily sensations or action-tendencies (e.g., fight-flight or freeze)), or only partly signified. The different symptoms described in the diagnosis of "Post Traumatic Stress Disorder" (APA, 1994), may in this context, be seen as lower-level mentalisation, which functions as protective devices in the attempt to avoid images of unnameable frightening experiences. In her theory, Matthis (1997, pp . 257–58) distinguishes between first, second and third grade symptoms. Third-grade symptoms are symbolic expression for something, e.g., a conflict, a memory etc. First-grade symptoms are concrete expressions of an underlying condition (e.g., appendicitis). Second-grade symptoms are experienced as alternating between first and third grade, that is, both as a direct concrete expression of something that is wrong and has to be fixed and maybe an expression with an underlying meaningful context. My experience is that the severely traumatised person experiences themselves in this uncertainty, not knowing what is going on and with doubts whether there can be any meaning assigned to their symptoms and sufferings.

In the above example, the therapist was mainly affirmative, but he also introduced a possible time-dimension for "finding meaning". This seemed to help the patient to conceptualise the idea of a future, although tentatively. The therapist's attitude may be seen as a basic and very common culturally determined response to pain reflecting a mother's holding attitude, which contains the possibility, that pain will disappear with time. It also represents the decisive function this primary relation has in providing a secure deictic (oriented in time and space) structure for the existence.

Mentalisation is here concerned with the process of transforming bodily excitation into mental representation in a cultural context where a sign, e.g., bodily pain, is transformed and given meaning in a process where the other is the source for the logical "intepretants" in Peirce's sense. One could say that the other is, in a very basic sense, necessary for giving experience meaning. In the context of psychotherapy, it is a relation where the therapist "gives" and the patient "takes in" and eventually is able to transform and use what is taken in.[4] (This process is, of course, reciprocal.)

The above is based on a model of a holding mother-infant relationship. This is, as is well known, a relation that may be disturbed by defensive processes and deficit ability to relate. On a higher level of mentalisation, the main concern is on how to relate to another and be able to experience oneself and the other as separate persons, that is, understanding in terms of mental states (Fonagy & Target, 1997). The dialogic process where culturally mediated signs, both verbal and non-verbal (imagery, sub-symbolic bodily signs etc.), are used for continuously making experience mental and thereby possible to think about and integrate is a part of this second aspect of mentalisation. The historisation of experience and the ability to construct a personal narrative of overwhelming experiences is dependent on this and is thus a later achievement in psychotherapy.

For the traumatised person in exile, the capacity for mentalisation (in both meanings described above) is important as part of two important processes facing them in exile. The first concerns the adaptation to and possible reorganisation of an inner reality that has been shattered by atrocity and the second concerns the adaptation to a strange (and often hostile) environment.

I will therefore, in the following, discuss these two aspects, the comprehension of which also is indispensable for understanding and handling the psychotherapeutic process with traumatised patients from foreign cultures.

Trauma and its after-effects

The concept of trauma is in psychoanalysis connected with overwhelming experiences. These have been largely modelled on the ego's reaction to acute events. In environments where people undergo repeated overwhelming experiences, often in a very aggressive, hostile and anxiety-provoking context, e.g., political prisons where torture is a rule, there are continuing forces that destabilise body and mind. The ability to cope or survive varies and different coping and adaptation strategies develop, which will determine the aftereffects. It is, however, difficult to separate the acute reaction from after-effects, as there is, in such milieus, a persistent process over time of overwhelming experiences, coping and adaptation and again maltreatment. The way of coping will again determine the reaction to new acute traumas. Living in an aggressive and hostile environment over time has thus to be studied as a separate factor that provokes coping strategies, defences and possibly personality changes. In the acute phase, the defences are principally set out of function. That would be a traumatic moment sensu strictu. This will immediately provoke defence and coping, and in a hostile context, these may become chronic in a special way.

The "reality factor" is important during the overwhelming experience. That is, what happened and how. This "reality factor" will, however, be subjectively apprehended. This subjective factor is relative during an overwhelming experience, dependent on age, developmental stage, context and support. The adaptations afterwards will increasingly be influenced by the subjective factor. Perception of and coping with experience afterwards will be determined by this subjective vulnerability. It seems, however, useful to distinguish between the immediate effects of traumatic conditions and the long-term adaptations, which may also be called survival strategies. The last concerns the mind's attempt to accommodate a changed inner psychic reality and a changed view on life and the external world. Aggressive forces in the social reality may, of course, make the distinction between the inner and the outer fragile.

There are thus (at least) two areas of importance:

1. The understanding of the traumatising process
2. The after-effects: the phenomenology of the post-traumatic conditions and the understanding of what kind of defects in the

mental processes produces the variety of changes following trauma. That is the adaptation of the mind to the fact of having experienced atrocity

The understanding of the traumatising process

Dissociation is an essential mental process in the adaptation and surviving during trauma when problem-focused coping (van der Kolk & Fisler, 1995, p. 304) is not possible. Dissociation produces the experiential quality of a mental flight. In a situation where the victim has no possibility to escape or to fight, there seems to be a surrender of one part of the personality to the atrocity while another part (or parts) is attempted preserved or saved as relatively unaffected. It involves compartmentalisation of experience and is thus anti-integrative (Bucci, 1997). This may take many forms such as fantasy travels, numbing of feelings, not experiencing the body, alternating mental states, de-realisation and depersonalisation to catatonic re-actions. These strategies may be seen as attempts to avoid the over-whelming of the ego by too many stimuli or attempts to preserve a stimulus barrier (Freud, 1920). The immediate consequence is that the experience is partly withdrawn from being represented and pro-cessed ordinarily. Instead, the experiences are recorded as raw sense-expressions, bodily sensations or more or less primitive relational models or emotion-cognitive schemas (Horowitz, 1986) dissociated from the organising influence of symbolic modes (Bucci, 2000).

Krystal demonstrated two models or theories of trauma in Freud's early approach (Krystal, 1978). In the first model, unbearable affects develop during the traumatic situation leading to the repression of perceptions and representations, which thus become unconscious. Affects are stifled and the experience cannot be worked through. The other model considered that ideas that were incompatible with the conscious ego, that is, unacceptable impulses, broke into conscious-ness ego and caused helplessness and set in motion defensive pro-cesses. The first model considers the representation of the experience as leading to a too strong affective reaction. The other underscores the incompatibility of the representation of the event. Both models were held in parallel until they were reconciled in the new theory of anxiety presented in 1926 (Freud, 1926b), where anxiety functions as a signal and when repression fails, anxiety may progress towards automatic anxiety compared with the situation of infantile trauma (Krystal, 1978, p. 83).

While infantile trauma is characterised by the development of automatic anxiety, a condition in which the ego is not developed and there are no possibilities to deal with (binding) impulses and excitations and the infant is thus rendered helpless, in adult trauma of the massive kind several ego-functions may remain intact. The infant becomes overwhelmed by affects without owning the adult's possibility to make use of defensive mechanisms and coping strategies and experiences a state of mortal terror or a biotraumatic situation (Stern, 1968). In contrast, the adult, owing to the existence of some integrity in ego functions, including the ability to dissociate, is unable to feel the almost complete regression and terror an infant may feel. The adult ego may, because of this, to some degree maintain a stimulus barrier and maintain an observing ego.

We may now specify this remaining integrity of the adult ego during the traumatising process as concerning the mentalising function. The observations related to signal anxiety show how early representation of stressful experience may function as models that may be unconsciously activated later, producing signal-anxiety, which may make the ego able to take defensive measures. In this way, mentalisation of early stressful situations may protect the ego from being overwhelmed. The mentalising function may be conceptualised as an aspect of the stimulus-barrier.

For the adult, the central factor in the traumatic experience is then the surrender in total helplessness and hopelessness in the face of a perceived mortal danger while for the infant, the experience of mortal anxiety dominates. Compartmentalisation of experience may produce a partial rescue for the adult but at the cost of often total surrender of the victimised part of the personality.

It is obvious that these statements must be tempered by consideration of the victim's age and mental development, the intensity, duration and character of the overwhelming experience and the circumstances during and afterwards. It is further obvious that the problem of metabolising affects lies at the heart of both infant and adult trauma and that the adult's surrender is merely "observed" by the more or less independently observing ego. This reasoning may help, however, to understand the surrender to the "internal torturer", characteristic of the post-torture condition (Sironi, 1995). This concerns those who repeatedly experience a return to the horror of atrocity by, for example, hallucinating the torturer. The first stage of this process is, as a rule, some factor (sign) in the surroundings, e.g., a smell, darkness, which reminds of the mortal danger and anxiety. The re-creation of the relation to the perpetrator is then a reproduction of the surrender. (The dynamic reasons for reproducing the torturer lay in the hope of achieving some control (even if only magically hoped for) because the total dependence on the torturer made him/her the only one capable of freeing the victim from pain.)

According to Krystal (1978), trauma results in a de-differentiation of affects, that is, "a loss of ability to identify specific emotions to serve as a guide for taking appropriate actions" (van der Kolk, 1996, p. 193). Trauma involves the body as well as the mind and affects as well as thinking and language. The regulation of affect becomes central and dedifferentiation of emotional meaning towards more and more primitive emotion-meaning schemas may be observed.

Affects do not in themselves need verbalisation to be known to consciousness and thus differentiated (Chiozza, 1999). The problem is not the naming of affects but the differentiation via working through emotional experiences. On one end, there are the transformative processes that change bodily excitation to mental qualities and on the other end, there is the culture as "supplier" of adequate schemas and symbols for making the emotional experience meaningful.

In man-made traumas, such as torture, both these aspects are attacked. The bodily pain inflicted may be the least devastating part of the experience, but the "automatic" anxiety produced by the mortal danger and the unpredictability of the situation, becomes devastating because it is not possible to link to representations other than very primitive fantasies. Being humiliated and dehumanised often produce a profound feeling of loss of hope and belief in oneself and others. Further, meaning and values are attacked, which makes orientation in time and space very difficult and reorientation through the use of culturally defined symbols impossible for many. The positive effect of being a "warrior" who expects the worst and thus is able, to a certain degree, to find meaning during torture has been amply demonstrated and confirms this reasoning (Basoglu, 1992).

There are few studies on massive traumatisation in adolescence. In my experience, this period is not to be equated either with infantile or adult trauma. Because of the strength of the drives and the relative weakness of the ego, it may resemble childhood trauma, and since the functioning of the ego may be relatively intact, it may resemble adult trauma. The main distinction lies in an understanding of identity formation in this period (Leuzinger-Bohleber, 1996) and in considering adolescence as the second separation-individuation period. Trauma interferes here with important developmental processes; the formation of the ego-ideal, the reworking of early attachments, the consolidation of gender and sexual identity etc. (This is illustrated in vignette 2 below).

Survival and coping during a situation where problem-solving behaviour is impossible involves mental strategies that become maladaptive afterwards. The consequences are manifold and only partially understood. Affect pathology is central. Semantisation of affects may describe the process whereby bodily excitation is connected with mental representation, verbal meaning and eventually narratives (that is, increasing elaboration of emotional meaning). Chiozza calls this "secondary affect", which reflects a tempering of the affects through the thought process. Full discharge is called "primary affect". The gap between primary and secondary affect may then be seen to reflect the discrepancy often seen when the traumatised person can tell parts of a trauma story while at the same time be severely affected by raw unmediated re-experiencing. The process between primary and secondary affect also corresponds to the process of mentalisation where stimuli and bodily experience achieve mental quality. The regulation of negative affects seems to be most troublesome for surviving victims.

This brings me to the after-effects.

The after-effects: the phenomenology of the post-traumatic conditions

What is seen in the aftermath of such extreme experiences is the person's adaptation to a changed inner reality. The host of symptoms, signs and personality changes described in the diagnostic lists are in this perspective representing different ways a person tries to deal with a disrupted inner reality. This is often a long term and chronic endeavour, and the prognosis has been described as dubious (Eitinger, 1973, 1980; Krystal, 1988).

Affect pathology implies disturbances in the transformative capacity of the mind and de-differentiation involves a reversal of the ability to work through emotional experiences. When in addition, lack of trust and hope characterises the traumatised person's relation to others and culture and society in general, a significant, and, especially for the exiled, problematic source of development is hampered. The needed cultural support, both emotional and linguistic, tends to be rejected. While the traumatising process involves the de-differentiation of affect, the continuation of this in the post-traumatic phase concurs negatively with the lack of available cultural support. The situation may for the refugee become a replica of the situation during trauma, where, in the example of torture, there was a constant aggressive and oppressive milieu and often an accumulation of traumatic experience. A vicious circle of defence, withdrawal and suspiciousness tends to become stabilised. Several studies have demonstrated the predominance of dysphoric or negative emotion (anhedonia, anger, hate, fright etc.) in survivors, at least in clinical populations (Eitinger, 1980; Hoppe, 1968; Van der Kolk et al., 1996).

Perception of reality and even reality testing may be affected. The traumatised person may, for example, be able to perceive outer actual reality according to the reality principle while at the same time, or consecutively, undergo a full-blown anxiety attack. On the level of primary affect, the traumatised person still lives in a world of trauma (re-experiencing the torture chamber and the concentration camp with accompanying overwhelming of undifferentiated affects). Here the perceptual categories at disposal are fused with mnemic symbols of the past. The mnemic traces of a traumatic experience tend to be static and rigid and dominated by frightening basic preconception. Something dangerous may happen at any time. This seems to be one of the basic experiences of trauma. Traumatic states induced voluntarily by other people, such as torture, tend furthermore to draw internal relations to good objects into this vicious arena.

Loss or damage of basic trust is a well-known result of such experiences. This points to the dimension of the other as a supporter of self-regulating functions, including mentalisation. By this, I mean the regulation, in this connection especially of negative affect, by an internal and external dialogic process. In this process, the prototype of which is the mother-infant relationship, communication on an affective level helps the subject to regulate and integrate affects (as was seen happen partially in the above clinical example). Because the traumatised person often withdraws and isolates him/herself, the availability of others – when own resources fail – may become foreclosed.

Commenting on the tragic story of a young Cambodian boy searching for his identity Laub and Podell (1995) demonstrated the devastating effect of this foreclosure of the other:

> The wish for life elicits no response from the executioner. No matter how much the Cambodian boy wanted to live, the execution would have proceeded at its own steady pace. The erasure of this primary empathic bond, the refusal of this most basic human recognition is always at the nidus, the source of massive psychic trauma. The breakdown of trust in a functioning empathic external dyad led directly to the boy's loss of internal communication with the "other" in himself. Without this internal "other, there can be no representation" (Laub & Podell, 1995, p. 991).

The understanding of massive trauma is here placed in relation to the other, both internal and external, and to the categories of memory, representation, symbolisation and mentalisation. These are seen as a dimension of the same process, namely the process of re-establishing a personal history and identity through the restoration of the inner empathic relationship (Kirshner, 1994; Varvin, 1998). In other words, a possibility of historisation through a relationship with the other. The other is, in a developmental perspective, not only nurturing and safety providing, but also the one who may structure the world, make it meaningful and predictable through representing a symbolising function which is then internalised. This perspective coincides with the semiotic model for mentalisation given above (Matthis, 1997).

The pain of an emotional re-experiencing, indispensable for establishing the knowledge of one's own history, places the survivor in an almost impossible dilemma. To live with the trauma means it's constant "knocking on the door" through the typical phenomena of nightmares, re-experiencing etc. It may only be held at bay with great cost's for psychical well-being, restriction of affects, re-somatisation, impoverished relations to others, depression, all the anxiety symptoms contained in the post-traumatic diagnoses, hallucinations and possibly psychosis. The wish for help is present but confronted with the possible empathic other, the confrontation with the executioner may appear and create anew the horror of experiencing oneself as victim. What lies ahead is then a complicated process of mourning. One might then say that the survivor, in a more acute way than what is usual in psychoanalytic psychotherapy, is confronted with the kernel of problem in the meeting with a possible empathic other in the analyst.

Trauma and exile. The trauma of exile

Extreme or massive traumatisation affects the ego or the internal object relations, but in addition, it also affects the basic assumption that the world is a safe and ordered or structured place. Man-made atrocity may be explicitly aimed at, and have as its effect, the destruction of the bond to the cultural and social community as well as damaging or destroying this community itself. Torture has, as its direct aim, besides the retrieving of information (which more often than not is useless for the interrogator), the destruction or destabilisation of body and mind. The person is no longer going to be able to feel whole and sane again and no longer be able to look upon him/herself as an ordinary human being. This may promote a destructive process, which also profoundly affects the group or community and the basic social safety structure, holding the group together, is damaged. (Mass rapes is a dreadful example producing this effect.)

When the survivor is expelled from his cultural community, thus also losing contact with his close and loved ones, this may represent a double disruption of the social bond or link and may in itself lead to the alienation from self and others. The survivor may bear within him/her the experience of his/hers own social and cultural context being disrupted while trying to establish a footing in a new social and cultural context. The resources inherent in culture may then be lacking both on a social level (the significant others are not there) and also on a symbolic level (a mistrust and feeling of disappointment towards own culture). Ambivalence against both own and the new culture often leads to a feeling of living in limbo.

How the survivor is met is decisive for the prognosis. Keilson and Sarpathie's study on sequential trauma showed how an ignorant attitude when the child survivor returned made for a bad prognosis and many represented crushing of hope (Keilson & Sarpathie, 1979). This then became the new phase in the process of sequential traumatisation. Generally, it must be said that the relation between background variables, including earlier traumatisation, and the acculturation process in exile, is complex and dependent on a host of different factors. The end result, however, may be described as different careers where the relation to the culture of origin and the new culture determines the degree and type of adjustment. This has important consequences for psychotherapy in that psychotherapy with people from foreign cultures not only is a process of integration of past experiences but inevitably also becomes a process where work on integration into a new cultural setting becomes central. Table 7.1 presents typical migration-destinies.

One may, of course, see different degrees and combinations of these variables and the table should not be read as static. It is, however, easy to discern in the clinical setting where a given patient may be in relation to these aspects. The traumatised refugee who feels rejected and deserted may have few positive expectations and easily end up isolating himself. Alternatively, highly idealised expectation on how to be received with a strong need and claim for compensation necessarily leads to disappointment and possible withdrawal. The own culture may be defensively idealised, leading the refugee to see no positive possibilities in the new situation. This, together with social forces tending to isolate the foreigners in social enclaves, may lead to the creation of separate communities with little contact with the surrounding culture.

From the above, it is clear that a deep-rooted mistrust often accompanies the survivor. Because of the traumas, actual relationships

Table 7.1 Exile destinies (Berry, 1997)

	Relation to new culture: positive	Relation to new culture: negative
Relation to own culture: positive	Integration	Separation
Relation to own culture: negative	Assimilation	Isolation

may be experienced in terms of potential harmful inner object-relationships. Displacement and projection may then distort new experiences. The situation is complicated by not only the open hostility many will experience but also by the structural violence inherent in the refugee situation. That is, there are built-in hindrances for creative adaptation to the exile-situation. One obvious example is the position of learned helplessness that many develop after spending a long time in asylum centres and on social welfare. For many, this may be experienced as worse than the prison experience where "the enemy" at least was known (personal communication from several refugees). This may be reflecting the experiencing of not being met in the sense of being recognised, but only in the sense of being attributed. One is met as a stranger, an unknown and not as a person. This contributes to the alienation caused by trauma, as Fichte says, quite appropriately: "Kein Du, kein Ich" (in Muller, 1996, p. 64).

In the semiotic and mentalisation perspective, this points to the necessity that the meaning given to an utterance, a symptom or a sign, can not only be a designation of what it may mean but needs to involve a recognition of the subject of the utterance. Many refugees develop what may look like a paranoid condition. This may involve fear that some agent may kill them but also often ideation about the inherent animosity of the inhabitants in their new country, a belief that someday they will be sent back etc. These complex conditions have quite another dynamic than ordinary paranoid conditions in that it is, in fact, something "real" that is happening, which is dangerous for the self. I am putting real in quotation marks to underline that this real is, of course, subjectively appreciated but nevertheless is rooted in how the survivor is met. There is a real loss of reference and recognition. And, of course, this may also be at the heart of other paranoid conditions. As Freud said, in every paranoia, there is a reality kernel.

Some considerations on treatment

The foregoing adds up to an understanding of traumatisation as a complex process involving the mind and the body as well as the relational functions. Trauma affects in addition consequent experiences but may also "nachträglich" affect representations of early object relations. Primary attachment experiences may be redefined (Varvin

& Dahl, 2000), recreating an early experience of infantile anxiety and thus deepen the lack of trust in others. A treatment approach has logically to take this into account by giving priority to the creation of a trusting relationship in the safe setting in which symbolisation or mentalisation may come about. Clinical experience emphasises the difficulty or impossibility of symbolising and working through certain horrifying experiences and many refer to metaphors like black holes to describe the central phenomena of extreme traumatisation (Gampel, 1999; Gerzi, 2001; Pösteny, 1996). Research has also demonstrated the difficulties involved when traumatic experiences emerge during psychotherapeutic work (Varvin & Stiles, 1999).

Symbolisation is not the same as verbalisation (Bucci, 1997). In fact, most of the process of symbolisation may be non-verbal and be represented as images, sound and smell and as procedural memory. Serious trauma may also, nachträglich, affect the procedural level related to ways of being with others, that is, the basic organisation of the relational experience stored in implicit memory.

The relational (concerning holding and setting) and interpretative aspects of psychotherapy seem then to serve different but related functions. The former in establishing on a basic level a safe surrounding for the reparation of trust and belief in the empathic other, whilst the interpretative level provides the verbal aspects through work with the understanding of the traumatic effects in the explicit transference manifestations. The severely traumatised person may, in regressive states, tend to experience the encounter with the other in terms of the internalised version of the traumatic experience. Often one may see a fluctuation between levels of internal realities and corresponding ways of perceiving and interpreting others and the reality at large. The trauma-related way of experiencing reality is derived from the encounter with an extreme non-empathic and hostile environment. In this mental state, there is often a concrete perception of the other as dangerous. The basic experience of primary affects (Chiozza, 1999) threatens and may be defended against by avoidance and restrictions of emotions. It is not possible to perceive others as having intentions, desires and purposes other than what may be harmful to oneself. This is the background for the tendencies to acting (withdrawal, aggressive acts etc.), paranoid ideation and also somatisation as a way of using the body as a container for, among other violent emotions. I suggest, therefore, that what may be curative for these patients is not so much a focus on the trauma story per se, but alertness and interpretation of these shifts in the mental states and helping the patient to understand how the here and now is perceived and interpreted in terms of trauma-related malignant object relationships. This will include strong attention to the non-verbal and prosodic level of communication.

In the following, I will present two case vignettes with a focus on some aspects of the treatment setting and technique.

Elements of a treatment-model

In my experience, the psychotherapy setting acquires special importance with these patients because prolonged stays in prison and often prolonged periods of hostile environments have eroded the trust in the stability and predictability of the everyday activities necessary for stable psychic functioning. A severe problem of many desolated refugees is the difficulty of continuing or re-establishing self-assuring and self-caring activities in exile. Daily rituals and self-care (food, sleep) are often disturbed, thus also hampering the ability to attend sessions and to have confidence in its frames. Rituals functions as basic signs in the structuring of experience and may contain unstructured or fragmented experience (Bleger, 1967; Kertesz, 1966; Sas, 1992b). An impaired functioning in these areas may lead to confusion and disorganisation and possibly psychosis.

The frame or setting of the therapy may often become the focus of attention and may become an important aspect of what is therapeutic in work with traumatised patients (Salonen, 1992). The stability and the security, which this frame implies, can be internalised and help the patient to achieve a feeling of safety and predictability.

I would also include here the basic dimension of the meeting with an empathic other. Research on infant development has shown how this relationship, including good-enough mothering, creates an environment for the child, an "average expectable environment" in the words of Hartman (1958), and which is a necessity for the stimulation and release of the patient's innate tendencies for growth. Besides working through traumatic experiences, it is in psychotherapy important to mobilise these innate tendencies and help the patient onto a path of continued development at any age (Emde, 1990).

The model for therapeutic action proposed by Modell describes two levels of transference which distinguishes between interpretative verbal level and the more silent containing and stability providing aspects (Modell, 1990). Interpretation proper presupposes the ability to reflect on oneself and one's experience. In this mode, the patient may be seen to have an experience of primary intentionality. That is, be able to see oneself as the cause of the behaviour and influencing the environment. The task is then to discover the meaning hidden behind the overt expressions. The severely traumatised often do not find him/herself on this level of mental functioning. Important aspects of the overwhelming experiences have not been mentalised and has thus not acquired any meaning beyond the value put on by primary affect (e.g., good vs bad or dangerous). Acting on the background of intention and seeking the hidden meaning is not the question and the subject find him/herself reacting to internal and external stimuli. The meaning of behaviour is not established. Before establishing meaning, however, the ability to organise mental experience must be re-established. The therapist may become a helping ego, necessary for regulating and organising emotional experience. There is often a constant failure to perceive and integrate outer and inner reality. This defect in the mentalising function indicates failure in the processes of the mind that underlies the representative function of the mind[5] (Fonagy, 2001). The therapeutic strategy and interventions must accordingly be geared towards different levels of the transference:

Three levels may be proposed:

1. Interpretation proper aiming at insight. 2. Elaborated interventions aimed at stimulating the processes of the mind dealing with affective experiences. This would include interventions aimed at "learning" the patient about mental states and also showing that the therapist has a working mind and is able to reflect on the experience of the patient. This would be mentalising in a sense given by Fonagy (2001). And 3., mentalising proper. This includes the linking of raw experience with symbolic levels and also the function of the silent, containing aspect where the therapy and the therapist provide a holding frame necessary for the linking function. In the example with the African patient Mohammed, the therapist worked on the last two levels.

1. Dependent/Containing Transference (level two and three).

This corresponds to the therapeutic frame and creates an analogy to a protective parental relationship, a holding environment (Model 1990). Within this setting developmental conflicts and arrests may be actualised symbolically, meaning that those aspects of the personality affected in the regressive situation induced by the trauma, e.g., basic trust (Erikson, 1950), may be actualised in the relationship to the therapist. The other is in this mental state perceived as dangerous, incomprehensible or both. The following is an example of how the work in this dimension helped the patient to gain more coherence of inner experience. This patient was quite regressed and was in the beginning hardly able to perceive the therapist as a human being:

Vignette 2.

Faridah, a Middle-Eastern woman had been brutally tortured in her late adolescence. In exile she lived isolated and constantly haunted by re-experiences and hallucinations of torturers and torture scenes. After two years of therapy, Faridah, began to gain some confidence in the psychotherapeutic setting. She had, however, great difficulties in talking because of a severe stutter, which set in as soon as her feelings got stronger (fear, anger, fear of anger). She also felt that the therapist knew all about her, so that she did not have to say more and attempted to create a situation where the mere presence of the therapist was enough.

She tried to keep the therapist as the all-good, all-knowing protecting parent, but often became very disturbed when faced with the ordinary tasks of a patient in psychotherapy. She had great difficulties in attending regularly. In the first two years of therapy, the main focus was on work with basic trust, as the therapeutic setting had actualised the conflict between trust and mistrust. A gradual widening of the aspects of what could be talked about led to a more trusting relationship. This also included the start of slowly "assembling" different aspects of her personality and the putting together of a fragmented experience of herself and of her history.

The setting and the basic qualities of the relationship, the meeting with a potentially empathic other able to reflect on her mental states, was the most important, but also the most fearful experience for her in these first years of therapy. Initially she almost tried to sit on the lap of the interpreter accompanying her in the early part of therapy, showing extreme separation anxiety. Faridah was unable to give a coherent story of her life and gave only fragments of her trauma story. As the ability to experience separateness grew, she talked about herself more coherently, also remembering parts of her childhood experiences.

Having faced the torturers and executioners in a living hell for two years, almost in total isolation, she had survived by holding on to the memory of her younger brother who was two years old at the time of her arrest. He was the only living being whom she could think of in her loneliness who had not let her down. In exile mother and the therapist gradually came to be regarded with some trust. Her psychic life was, however, for the most part dominated or invaded by her prison-life, experiencing almost every other relationship in terms of torturer-victim relation, repeating the pattern of surrender whenever a nameless terror approached.

Being traumatised in late adolescence, the therapy also involved working with phase-specific problems about growing up, being a woman, and looking at the possibility of becoming a mother and other themes related to her development.

She suffered a severe narcissistic disturbance with fragmentation experiences and a tendency to psychotic functioning. She was most of the time "reactive", perceiving others in term of a potentially violent relationship. She seemed to rely on sensuous cues such as mimics, tone of voice etc. When arriving at sessions, she seemed frightened and fragmented. The technique developed with her (and other) patients may shortly be summarised:

a. Affirmation (Killingmo, 1995) of mental states and accompanying sensations and to relate these to present experiences. This counteracted the inevitable activation of torture related emotional schemes

b. Active use of countertransference and use of analyst's self as a reflective and feeling person towards whom she could relate (I think/feel that you became afraid for...). This seems to enhance the ability to perceive and ultimately think about own and others mental states

c. Historical cognitive-emotional reconstruction. Gives a framework for establishing boundaries between then and now, and by implication – the future

d. Maintenance of the frame and adherence to the "rituals" of the therapeutic encounter as they developed

Affirmation of psychic experience (Killingmo, 1995) may be the most important mode of intervention for long periods. Affirmation, in essence, confirms the other's subjective emotional state of mind and also affirms the right to have emotions and thoughts. This implies a basic level of recognition and may be critical when the traumatised patient tries to deny psychic reality altogether. Affirmation is a type of intervention that may be expressed in direct interventions such as: "This seemed to be the only possibility you had..." but may also be contained in the way of phrasing and the emotional climate.

2. The Iconic/projective Transference (level one).

This resembles the classical concept of transference. Here the therapist becomes the recipient of projections of different aspects of self- and object-images from the patient's internal world, such as the punishing father, the incestuously invested mother, and the patient as victim (or identified with the aggressor). With Faridah, the therapist could at times be experienced as the paranoid-aggressive interrogator from the prison, which could be interpreted accordingly as an "as if" experience. The following example contains excerpts from a therapy where work on all levels was important but where the direct work on reorganising the representation of the therapist in the transference became important.[6] For this patient, the setting was more of a silent frame for the therapy, and more could be done directly in the "projective" part of the transference early in therapy:

Vignette 3.

A recurrent theme in the therapy of this woman, which I will call Francoise, was the fear of being made helpless; a fear of being manipulated and put in a helpless position, that somebody did something which made her powerless. As we shall see this was a many-layered problem that had its roots in her torture-experience when being in a concentration camp in a South American country.

The following is a fragment of this analysis concentrating on highlighting an early precursor to what was later to be a major transference theme. I will then present a key-session and some of what lead up to this session, where this theme was especially focused.[7]

In the third session the following took place:

Therapist: (...) Yes, I don't know if you have any comments to our last meeting.

Francoise: Yes I think it was last Thursday / afterwards that I ,, tried really to find explanations.
why I had come here .
but I did not.. (childlike, helpless)
I feel that I in way try to find explanation, which is based, in my mental condition,
but the way I experience it so eh,
it is not like eh, (small laughter)
this thing about normal and abnormal is very much discussed but ...
. But is has not been such terrible things or such ..
which may be like,...
that I have been afraid of being crazy!, to say it like
that, (anxious voice)
but more like sorrow and depression,
and more a feeling like of eh hopelessness,
but not so much because of the mental condition
but because of physical pains (aggressive tone of voice)..

She was expressive and the prosodic qualities of her voice had distinct variations that were interpreted as markers of different voices in her inner dialogue (marked in the text). She struggled with why she had come to therapy. It was important to assure herself that she had not experienced something that would make her crazy and that, in fact, her problems could be attributed to physical pain.

This utterance became understandable in light of what happened later in therapy. She was afraid that it would turn out after all that she was mad or irreparably damaged (as the torturers had "promised"). The defensive and the complaining voices signalled the later marked negative transference, which was to become the axis of the transference relationship, especially around the time of the key session where some central elements of her torture-experience were re-framed in the transference.

Three quarter of a year into the treatment, it was possible to follow how the themes from the torture became more and more present in her mind at the same time as the negative transference became more prominent.

She became increasingly frightened and was quite overwhelmed by narratives from the torture. (I continue to mark the utterances in the text as above; bold = **childlike, helpless voice**, italics = *anxious voice* and bold and underlined = **aggressive tone of voice**):

Francoise: **yeah, because I feel I am punished by having such pains. But I don't know why, I, I, it is just meaningless.**
Therapist: mhm
Francoise: (small pause). I remember that those torturers were very keen on getting me to understand that **they would destroy me for the rest of my life.**
Therapist: hm
Francoise: / **it is out of question, either you kill me now or else I shall live, so // so I feel that maybe they are right after all** (cries heavily) (long pause).
Therapist: is this, thoughts like that (P cries heavily) which you may have in the back of your mind from time to time which makes you afraid, for coming, for in a way let go for..
Francoise: yes (cries) **I have had them for many years, I can't manage..**
Therapist: mh, mh, and then it has been important to put them, put it away or put it away, is it...
Francoise: (cries heavily), **I can't go on thinking about those things because I feel, forever, that they, eh, eh, are only words.**
Therapist: mh
Francoise: have after all a body which apparently is healthy and eh (sighs and cries) one can see
/ have said it only to make it feel worse, even worse, **they were angry at me because I** (sounds like a frightened

child) had fooled them
// they wanted to take revenge,
they hit me many times only to take revenge,
they knew it was nothing to get from me,
there was nobody they could arrest anymore [of her
comrades],
nothing, but they were (cries heavily)

Therapist: mh

Francoise: (cries heavily, for 60-seconds). That's why I am so
tormented when I get ill
so that is // (cries) that I maybe shall be so sick that I
becomes helpless, not able to manage // not being able to
participate in ordinary life, not, only (cries) as a ordinary
human being (cries heavily)

In this and the following sessions the therapist became more and more
involved in the patient's staging of an internalised relation to her torturers and this inner (pathologic) object-relation became increasingly
symbolised. The torturer-transference is marked in the key-session some
weeks later. The prelude to this session is a deterioration of her condition with strong suicidal impulses, which led the therapist to give her
anti-depressant medication. She reacted with, what felt to her, as a
psychosomatic catastrophe, with many bodily symptoms not compar-
able with ordinary side effects. What appeared in the preceding sessions
was the narration of the active participation of a medical doctor in the
torture, both advising the torturers of how far they could go but also by
giving her medication and trying to hypnotise her. She remembers the
torturers repeatedly saying they would destroy her for the rest of her life.

The therapist then interpreted her difficult relation to him in
connection with her relation to the torturer-doctor:

Francoise: (trembling in her voice), I experience that you also
maybe dangerous in that way (small pause)
but it is not necessarily the relationship between you and
me (pause)(sobs loudly)
I am so sorry it is like that

Therapist: but it is in any case something that is important for us to
talk about.

Francoise: (crying)(sobs) **I have problems with forgiving that /**

> **because / on misuse of power (sobs) by the help of a doctor**
> **who just stands there and says // but she can stand a bit**
> **more.**
> (cries,) **because it was a doctor who was there in // torture**
> **which was / with electricity which /**
> **standing by the door like (incomprehensible)**
> **bent like an arch, and come and make an examination**
> **and saying; "yes, it is possible a bit more"** (crying).

Therapist: mh, so there is something about this experience
which reflects in the feelings you gets about what is
happening here.

Francoise: (cries) I have / just connected these things, (..).

In this passage, she seems to move "in and out" of the experience and, in the end being able to reflect on this as an as if" experience in relation to the therapist. This theme was repeated and repeatedly worked with during the rest of the treatment. She experienced a marked improvement in her bodily pains and an increasing improvement in trust both towards the therapist and towards others. The prosodic aspect of her speech also changed, and the aggressive, complaining and childish aspects lost their prominence and a warmer emotional tone voice became prominent.

In the last utterance, she acknowledged that she had "connected these things", that is, connected therapy with torture and the therapist with the torture-doctor. This represented an insight where she was able (after repeated working-through) to differentiate mental representations of past and present situations and accordingly work on the projective transference level.

Conclusion

The distinction between levels may be fruitful from a heuristic viewpoint when discussing the psychotherapy/psychoanalytic process. They are aspects of the same process, but each level needs a different therapeutic strategy. For traumatised patients, deficit mentalisation is a major problem and a therapeutic strategy aimed at enhancing these processes has been described. A common theme is a recognition as a precondition for mentalisation. I think of recognition in the Hegelian sense, that is, affording the possibility of finding oneself through others in a reciprocal relation. The traumatised refugee often finds him/herself closed in relation to the own body. The traumatised must then be offered the possibility to find him/herself in the mind of the therapist. This involves the whole range of the psychotherapist's or psycho-analyst's symbolising and mentalising activity from reverie through "bindung" (German for "binding") and linking to the ability to help the patient to see him/herself and the therapist as separate desiring subjects. This involves, however, that the therapist takes on himself a part of this work of mentalisation. The countertransference may be difficult indeed as many of the utterances or symptoms of the patient are concrete expressions of the "mute suffering" (first- and second-grade symptoms in a sense given by Matthis) affecting the therapist on a bodily level. One may wonder about the nature of the motivation involved in enduring this emotional stress. Dinora Pines comments: (referring to her work with Holocaust survivors);

> ..., my experience of working with these massively traumatised patients leads me to believe that the analyst's omnipotent wish to rescue and repair those whose lives have been so ravaged may also contain the guilt of the survivor and a need to mourn the reality of the Holocaust and those who have been lost. Once these unconscious needs have been worked through by the analyst, the intense countertransference that accepts the patient's projections so openly cannot be maintained. Natural defences against the acceptance of another's pain come into play and inevitably distance the analyst from the patient (Pines, 1986, p. 203).

This may be a rather pessimistic tone to the possibility of sustaining work with these patients. It points, however, to a dilemma for trauma-therapists, which is not unlike the dilemma the patient is facing. To be open to the patient's projections creates intense and often non-verbalised primitive bodily reactions. The symbolising work relating to these reactions is a part of the therapeutic work. What Pines suggests, however, is that this may have an omnipotent tone and be motivated by survivor guilt, and, accordingly, when this guilt has been worked through, the capacity for openness may not be sufficient. I believe, however, that there is a whole range of motives and countertransference reactions involved that must be worked through, not all of them defensive.

Time does not consent to a thorough discussion of this complex theme. One might say that all this is a prelude to the integrative work of mourning so difficult for these patients. This work should not be restricted to the survivor as an atrocity and the work with its after-effects concerns the society as a whole. I will therefore end with a kind of moral-political imperative; – seen on a larger scale, if atrocities are not worked through both in the consulting room and society at large, they may be repeated with devastating consequences in social reality (Varvin, 1995; Volkan, 1996).

Notes

1 Published in German: Die gegenwärtige Vergangenheit. Extreme Traumatisierung und Psychotherapie. Psyche - Z Psychoanal 54 (09/10), 2000 and reprinted here in an updated English version with the kind permission of Psyche.
2 I present the passages in stanza form, following principles suggested by Gee and others (Gee, 1986; McLeod & Balamoutsou, 1996). The sessions have been tape-recorded and transcribed using the standards developed by Mergenthaler and Stinson (1992). I have, however, not reproduced all details in the text. Many of the therapist reinforcers (hm, uhm etc.) have been omitted.
3 (...) signifies that a part of the dialogue has been omitted.
4 Important critique has lately come from cognitive science concerning the impreciseness of this conceptualisation.
    Models have not yet been developed that account for the interaction of cognitive functions with somatic, including visceral events, but the epistemological framework is in place to develop such theories. The type of abstract model that Freud sought to develop for psychoanalysis, and that we now seek to develop in the context of cognitive science of today, must be a model of emotional information processing, not information processing only, and must account for the relationship among motoric, perceptual and visceral functions, and the interactions of these with language and abstract thought. (Bucci, 1997, p .62).
    Bucci's general critique of psychoanalytic theory and models are mainly that the theoretical constructs are loose, with internal inconsistencies and not anchored in reliable and valid data. Or, as she says, while acknowledging the need for a scientific theory to be built on a "framework of hypothetical constructs", the danger is... *the kind of reification that has proliferated in the psychoanalytical theory, with endless multiplication of empty theoretical terms* (Bucci, 1997, p. 66). Her argument is based on the endeavour to build theory on sound empirical research. Although I concede in this, the concern of the present paper, while acknowledging the need for further empirical research, is to clarify some concepts. This may lay ground for further empirical research.
5 It should be mentioned that there are increasing evidence for functional and even structural damage in the function of the brain on a neuro-physiological level underlying the failure of these processes (van der Kolk et al., 1996). It is an empirical question whether psychotherapy may influence these dysfunctions and perhaps stimulate other areas of the brain when there is structural brain damage.
6 I am grateful to the late Dr Carl-Ivar Dahl for providing material from this therapy. The therapy process has been analysed in-depth with qualitative methods (Varvin, 2003a).
7 I present the passages in stanza form as described in endnote 2.

Chapter 8

The influence of extreme traumatisation on body, mind and social relations[1]

Introduction

The after-effects of psychic trauma are, by now, one of the larger health problems in the world. In addition to psychic trauma caused by accidents and natural disasters, man-made traumatisation system-atically directed against other human beings (e.g., rape, torture, war atrocities) are endemic in many parts of the world. State-organised violence, war and terrorist attacks create traumatised individuals, disrupted families and destabilised groups and communities. The civil population becomes, more than ever, victims of wars, which have produced more than 40 million refugees (including internal refugees),[2] many of whom have been severely traumatised.

Violent and aggressive milieus as concentration camps and inhuman prisons with torture implicate harm done with malignant intention aiming at destroying the personality of the individuals and the coherence of the group or family, and it is often carried out in a malignant political context of persecution, power struggle, ethnic cleansing, etc. Living under these conditions may produce long-lasting adverse effects in the personality (Eitinger, 1964; Herman 1992; Niederland 1981; van der Kolk et al., 1996). The effects are complex, involving psychic and somatic aspects as well as the family and the groups to which the person belongs (Allodi, 1980; Hjern & Angel, 2000; Miller, 1996). These types of extreme trau-matisation cause destabilisation in the capacity for symbolising emotional experience including giving meaning to life after the trauma (Tutté, 2004). These post-traumatic conditions pose major problems for analysts in clinics and in their private consultation rooms. In line with this, consider the following vignette.

DOI: 10.4324/9781003206057-8

Clinical vignette

In her teens, Fatima was arrested at school in a Middle-East country for having voiced support for the former leader of the country. She was incarcerated for four years, most of the time in isolation receiving no visits from family or others. She was exposed to endless and meaningless interrogations, repeatedly threatened with execution and tortured heavily both physically and psychologically. During her stay in prison, she almost lost all hope of surviving and felt everybody had deserted her except her sister who was three years old at the time, and she became a good internal object for Fatima when she was in isolation. "She could not be made responsible for not helping", Fatima said. Fatima was "sent" to a Nordic country as a refugee after release from prison and lived alone with no friends and only sparse contact with her family (mostly by telephone). She had to live in hostels with criminals and drug addicts for longer periods of time, until, after several years, she managed to find secure housing.

Without personal contacts, no reference to her own culture and marred by invalidating post-traumatic symptoms – including cognitive disability, hallucination, anxiety attacks and chronic anxiety and nightmares (in addition to somatic problems caused by the torture) – she struggled to achieve coherence in her daily life. Her psychoanalyst, who was, for a long period of time, her only stable contact, strived with her to find points of anchorage in her inner life, bedrocks for possible psychic development in which object-presentations could be anchored in words and symbols rather than bodily sensations and fragmented images. The transference to the analyst presented itself by oscillations between hope and disillusionment. A wish to be the omnipotent saviour characterised the analyst's countertransference, especially in the beginning of treatment. That fantasy became later understood as a defence against a deep sense of hopelessness when he was constantly confronted with the patient who lacked almost all inner and outer resources. The patient's inner involvement with perpetrators soon appeared in the transference and confronted the analyst with additional stress. The analyst's ability to symbolise his own countertransference reactions was, at times, extremely difficult. Treatment of patients like Fatima needs a collaborative effort that includes social and physical rehabilitation. The breakdown in the cohesiveness of her mind, and thus in her ability to make sense of her daily life, remained, however, the most difficult condition to understand and to treat. We believe that cases like Fatima's demonstrate the need for a widening of the scope in our psychoanalytic theories and for more comprehensive and in-depth research strategies that can gain knowledge which ultimately can help the clinician when working with extremely traumatised patients.

Our paper describes a psychoanalytic and psycho-semiotic research strategy (Rosenbaum & Varvin, 2002; Varvin & Rosenbaum, 2006) that investigates dimensions according to which meaning-making may be established and unfold itself in the analysis. This approach makes it possible to study how traumatic experiences affect the ability of the mind to structure internal relationships as these are revealed in the patient's utterances, narratives and ways of being (Varvin, 2003a). The model on which this approach is based has significance also for the understanding of psychopathology in psychoanalysis, and we hold that it has special value for conditions where there are major disruptions in the mind–body relations on several levels as is the case with many traumatised patients having been exposed to man-made trauma (Varvin & Rosenbaum, 2003a).

The influence of trauma

Freud

In Freud's attempt to address the models of trauma, he struggled with at least four problems. Firstly, he went against the idea that trauma arises solely because of the objective presence of a danger without any participation of deeper levels of infantile mental functioning. Secondly, he struggled with the idea that fear of death was the causal agent of the traumatic anxiety. Rather he regarded fear of death as analogous to fear of castration and separation so that the traumatic situation to which the subject was reacting was that of being abandoned by a protective superego, losing the object's love or losing the object itself, and thereby losing safeguards against internal and external dangers. Thirdly, he worked on the question of quantity – both the massiveness of external stimuli in the trauma, and the inner excitations impinging upon the mental apparatus. Fourthly, he connected psychic trauma with the immediate effect of the experience of helplessness (1926).

Implicit in Freud's reasoning is, thus, both an economic (a "too much" of forces of the id overwhelming the ego) and an object-relational perspective on trauma. Freud's arguments included both the concept of primal repression (Urverdrängug) and the concept pair of binding (German: Bindung) and unbinding (German: Entbindung). Binding furnishes the formation of coherent, homogenous unities; it binds the quantities of somatic excitation as representations at different levels of symbolisation in order to master them. Unbinding, in opposition hereto, due to an excess of destructive stimulation, affects the representational system including the primal repression to the extent that it causes a breach in the boundaries that function as part of the fundamental protective shield of the ego. The breach of the boundaries may accordingly threaten the unity and identity of the ego. The helplessness characteristic of psychic trauma is the consequence of massive unbinding of painful and destructive excitation. The unbinding process that underlies this helplessness leaves memory fragments or ideational memory traces of the experience unbound in the internal reality. Such traces or "foreign bodies" with excessive unbound affect may be damaging to the internally binding function (the stimulus barrier) and can as such produce symptoms of dissociation and a persevering illness-experience.

This description may be seen as Freud's early conceptualisation of dissociative processes of the mind. The accompanying disturbances of the balance of the basic emotions (Damasio, 2000) represent a most disturbing feature of the post-traumatic conditions.

Object-relation theory positions

Freud thought of the metaphor "stimulus barrier" from mainly an economic point of view. In object-relation theory terms, the stimulus barrier may be conceptualised as a representational system establishing a good enough empathic and protecting internal object relation, which may function as a barrier and protection towards excessive and destructive anxiety and anger. In the dynamics of the modes of the experiences – shaping the interplay of the depressive position, the paranoid–schizoid position and the autistic–contiguous position (Ogden, 1989) – the normal binding inherent in the stimulus barrier (the protecting, empathic internal object) tips the balance of this generative dialectic interplay of modes of experience towards the dominance of the depressive position. Psychopathology may be seen as a collapse of these three modes of experience. Excessive unbinding is, then, the result and may be experienced as a failure of the inner protecting object. In severe traumatisation, the balance of the modes of experiences may tip towards the paranoid–schizoid and the autistic–contiguous experience, which in addition may lead to the demolishing absence of the mutuality of the generative dialectic interplay of the positions, as described by Ogden:

> Collapse in the direction of an autistic–contiguous mode results in a tyrannising imprisonment in a closed system of bodily sensations that precludes the development of "potential space".

> Collapse in the direction of a paranoid–schizoid mode results in a sense of entrapment in a world of things-in-themselves wherein one does not experience oneself as the author of one's thoughts and feelings; rather, thoughts, feelings and sensations are experienced as objects or forces bombarding, entering into or propelled from oneself.

> Collapse in the direction of a depressive mode results in the experience of a subject alienated from his bodily sensations and from the immediacy and spontaneity of lived experience (p. 136).

The unbinding force of traumatisation may, thus, lead to destabilisation in all three modes of experience. The common features of chronic post-traumatic states reflect this with a dominance of somatic pain syndromes, paranoid ideations and intractable states of depression marked by a feeling of hopelessness (Krystal, 1978, 2001; Shalev et al., 1998).

Psycho-semiotic perspectives

Disturbed structures of the internal subject–object relationships manifest themselves in the patients' discourse and symbol-formation, and their ways of relating to others socially, emotionally and in fantasy. The analysis of the structure of different dimensions of the patient's internal and external relationships, and his capacity for symbolising these, is the focus of the rest of this paper.

Outline of dimensions of symbolisation

A model of symbolisation must take into account three basic dimensions in the person's relations to the world: the body–world dimension, the subject–group dimension, and the subject–discourse dimension. The three dimensions are ways of cognising, conceptualising and relating emotionally to the world.

In the body–world dimension, human beings are linked together in bodily feedback and mirroring responses that are immediate and to a large extent (radically) unconscious. Event perception, mapping and capturing interplays and inter-gestures in simple and complex sets of relationships, mirroring, imitating and miming routines – all these functions characterise the dynamics of the body–world dimension. The subject's experience of the world is emotive, psychophysiological and temperamental. Tone of voice, facial expressions, eye movements, manual signs and gestures, postural attitudes, and other action patterns express aspects of the body–world relationship.

Subjectively, the analysand (and the analyst) may feel warmth, coldness, sadness, abandonment, anger, bitterness, emptiness, fullness, confusion, calmness, balance/unbalance, etc. In general, it is an egocentric episodic view of the world.

In the subject–group dimension, the self is linked affectively to internal group formations (Freud, 1921). These are internal matrices of object relations in which the individual subjectively (unconsciously) identifies himself. The self experiences unconsciously itself as a member that is both unique (with traits of one's own, feeling that one has a special value to others) and at the same time similar to others (carrying traits similar to others, being an average and exchangeable subject, and thus being of equal value as others to "the group as a whole"). One may conceptualise these internal links as "a basic group mind" which is a fundamental capacity of our human being, and which is the foundation for the asymmetrical links between subject and other. Intersubjectivity (linked with the assumptions and desires of others) and inter-intentionality (recognising others' intentions) belong to the subject–group dimension.

Questions that organise the awareness and emotionality of the self are for instance: "How am I anchored and mirrored in the group's desire and beliefs?"; "What do I mean to the group?"; and "How am I attached to and part of the group and how am I appreciated and integrated by the group"?

The subject–discourse dimension encompasses the subjective relationship to the socio-cultural knowledge and experience. Cultural perspectives – the personal and identity-shaping stances relating to politics, ideology, education, ethics, moral conduct and religion – are the main organisers of subjectivity and intersubjectivity of this dimension. The cultural discourses are inscribed in the mind, and the personal and identity-shaping stances are expressed overtly or tacitly, in accordance, or discordant, with the inscriptions. Human interaction in this dimension always takes place with reference to converging and diverging myths, narratives, ideologies, paradigms of beliefs and patterns of argumentations.

Human brains seem immediately minded for carrying out the functions of the body–world and in part the subject–group dimensions. These only require, to a limited degree, a verbalised language-supported sign-system, but they do rely heavily on mimetic representation (Donald, 2001). In contrast, the subject–discourse dimension and other parts of the subject–group dimension is founded on the premise of symbolic systems. The existence and function of the symbolic systems make it possible to create and regulate the rules of communication and other symbolic inventions. The integration of myth, narratives and written language functions as an external symbolic storage system (Donald, 2001) – liberating the mind from the limited knowledge we can gain by investigating the brain's biological memory systems and giving thinking new options and an ethical dimension.

Dimensional dynamics: a model

Whenever a person is expressing himself towards others, or otherwise relating and interacting with others, all three dimensions – the body–world, the subject–group, and the subject–discourse dimension – display specific characteristics that can be observed in the person's narrative speech, in self-awareness and in self-reflection. Furthermore, the dimensions are dynamically closely related. Thus, the dimensions both interrelate and function in their own right (see Figure 8.1).

On each level, attractors make the subject move dynamically between opposite poles. The three levels are constantly interacting. Each level has its own dynamic patterns. On each dimensional level,

subject - discourse dimension

Eros
Integrating thinking
Tolerance

Thanatos
Fundamentalistic,
rigid ideologies

Body - world dimension

open
near
Warm
calm

closed
distant
Cold
uneasy

**Subject - Social group
dimension**

Mutuality
Interdependency
Group-perspective

Intrusion, avoidance
Solipsism
Self-perspective

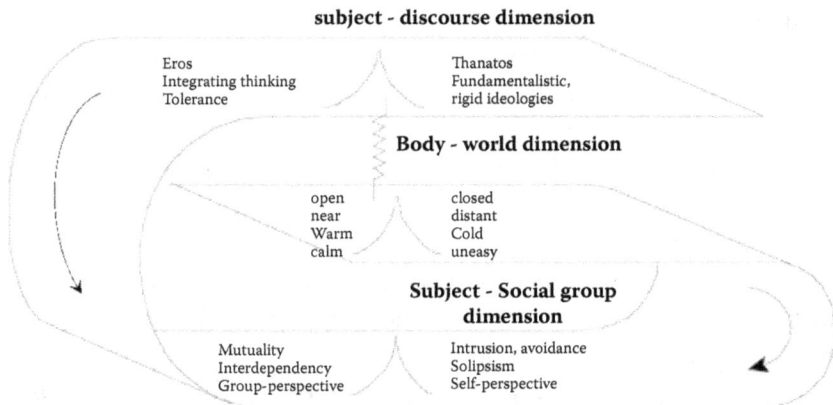

Figure 8.1 Three dimensions in the person's relating to the world here
Upper level: subject–discourse dimension.
Middle level: body–world dimension.
Lower level: subject–group dimension.

the subject is under influence of attracting and repelling forces, re-presented non-verbally and verbally, involving emotions such as anxiety, anger, dependence, isolation and shame, and forces such as threats, aggression, sexuality and the need for stimulation and nourishment. These forces produce and govern interactions in reality (that which takes place between conscious minds) and inter-subjectivity in fantasy (that which is in play between unconscious modes of subjectivity). The attracting and repelling forces drive the subject into adaptational modes, adapting to the internal and ex-ternal conditions, but also into conflicting dilemmas of existence.

Conflicts and frustrations are natural and basic to the human mind. They are states of mind that usually accompany problem-solving, suppression, repression, and even more primitive defence strategies, but they are at the same time preconditions for bringing the person to make choices and take responsibility. Conflicts and frustrations are not always totally dissolved and extinguished from the mind. Often, they "stay alive" and create a state of ambivalence in the subject as to whether it shall prefer one stream of thoughts or actions instead of another. Actions or symbol formation are the mind's "answers" to the existence of the basic conflicts and frustra-tions.

Such a conflict between the attracting and repelling forces in the mind can be illustrated by material from a session with an analysand traumatised in childhood:

> The analysand felt that the analyst in the previous session behaved unempathic, unaccepting and in a rejecting manner. The analyst herself was not consciously aware of having harboured feelings of a similar kind. Reacting on his perception, the analysand was right from the start of the actual session immediately filled with anger and had a preconscious wish to attack the analyst. On the preconscious level, he had a counterattacking impulse revealing itself in a conscious wish for "flight". The wish for attack and the wish for flight thus indicated the existence of repelling and attracting forces. The double bind of the anger and fear kept the session in a tense atmosphere, sustained by the silence of the analyst which did not help the analysand to insight.

The meeting of human beings with other human beings, or rather with otherness, always implies the existence and influence of both positive and negative values. That is, attracting and repelling forces in the mind of each of them are working in their joined effort to create meaning to their encounter and create meaning to what they are saying and not saying. The subject is attracted to or repelled by divergent representations of otherness. This dynamic between subject and otherness is a core constituent of the functions of each of the three dimensions in the above model. Each dimension has its own psychodynamic patterns. The subject may swing rhythmically, based on the atmosphere of the situation, between closeness and distance, balance and imbalance, warmth and coldness; or between feeling "part of" or "neglected", "ego-centred" or "other-centred"; or between "having integrated oppositional viewpoints" or "being fundamentalistic".

Dynamics of states of stability and instability

The relation between subject and otherness does not only affect each singular dimension, but also the interrelations of the three basic dimensions (see Figure 8.1). The analyst may observe this in the patient's entrance into the room, the atmosphere and music of the beginning of the session, the ways the patient expresses his different thoughts and feelings (rhythm, tone of voice, pauses, etc.), in the unfolding of the narratives of the patient (different themes functioning as attractors and repellors). In the following, we exemplify the three dimensions and their interrelation in general, and we describe the dynamics by distinguishing "states of stability" and "states of instability".

In the first dimension, the body–world dimension, the dynamics concern the immediate bodily relation on an emotional level to other physically or imagined present bodies – be it the analysand and the analyst, or the analysand talking about meeting somebody else. Let us imagine the situation in which one person meets another with whom he is acquainted. In states of stability, the subject may experience emotions of warmness–coolness, openness–closeness and intimacy–distance. Usually, one or the other condition will dominate the relation, and the specific atmosphere in the moments of meeting. If unconscious oscillations between these poles of emotions take place without affecting the conscious sphere of attention and cognition, then these trajectories are managed and controlled. In this body–world dimension, important non-verbal, affect-regulated, emotional processes are at the base of the expressions of the mind. The possibility of integration of these emotions is linked to the capacity to establish, and to preserve already established, internal object relations with a positive valence, based on the subject's trust in his enjoyment, excitement, surprise and the absence of long-lasting states of anxiety.

In states of instability, the subject is disabled in its effort to concretise or symbolise the sensations of its body. Neither solid anchoring nor integration of the fantasised emotional scenarios into meaningful narratives take place. Singular emotions appear unintegrated. Self-support and self-soothing may be transformed into greedy dependence, adhesion or fusion with the other, or it may adversely be transformed into fierce rejection, unemphatic distancing or total isolation and coldness.

The second dimension, the subject–group dimension, concerns the identifications and the internal bonding that takes place in the person's mind in relation to the group. The salient theme of this level is how the subject grounds its identification in a group-structure (family, subculture), externally as well as internally.

In states of stability, the subject reflects itself not only in the mirroring of the other but also, and even more, in the mirroring of the group matrix. One learns from the group-as-whole as well as from its singular members and acquires the ability to empathise and take the other's perspective within the framework of the group. This means that the person understands, persuades or is taken away by the other's view, and more importantly is able to view the matter from many possible standard views and establish a consensual validation.

When the subject finds itself in a state of instability, then the self and the group cannot cognitively act as foreground and background for each other. The group becomes a devalued or idealised part of the self (projective identification) and the trust in the group is lost. Empathy is reduced to egocentricity, intimacy perverted to intrusion or exploitation, and care is turned to neglect. Consequently, the self no longer experiences itself as a part of a group but may instead experience an irreversible loss of that aspect of personal identity that is related to the group, or to the family. In societies where the family and the group (the clan, the tribe, the subculture, the group-based belief, the small community) is the grounding unit of culture, and where belonging to such a group is of fundamental importance both for personal and social identity, disturbances of this interdimensional kind may have grave internal disorganising effects.

The third level, the subject–discourse dimension, signifies the subject's relationship to culture in the broadest sense: myths, philosophies, ideologies, ethics, jurisdiction and other social discourses transgressing the frame of the group. The narratives of the culture are not necessarily stable over centuries, but stable enough to produce converging and diverging myths, societal narrations, ideologies and paradigms of beliefs and argumentations, which may last decades.

In states of stability, the subject understands that the cultural discourses are divergent and contradictory and that this paradoxically is a creative force of culture. However, the outcome of the paradox may also be that the subject becomes attracted strongly only to one pole, or one type, of the cultural discourses. Isolating religious or ideological ideas and turning them into the only truth about mankind and society is an example of this cultural one-sidedness. In general, the subject's modes of relating to a multiplicity of opinions with differences and divergences, and to the expressions of social passions based on "higher principles", are part and parcel of the subject–discourse dimension.

Also included in this dimension are the subject's beliefs and fantasies of being grounded in narrative time, including experiential or deictic time (seeing the present in relationship to past and future), and existential time (inchoate, enduring, associative, dreaming).

The subject–discourse dimension transforms the group mind, giving rise to the possibility for the subject to step outside the group, construct unexpected viewpoints, acquire a dialectic reasoning mind, and still be a part of a cultural movement. Ideally, group intentions as a whole can be observed side by side with the subject's own intentions, even though the latter may run counter to the group intention.

States of instability may be seen as the outcome of totally fragmented societies or societies governed by terror and extreme fundamentalism. A fragmented society may induce mind states of polarities, encapsulation of sub-groups and contra-groups, ghettoisation and other enclosures, isolation and non-engagement. A society with extreme fundamentalism may be characterised by other patterns of the mind: minimal degree of role-differentiation, anonymisation, totally uniformity of beliefs, excessively diffuse quality of interaction, etc. The communication is incoherent either in the form of "bureaucratese" (impersonal, excessively abstract, euphemistic) or in the form of "cult-speaking", and the meaning conveyed is either fragmented, based on partial-object relations or stamped by signs of evacuation (Hopper, 2003).

The model in toto, thus, attempts to give a comprehensive picture of the subject's relations to itself and the world on a bodily–emotional level, on a group level and on a societal–cultural level. It depicts a system of interrelated dimensions. "Maladies" in the dimensions of subject–group or subject–discourse may cause disturbances on the person's ability to regulate emotions in a dyadic, body–world dimension. The persecution of a minority group, or ethnic cleansing, changes the way the group's identity is formed and maintained, and it has grave effects on personal and intimate relations, e.g., childrearing, caring for the ill, etc. (Lavik et al., 1996).

Trauma and post-traumatic states imply disturbances in each dimension of the model, as well as disturbances in the dynamic relation between them. The terrifying, deadening and numbing experiences produced by extreme trauma affect the individual in its relation to impressions of the surroundings as well as in its relation to the group and the culture. State-organised violence, including torture, is a sign of perverted dynamics in all dimensions, and the consequence for the individual is often enduring disturbances in his relations to the other, the group, and the cultural discourse. State-organised violence has severe repercussion on the subject–group relations as well as in the body–world dimension. Being exiled, after being exposed to state-organised violence and torture, may magnify the difficulties of symbolising the past, the present and the future for the individual survivor, and may make the situation more difficult because of lack of social, cultural and human support in the new country to which the survivors arrive.

In the following, a case of psychoanalytic therapy with a severely traumatised refugee from a persecuted minority group in a country with state-organised violence illustrates the analytic function of the model.

Clinical material

Background and trauma story

Hassan came from a Middle East country to the Nordic countries after having been in a desert refugee camp in a neighbouring country for almost four years. He aligned this experience with the inhuman experience in the prison in his home country. He was exhausted and suffered serious psychic distress as well as physical disabilities and sequels after being maltreated for prolonged periods. His trauma story had begun when a dictator had come to power when Hassan was in his teens. He and his family were seen as opposed to the regime and were constantly persecuted. In his late teens, his father was executed by the regime and his brother disappeared under unclear circumstances probably having been killed by the government. He became politically active at the university and it became an insurmountable blow to his feelings of existence when his fiancé was arrested because of her relationship with him, raped by the police, and then committed suicide as a consequence of this. He was arrested twice and tortured beyond imagination on both occasions both physically and mentally. He was, among others, shot through his arm in order to make it impossible for him to practise sports again (and received no medical help afterwards). Once, agents from the government attempted to kill him when he was walking in the street with a relative. The relative died from the shots and this experience, and several experiences of mock executions, were later the roots of his "experience of being killed", or an imminent fear of being shot, almost feeling the bullet piercing into his chest. He thus had feelings of being totally unprotected and living in a state of persistent insecurity.

He was relieved by at last coming to a seemingly peaceful place but his life in exile proved to be more difficult than he had expected. After a period in the reception centre, he got a room in a hostel – together with drug addicts and alcoholics. His journey of survival in exile started here. He was then in the mid-thirties. His twice-a-week, face-to-face psychoanalytic therapy began at this time and came to play an important part in his life for the following six years in which the analyst became one of the few stable contacts in his fragile network.

Session material

Hassan brought only fragments of his story to the sessions. By listening carefully and collaboratively weaving the parts together, the analyst managed to get a picture in his mind in which his associations could function.

In the early sessions, the analyst got the impression that Hassan grew up within a traditional, well-organised community and that there was little social unrest or wars in his early childhood. He spoke of being the eldest son of a clan leader and part of a minority group in his country. He was a longed-for son, born after four sisters and was raised as the one supposed to take over the leadership of the clan and from early on, he had to follow his father on official business.

He told the analyst how he had spent his childhood in a large family and achieved a privileged protected status as the first-born son. He described his mother as all loving and caring, which he contrasted with the ambivalent relationship he had to his father. On the one hand, father was idealised and, on the other, he was feared and denigrated. The split and ambivalent feelings towards his father corresponded to the ambivalence in his self-image: on the one hand, he enjoyed having a privileged, prince-like status and, on the other, he felt estranged from his friends, like an odd guy who was apart. In his late childhood, due to his privileged status, he felt estranged both from his friends and from father who at times was physically threatening when he misbehaved. At that time, he felt vulnerable and easily injured. "And nobody did anything to help" was a recurrent theme of his childhood story, which also, later in therapy, became a prominent theme when talking about his suffering and the sufferings of his people. He did well in school and in sports, and, in spite of his vulnerability, he described himself as ambitious and proud, reacting strongly to defamatory behaviour by others. In his listening, the analyst noticed the ambivalence, and the narcissistic vulnerability paired with grandiosity. The analyst also felt how Hassan struggled to establish a secure relationship with him. Non-verbal interactions proved to be of great significance for Hassan who closely observed the analyst's emotional communication (facial gestures, tone of voice), but often misjudged the enunciations as signs of the analyst's disengagement, ignorance or animosity. The communication in the body–world dimension of the analysis thus became an absolutely necessary entrance to the analysis of the traumatic experiences and their undermining of Hassan's narcissistic feelings of identity that threatened to make him unsociable (subject–group dimensional problems).

In the initiating phase of the therapy, Hassan also presented a detailed account of how he by chance disclosed his father's transgressing of rules of the clan that would have been disastrous for the father had it become known. Hassan felt afterwards that his father was dangerous for him and he was afraid his father wanted to kill him. This disclosed oedipal relationship was tacitly emphasised by his obligation to participate in the leadership of the clan. This made him estranged both from his father and from his friends. At the same time, he talked of his immense longing for his father who was always busy. Behind Hassan's harmonic childhood experiences as he described them, the analyst could hear a story delineating a clash between his assigned cultural position (affecting both the discourse and group dimensions) and his immediate emotional relations to others (body–world dimension). This clash has a parallel in the internal conflict between Hassan feeling himself as a coming leader while experiencing a threat to his safety. The analyst sees Hassan's later idealisation of his relation to his father as a defence against this threat. The split in the father image was thus later reinforced by the violent meeting with the cruel dictator forcing him to submission, and it reappeared repeatedly in the transference in which Hassan's perception of not being understood was felt as subjecting himself to the power of the analyst, while at the same time being entitled to be saved and in the powerful position he once was assigned.

Several times during the first part of the analytic treatment, Hassan returned to the persecution of him and his family, his political activity at the university and the insurmountable blow when his fiancé was arrested, raped and then committed suicide as a consequence of this. Also recurrent was the physical and mental torturing and how he was shot through his right arm in order to make it impossible for him to practise his sport.

The analyst was constantly impinged upon on a bodily level by these descriptions of torture, impotence and anger, even though these descriptions often were expressed as culture- and group-bound. He also observed Hassan's attempts to deny guilt and his flight into the role of the victim, and his feelings of being treated as a nonhuman. Both the emotional nourishing-seeking aspects of the transference as well as the identity-supporting aspects suffered temporarily by these countertransference reactions. An interpretative strategy taking into consideration the failure of culturally assigned role as the protector slowly helped him to start mourning.

Early in the therapeutic process, Hassan described a feeling of being alienated. He had extreme difficulties in trusting people and lived much of his life alone, having only a few friends. In his internal and external exile, the relation to his group was dominated by withdrawal. He felt he had failed his assigned task and felt shame, and, as a consequence, he worked for longer periods in "splendid isolation". In long periods of his therapy Hassan's mind was dominated by experiencing persecutors everywhere, also in his home. He felt that people were following him everywhere, and the fact that they did not watch him became a proof that they had done so, and that they now pretended that they did not notice him. He seldom left his house, and if he did, he was forced to take detours, which made his arrival at sessions quite irregular. This existential insecurity and anxiety come to expression in fragmented forms of speech:

> Yeah, I am afraid really ... I don't know how to explain how I feel, and that's a problem ... Maybe I am more than afraid, something more, if you are afraid for something you know, you

are afraid from for example the car, then you know that this is the car and you go away, but if you are afraid for something you don't know, I don't know what it is I am afraid of.

In the later part of therapy as he got a clearer picture of past dissociations, he described himself as living in three worlds:

1. The world of his past in which he would live, as he explained, in the world as it existed before his traumas, and would be able to relate to his father, his mother and the rest of his family. His descriptions of this world had an idealistic and almost delusional character, especially regarding his relationship with his father
2. The present but imaginary world that was the world of persecution. In this world, he could be killed at any moment and had to take all sorts of precautions. He would in this state of mind be in contact with memories of prison life and be very occupied with the real and ongoing persecutions in his homeland. These perceptions and memories could realise themselves in actual perceived scenes of seeing or hallucinating attack persecutors, nightmares, etc. This "world" dominated during a longer period, but, as therapy developed, it grew more distant and lost much of its character of presence. It lost, in other words, much of its delusional character
3. The world "in between", as he called it, consisted of his daily life when life experiences approached the normal, and as may be understood from the expression "in between". It was not at all a stable experience

In the analyst's mind, the imaginary world implied a "withdrawal" from the normal dialectics of the attractors of the body-, group- and culture-dimensions to an exclusive identity in the negative valences of these dimensions (depletion, distance, coldness; feelings of intrusion, avoidance and isolation; social self-destruction—see Figure 8.1). This "withdrawal" diminished clearly in all three dimensions during therapy.

The nightmares and re-experience decreased and his social competence increased. The "internal world" concerning his childhood (the world of his past), which appeared in an idealised version as a retreat to a paradise position of an idealised self with idealised parents, represented in the analyst's mind a defensive solution bringing the three dimensions "in order". This was a brittle construction, and the concomitant idealised transference provoked countertransference feelings of estrangement, fatigue and aggression. It represented for Hassan, however, a safe haven, needed when his "internal prison world" threatened to take over. During the course of therapy, the struggle between the "safe haven" and the "prison world" was always a motor of the projective identification and countertransference movements of the dynamics between Hassan and his analyst.

He gradually increased this territory both internally and in the external world. He established a lasting intimate relation where he could have emotional support and achieved also a belonging to a new group in exile, a family of the country he lived in. This implied a step in a gradual reorganisation of his relation to discourse and culture in that he established more realistic goals regarding what he was able to achieve as the designated leader of his clan and also gradually achieved a more secure position as an exile belonging to two cultures. In the end, he got a small apartment and a little car. He established a stable relationship with a woman and had a child.

Concluding remarks

The analytic process in Hassan's case can be divided in four broad phases which may overlap.

Firstly, a phase of relative bodily–mental security and relief, based on meeting understanding from the analyst and the raise of a new hope of regaining health. Secondly, a phase with disappointment and disillusionment in the patient, accompanying the empathic failures of the analyst. Accordingly, Hassan became depressed and felt little hope for the future and harboured suicidal thoughts. Third, a long phase where paranoid anxieties dominated and where he for long periods was hardly able to go out of his flat. He organised his life around the expectation of meeting an assassin at any moment. This was understood by the therapist as an attempt to make his existence more predictable, and interpretations along these lines seemed to calm him. The fourth phase was marked with renewed hope where Hassan's ability to symbolise and integrate his traumatic experiences improved and he became gradually able to establish a reasonable decent existence in exile. The background of the "uncanny" was gradually replaced by a feeling of safety even though he still remained vulnerable.

Treatment of cases like Hassan's involve attention to complex transference–countertransference situations, his fragile ego-structure and to a life situation that was characterised by multiple losses, lack of anchoring in own cultural and social setting and demanding accommodations to new life circumstances.

A key process in the therapeutic endeavour is to re-establish the capacity for symbolisation that has been restricted, disordered or damaged as result of the traumatisation. Trusting, caring and comforting self-object relations from the life period previous to the trauma must be reintegrated with the fragmented and encapsulated debris of the disturbed mentalisation of the trauma. If reintegration fails, imminent catastrophic states of mind may temporarily numb the mind function with the experience of disaster as a consequence. Based on the need for developing rational approaches to the treatment of severely traumatised patients, as well as strategies for prevention, the preceding analysis has attempted to see trauma and traumatisation in a structural perspective. The helplessness of the ego, described by Freud, has been seen as affecting the body–world, the subject–group and the subject–discourse dimensions. When destruction affects all these dimensions, the stage is set for destabilising processes on an individual as well as a group level.

We believe that our structural analysis of the traumatic experience can shed some light on the complicated effects on the psyche on relational functions of the traumatised person. Not only may ego functions be disturbed. We can observe that identity and capacity to maintain relations are heavily dependent on the subject's relations to the world on the three dimensions analysed in this paper. In the therapeutic process, we think this is reflected in the transference–countertransference relationship where the bodily, non-verbal and the verbal interpretative levels interact in complicated ways. An understanding of these processes may help the clinician in the necessary but complicated tasks the treatment of these patients represents.

Notes

1 Published in: *Int J Psychoanal.* 88:1527–1542 Copyright © Institute of Psychoanalysis, reprinted by permission of Taylor & Francis Ltd, http://www.tandfonline.com on behalf of Institute of Psychoanalysis.
2 In December 2020, there are approximately 80 million.

Chapter 9

Psychoanalysis with the traumatised patient

Helping to survive extreme experiences and complicated loss[1]

Introduction

Traumatised persons struggle with mental and bodily pains that are difficult to understand and difficult to put into words. The pains may be expressed as dissociated states of mind, as bodily pains and other somatic experiences and dysfunctions, as overwhelming thoughts and feelings, as behavioural tendencies and relational styles, as ways of living and so forth. The effects of both early and later traumatisation may show itself in many diagnostic categories where the symptoms characterising PTSD is only one form. Traumatisation may be a causative and/or disposing factor in many psychopathological manifestations: depression, addiction, eating disorders, personality dysfunctions and anxiety states (Leuzinger-Bohleber, 2012; Purnell, 2010b; Taft et al., 2007b; Vaage, 2010; Vitriol et al., 2009).

What is common for these manifestations of traumatisation are deficiencies in the representational system related to the traumatic experiences; the traumatic experiences are painfully felt and set their marks on the body and the mind but are poorly contained in words. They are not or deficiently symbolised in the sense that they cannot be expressed in narratives in a way where meaning can emerge that can be reflected upon. They remain in the mind as dissociated or encapsulated fragments that have a disturbing effect on mood and mental stability (Rosenbaum & Varvin, 2007a).

As a rule, extreme traumatisation (like rape and torture) eludes meaning when it happens and it also precludes forming an internal third position where the person, in his or her own mind, can create a reflecting distance to what is happening. The inner witnessing

DOI: 10.4324/9781003206057-9

function, so vital for making meaning of experiences, is attacked during such extreme experiences hindering the individual from being able to experience on a symbolic level the cruelties they undergo.

Psychodynamic treatment approaches

In this paper I will discuss how people may live through extreme and prolonged traumatisation and also how they try organising their lives in the aftermath and how their way of struggling and coping may manifest itself in the therapeutic or analytic process. A main point is that the analyst, when taking on the task of treating such traumatised patients, inevitably becomes involved in the not-symbolised, fragmentary and as a rule strongly affective scenarios related to the patient's traumatic experiences. This happens from the first encounter with the patient and is mostly expressed in the non-verbal interaction between the patient and the analyst. It may take long time before these manifestations may be given a narrative form that in meaningful ways relates to traumatic and pre-traumatic experiences, and it implies hard and painful emotional work from the patient, and also from the analyst to achieve this end.

There are several therapeutic approaches at present for the treatment of the seriously or extremely traumatised persons. There is, however, a lack of research on outcome, on how different approaches works for which patients in what situation a certain therapy may help. In this presentation I will focus on psychoanalytic treatment. I have, in my own research and clinical practice which has seen good results of this approach, an example of which I will demonstrate in this article. It is perhaps a paradox that many traumatised persons prefer psychoanalytic treatments in spite of recommendations for many evidence-based, often exposure-oriented or trauma-focused, therapies (Van der Kolk et al., 1996). This user-based view on the advantages of psychoanalytic approaches was, moreover, confirmed by Schottenbauer and co-workers who demonstrated essential beneficiary aspects of this approach. Firstly, they found in metastudies that evidence-based treatments had high drop-out and non-responder rates (M. A. Schottenbauer et al., 2008). They argued further eloquently for psychodynamic therapies as suitable for the treatment of traumatised persons for the following reasons (M. Schottenbauer et al., 2008):

- Psychodynamic approaches address crucial areas in the clinical presentation of PTSD and the sequels of trauma that are not targeted by currently empirically supported treatments
- They may be particularly helpful for complex PTSD as they target problems related to the self and self-esteem, ability to resolve reactions to trauma through improved reflective functioning and aim at the internalisation of more secure inner working models of relationships
- They work on improving social functioning
- Psychodynamic psychotherapy tends to result in continued improvement after treatment ends

Patients with complex trauma often live in difficult social, economic and cultural situations and treatment needs thus to be integrated with rehabilitation procedures and often with complicated somatic treatments. This holds true not only for many traumatised refugees, but also for complex family-based traumatisation. Treatment and rehabilitation need therefore often to be conducted by a team and when and how to implement psychoanalytic therapy, has to be carefully evaluated and will need constant support from the team and social services.

Trauma and the social context

For these not symbolised and insufficient symbolised experiences to approach some integration and given some meaningful place in the individual's mind, they need to be actualised and given form in a holding and containing therapeutic relationship. This implies that the analyst must accept living with patient in areas of the mind that are painfully absent of meaning and at times filled with horror.

As a rule, however, this is not sufficient: without acknowledgement of the traumatic events at the societal, cultural and political level, the individual and the group's work with traumatic experiences may be extremely difficult. Without affirmation on the social and cultural level, the traumatised person's feeling of unreality and fragmentation connected with the experiences may continue.

This was the case for many after the World-War II in the West, where the official attitude to a large degree was that one must go on living and put the past behind. In Norway this had devastating and often fatal consequences for many warship sailors who had endured extreme traumatisation and hardships while being constantly attacked and torpedoed by German submarines (Askevold, 1980).

One should remember also that what may contribute most to the personal suffering of survivors seem to be to observe others being maltreated and killed and not being able to help or protect. This underlines the importance of Niederland's seminal papers on survival guilt (Niederland, 1968b, 1981), a theme that came in the background in the trauma literature for many years but was highlighted clearly by the youth surviving the Utøya massacre of July 22, 2011 in Norway.

The dynamic and structure of extreme traumatisation

How trauma affects a person depends on the severity, complexity and duration of the traumatising event, the context, whether intrafamilial or external and the developmental stage. Central is the way in which traumatisation affects internal object relations; for example, whether earlier traumatic relations are activated and the perceived support after the event and the treatment offered.

Here, I will concentrate on adult-onset trauma and give one example from a traumatised refuge in psychoanalytic therapy.

Phenomenology of traumatisation

Being traumatised is an experience of something unexpected that should not happen. It creates an internal situation of profound helplessness and an experience of being abandoned by all good and helping persons and internal objects. The feeling of helplessness and being abandoned may be carried over into the posttraumatic phase. A deep fear of an impending catastrophe of helplessness where nobody will help, or care may develop. An inner feeling of desperation and fear of psychosomatic breakdown with fear of annihilation may ensue and much of posttraumatic pathology may be seen as defence against and an attempt to cope with this impending catastrophe, which in fact already has happened (Winnicott, 1991).

Human made traumatisation influence internal object relations scenarios in different ways. Early traumas that bear more or less similarity to the present traumatisation may be activated making the present trauma imbued with earlier losses, humiliations and traumatic experiences. Even an early safe-enough relationship may be coloured by the later traumatising relationships when for example a too authoritarian father may be fused with a torturer thus almost deleting the good enough aspects of this relation. Unbearable losses may bring the traumatised to forever seek a rescuer or substitute in others, as happened with Fatima, to be presented later.

Complicated relations to the traumatising agent/person, the circumstances and other relations involved may thus ensue and these may be actualised in the transference. Identification with aggressor is well known.

The traumatised person internalises important aspects of the traumatising scenario in the form of self-object relation which may be more or often less differentiated and/or fragmented and in different ways self-negating. As we shall see, the actualisation of these may in the analytic process take dramatic forms.

Relation and symbolisation

One salient task in psychotherapy with traumatised patients is to enhance a metacognitive or mentalising capacity that can enable the patient to deal more effectively with traces and derivatives of the traumatic experience. This implies helping the patient out of mental states characterised by concreteness and lack of dimensionality.

During traumatisation the ego meets an overwhelming abundance of stimuli and impressions. The regulating functions of the mind breaks down and the processes of the psychic apparatus are pushed towards states of extreme anxiety and catastrophe (Rosenbaum & Varvin, 2007a). Mental traces of such traumatic experiences are "wild" in the sense that the person has no capacity to organise and deal with them; no inner container in a relation to an inner empathic other that can help give meaning to experience (Laub, 2005a).

There is an experience of loss of internal protection related to the internal other – primarily the loss of the necessary feelings of basic trust and mastery. An empathic internal other is no longer functioning as a protective shield and the functions that gives meaning to experience may no longer work. Attachment to and trust in others may be perceived as dangerous reminding of previous catastrophes. Relating to others, for example in psychoanalytic psychotherapy, may be felt as a risk of re-experiencing the original helplessness and a feeling of being left alone in utter despair. Withdrawal patterns may be the consequence, creating a negative spiral as withdrawal at the same time means the loss of potential external support (Varvin & Rosenbaum, 2011b).

The effects of trauma may thus affect several dimensions of the person's relations with the external world and give disturbances on the bodily-affective level, on the capacity to form relations to others and the group and family and on the ability to give meaning to experience. The last is dependent on the social and cultural meaning-giving functions which under normal circumstances provide affirmative narratives, e.g., stories told by elders, scientific explanations, psychological theories and political acknowledgement and leaders' acknowledging the historical circumstances of the atrocity.

The traumatised person is living with historical experiences that are not, or poorly, formulated but painfully and non-verbally represented in the body and in the mind. The task of therapy is to allow these experiences to emerge in the transference relationship so that words and meaning can be co-created even if the experiences themselves by all human standards are cruel and devoid of meaning.

The traumatic experiences must thus become actual in the therapeutic relationship. This may happen when the analyst is drawn into relational scenarios where he/she becomes part of the emerging trauma related scenes that the patient hitherto has struggled with alone.

I will in the following demonstrate one aspect of psychoanalytic therapy that may be an important step in this symbolising process

Actualisation, projective identification and enactment

The traumatised patient will, from the start of therapy, involve the analyst in a non-symbolised and unconscious relationship where the patient communicates by acting out and in this way present important aspects of their traumatic experiences (Varvin, 2013b). In this way, trauma is present from the beginning of the contract. "Trauma" is not something that comes later when a trauma narrative is told.

What the patient communicates touches the analyst and may hook on to unconscious, not worked through material on his/her side resulting in action that at first sight is not therapeutic, therefore named countertransference enactment (Jacobs, 1986).

Such enactments on the analyst side may, however, be a starting point for a possible process of symbolisation and making conscious of these implicit experiences (Scarfone, 2011).

It should be underlined that an enactment actually involves a collapse in the therapeutic dialogue where the analyst is drawn into an interaction where she/he unwittingly acts thereby actualising unconscious wishes of both him/her-self and the patient. It may be a definable episode in a process with more or less clear distinctions between the pre-phase, the actual moment and the post-phase but may also be part of a prolonged process in therapy (Jacobs, 1986). Enactment appears thus as an unintentional breakdown of the analytic rule of "speech not act", and this may imply a new opportunity of integration or it may hinder the analytic process when it goes unnoticed or unanalysed.

Enactments may come as a total surprise but can also be identified in, for example, fantasies, thoughts and feeling states beforehand (Jacobs, 2001). Most often it is a surprise, and the analyst suddenly finds himself doing something that is out of the ordinary and not in accordance with the usual practice of psychoanalytic psychotherapy. It is only afterwards that it is possible to look at what happened and then, if things go well, be able to understand which processes were at work.

In the context of trauma, enactments may represent a possibility for symbolising material related to traumatic experiences. Scarfone holds that "remembering is not, when it works, a simple act of 'recalling' or 'evoking'. It implies the transmutation of some material into a new form in order to be brought into the psychic field where the functions of remembering and integration can occur" (Scarfone, 2011).

Enactments can thus in connection with trauma be seen as actualisation of relational scripts or scenarios where unconscious, not symbolised material are activated both in the patient and in the analyst. This is seen as an unavoidable part of the analytic interaction and the outcome depends on the analytic couple's ability to bring the enactment into the psychic field.

The pressure is usually understood as starting from the patient, although mutual or reciprocal pressure may be seen (Mc Laughlin, 1991, 1992) where analysts conflicts reinforce the patient's tendency to act. An unconscious fantasy is actualised in the transference, the pressure is mediated via projective identification and the analyst "acts in" due to unresolved countertransference problems.

I will try briefly to illustrate aspects of these processes.

Loss and trauma – a case story

Fatima, a woman in her late thirties, came to Norway as a refugee from a country in the Middle East nine years prior to treatment. She was in psychoanalytic psychotherapy face-to-face, two – three times a week, for one and half year.

She reported a relatively happy childhood, being loved both by father and mother and her siblings, and she had managed to get an education as well in spite of a culture that did not favour women's education. She was married and was working as clerk when she was arrested because of participating in a non-violent political organisation together with her husband. At the time of her arrest, she was pregnant in the last trimester. She was maltreated physically (including beatings on her pregnant womb) and psychically (threats, seclusion etc.) and suffered from malnutrition and lack of proper medical care when she became ill. Her husband was arrested at the same time and was tortured to death some months later. She was allowed to go to a public hospital to give birth, and an escape was arranged for her shortly thereafter. While she was living clandestinely, her child died of an unknown disease, probably caused by the torture, maltreatment and lack of adequate medical care during her stay in prison.

After the death of her child and husband, she lived clandestinely for about one year before she fled from her country under difficult circumstances. During this time, she experienced additional serious traumas. When she arrived in Norway she was not believed by the authorities. She was put in prison and sent back to a third country where she had to live under very poor conditions for some time before she again was allowed entrance to Norway.

She arrived in Norway severely depressed and suicidal and had serious eating problems in addition to post-traumatic symptoms and psychosomatic symptoms. In the years in Norway, she suffered almost continuously from nightmares, re-experiencing, avoidance behaviour, somatisation, and psychosomatic illness and recurrent depressions. In spite of this, she managed to settle and achieve a considerable degree of integration in the community. She lived alone and had friends but no intimate contact with men. High levels of activity, lots of helping others, and little time for herself, seemingly reflecting a need to act rather than feel, characterised her life in exile.

Fatima had to a large extent mourned her husband, for example, performing grief-rituals on his birthday. The loss of her child was not a problem she presented when seeking therapy and it remained silent during the first part until it emerged in a quite dramatic way in a session after a week's break in the treatment.

She arrived on time at the session, out of breath as she had been running believing she was late. Her first remark was. "I lost the bus" (A common expression in Norwegian when coming late for the bus, and here also indicating the theme of loss). In the first part of the session, she spoke in staccato manner evoking a strong need in the analyst to help and support her.

She talked about her loneliness during the break, the need to have someone to lean on, to trust and who could be close to. The analyst affirmed her feeling of loneliness; something that set in a counter movement where she referred to a progressive friend who maintained that one could easily do without the support of a family. Her own family and her close relations to them and also her ambivalent feelings towards them had been a theme throughout the therapy. In this section of the session the analyst's interventions also became intellectual with lack of affective resonance. The analyst did in this way join the patient in an enactment attempting to ward off painful material.

Then a shift occurred when the analyst remarked, remembering her earlier clearly stated affection for her family that they surely would have liked her to establish a family in exile. She then became silent for some minutes and said crying:

Yes, I have been thinking if I had my son, he would have been 13 years old and ..

She cried a lot and seemed distant, obviously re-experiencing scenes from the past. She then haltingly in short sentences, and after encouragement, talked about the birth of her child, how happy she had been when she heard the child cry. It felt like a victory. Also, the dangers came to her mind and she was frightened and desperate in the session. She did not manage to stop crying as she left.

This was a breakthrough of memories, or rather memory-fragments, which came as surprise for the patient (and for the analyst). It was a re-experiencing "like a film" of the trauma-scenario, a broken narrative.

She was physically ill during the night and when she came the next day, she was still quite affected and it gradually became clear what had happened before and during the previous sessions, which in fact represented an actualisation of the drama when she lost her child.

Three consecutive nights before the key session she had had the following dream, which she told, realising the connection with her child's death:

> And then suddenly I get all; I feel I, I got like; I had / I did not tell you,

> I dreamt for three nights [before the key session] that I cried.., I was very narrow in my throat and, and had like saliva around my mouth. It's like a; then I thought like, what is it that makes me feel. I don't get enough oxygen and (heavy breathing), when I, eh, was in the middle of crying, when I woke up.

She then could narrate how her child died:

She was living clandestinely under poor conditions. Her child got fever and had increasing difficulty in breathing. In the end the baby died in her arms due to lack of air (asphyxia). Her despair and grief were abruptly interrupted by the dangerous circumstances, which demanded that she moved on. Her baby was buried in haste and the harsh tone among her comrades stopped any attempt of her for emotional reactions.

We can now reconstruct aspects of what happened in her therapy.[2] She had a markedly positive, almost idealising transference towards the analyst. In the break she had felt utmost loneliness, and this had evoked in her unconscious memories of her child, as well as other persons she had lost (her husband and also her father when she was in exile). In the session she came out of breath with a feeling of loss (expressed in her first remark: "I lost the bus"). The counter-transference was characterised by a desperate wish to help but then a felt helplessness, which resulted in distancing and intellectualisation on the analyst's side.

In hindsight it was possible to identify several episodes earlier in the therapy where the theme of loss had come up and also where dead children had been mentioned. This had obviously been small attempts by the patient to bring maybe her most painful experience into the therapy, but she then backed away and either intellectualised or dropped the theme. The analyst had colluded with this and also avoided the theme of loss, which had connection with the analyst's own problems and some unresolved issues concerning his own losses. These countertransference problems were possible to identify, understand and reflect on only when analysing the sessions afterwards.

The theme of loss became, however, more acute for her in the break preceding this key-session. She had obviously during this time, partly unconsciously, lived through and been occupied with her tragic loss and identified with her dead child and, by projective identification, the analyst got the role of the helpless helper pushing him to act according to the role assigned to this part. This interpretation was supported by analyst's subjective counter-transference reactions (i.e., feeling solicitous but helpless).

The relative abstinence in the session allowed her to start symbolising her traumatic loss. The dreams were obviously a signal of an unconscious preparation for re-experiencing the death of her child, in which she gave voice to the part of herself that identified with the child trying to survive.

As the loss theme was elaborated, Fatima began to integrate the loss of her child with her other losses – her husband's death, her father's death some years ago, and also other deaths. Thus, the emergence of the loss of her child brought with it memories of other losses, which she then worked to integrate and mourn during the rest of the therapy. She also had to face her guilt for not having been able to help her child, which may be interpreted as a survivor guilt.

Needless to say, this was a hard and labourious process also for the analyst who had to work on his own unresolved issues. The work was completed, and the treatment did make a difference in her life; she was no longer depressed and had less somatic pain and, more important, she started a new way of life. She was no longer the tireless helper; she took time to care for herself and relax and she managed to establish a relationship with a man.

Discussion

Fatima's experiences in her therapeutic process reflect complex interactions on a verbal and nonverbal level. Traumatic experiences are present in the mind and body of the traumatised in different ways, all seeking expression in communicative styles and ways of being in relation to the analyst. They may dramatically involve the analyst in processes that touch the analyst's own unresolved or partly resolved issues and draw him into a process of acting instead of thinking and reflecting. The transference-countertransference situation may push the analyst to become involved in a relational scenario that, as a rule, is possible to understand and interpret only after the fact. In the sequence presented from Fatima's treatment, the analyst became the "helpless helper" in the transference and defended against this feeling by joining the patient's intellectualisation. The transference situations vary, and different personas from the patient's internal world may appear in the transference as, for example, the perpetrator, the dehumanised victim and so forth.

It is argued that countertransference enactment may be a central vehicle for unsymbolised trauma related material to emerge and that when this happens, an opportunity may appear for the "unthought known" to be heard and contained in a joint created narrative that relates present suffering to past misery. A time-dimension can then be established in this area of the psyche, which also makes reflection possible. The precondition is attention to countertransference reactions and fantasies and the analyst's capacity for containment and gradual reflection and working though of the personal part of his reactions.

What happens is a mostly unconscious "mis en scene", which may happen over longer time in therapy. What we saw in this example was a more acute reaction of the analyst, but also that avoiding the loss theme probably had been going on for a prolonged part of the treatment.

One may speculate that similar processes are at stake in so-called trauma-focused therapies (Kruse et al., 2009). These do not, however, reflect on transference and countertransference processes. It is an open question then whether psychoanalytic therapies may have more lasting effects, as claimed by Schottenbauer et al. (2008), due to the working through of traumatisation in the transference. This may focus trauma-related experiences in their rootedness in the personality, which implies work with both personality functions and relational aspects.

This may especially relate to the work nonverbal aspects of communication, as the most important aspects of relational traumas, are non-verbal and only partly symbolised (Packard et al., 2014). Traumatised persons' experiences represent a partial foreclosure where parts of the symbolic function are undermined. This contrasts with the almost total undermining of the symbolic function in many psychotic conditions. Foreclosed signifiers are not integrated in the subject's unconscious, so they tend to re-emerge from outside, in "the Real" (Lacan, 1977). Another way of saying this is that they appear as beta-elements and sometimes also as bizarre objects experiences as coming from the outside through for example hallucinations (Bion, 1977). These mechanisms may also be reflected in a traumatised persons' attention and concentration problems and their difficulties in organising impressions in thoughts (van der Kolk, 2014). Many traumatised persons have, moreover, the experience that language was perverted during torture and other atrocious situations. The consequence of this is that they, to a large degree, have learned to rely on non-verbal communication. In torture, for example, day-to-day expressions are often used for the most gruesome torture practices, confusing communications are used to break down people and so forth.

The fact that so much of the focus in interpersonal relations with severely traumatised patients relies on non-verbal dimensions may explain to a certain extent why many traumatised patients feel safe in "psychoanalytic context" and also why psychoanalytic therapy works when the patient and analyst have different cultural backgrounds and different native languages. As Erik Homburger Erikson stated poignantly many years ago regarding communication with exiled and immigrants: They do not "hear what you say, but 'hang on' to your eyes and your tone of voice" (Erikson, 1964, p. 95). Apart from this, one must underline that psychoanalytic therapy is in itself a culture-sensitive approach in that utmost care is done to understand patients on their background of their personal and cultural contexts.

Massive traumatisation creates destabilisation of the basic structures of human relationships:

- on the level of intimate relationships where intrapsychic and interpersonal functions concern regulations of emotions, primary care functions and basic identity issues
- on the level of the individual relations to the group where personal identity and developmental task are negotiated
- on the cultural or discourse level, where narratives are established that give meaning to and stabilises relations and developments on the individual and group levels (Rosenbaum & Varvin, 2007a)

Any approach to patients who have been traumatised in a violent social context, such as wars, mass persecution and genocides, must therefore be sensitive to, and take into consideration the dimensions of social and cultural influences on development, psychopathology and health-sickness behaviour.

The last hundred years of history has moreover shown that social forces repeatedly have neglected traumatised persons and groups and even treated them as malingerers as was seen during World War I. This lack of social support and recognition has been devastating for many. Treatment of traumatised patients can therefore, with great difficulties, only work in a social/cultural setting where traumatisation is not acknowledged and worked with at other levels in society.

Notes

1 Published in: *International Forum of Psychoanalysis* 2016; Volume 25.(2) s. 73–80. Reprinted here with the kind permission of International Forum of Psychoanalysis.
2 The therapy process was analysed longitudinally using Assimilation Analysis. This analysis tracks the development of problematic experiences throughout therapy through a qualitative procedure using narrative and procedural aspects of the therapeutic dialogue (Varvin, 2003a; Varvin & Stiles, 1999).

Part III

Research

Introduction

Research has had a troubled position in psychoanalysis. Later years have, however, shown an increasing interest for and also acknowledgement of the value of research for psychoanalytic understanding and practice. A dominant paradigm has, however been a rather positivistic approach with reliance of replicability, controlled trials and experimental studies. Qualitative research strategies have been downplayed in the psychoanalytic research community. This is in my mind rather paradoxical as this research strategy is much closer to psychoanalytic theory and thinking and closer to psychoanalytic practice. Freud characterised research in psychoanalysis as a "Junktim" approach: healing and research go hand in hand (Freud, 1927). In many ways, qualitative research strategies are close to realise this aim.

In my opinion we need the whole range of research strategies in psychoanalysis. Psychoanalysts need to learn to read research articles and conversely, researchers need to appreciate the unique data achieved in the psychoanalytic situation. Because the language of research, especially in positivism, is different from our clinical discourse, dialogue between clinicians and researchers has proven to be difficult and has resulted in misunderstandings and resistance against research amongst analysts and often rejection of psychoanalytic theory among researchers.

It is worth remembering, however, that the main goal both in clinical psychoanalysis and in research in the clinical field is to create the best possible knowledge base for treatment. The "evidence movement" is an attempt to answer this need. In recent years, the claim for

DOI: 10.4324/9781003206057-103

evidence-based practice has resulted in promoting only a part of this endeavour, the controlled trial, as the "gold-standard" of what counts as research on outcome of treatment. This is in sharp contradiction to the original, and in my opinion a much more useful approach to make clinical work evidence-based formulated by co-workers in the 1990's (Sackett et al., 1996). Evidence-based-medicine (EBM) was designed as a way to organise the best evidence with which to answer clinical problems by using knowledge from there sources: clinical experience, research and patients' preferences, and to use this critically in a clinical situation and then to evaluate what was clinically relevant and useful.

In this section I bring two articles. One resulting from a collaborative research with psychoanalytic practitioners and researchers on the study of the dreams of severely traumatised persons from the Balkan wars. The aim of this article is, among others, to show how formal research may influence our theories on dreaming and also help the clinician in working with traumatised patients dreams.

The other article is an attempt to create a genuinely psychoanalytic method for research in clinical situations. A qualitative method has been developed and its application on clinical material is demonstrated.

This part of the book is a modest attempt to show how formal research may be useful both for developing psychoanalytic theory and for clinical work with patients.

Chapter 10

When dreaming doesn't work

Traumatic dreams, anxiety and the capacity to symbolise

Introduction

In this article we will present laboratory-based dream research. We will argue that this research may inform clinical work with dreams and possibly change theory. A dream dreamt in a laboratory setting and a dream dreamt during a psychoanalytic process do not, however, necessarily express the same underlying process. The latter will, to a large extent, be determined by the specific and actual transference-countertransference situation, in contrast to a laboratory setting where transference reactions usually are not accounted for. In our research it became apparent, however, that those volunteering to participate in the laboratory dream research did have expectations and transferences that were displayed in relation to the setting and the interviewers. A wish for security was obvious in many cases and many had also "unfinished business" that in one way or another appeared as themes in dreams and associations to the dream. This was especially visible in individuals with chronic post-traumatic states who often struggled with long-standing guilt and problems with aggression.

The knowledge gained from the research presented here strives to give insight into significant mental processes that are affected by traumatisation and thus contribute to psychoanalytic trauma theory and to a better understanding of how therapy works. Furthermore, the two methods applied for the analysis of traumatic dreams in this research deepen the understanding for affect-regulating processes, deducible from manifest dream content (the Zurich Dream Process Coding System, ZDPCS by Moser & von Zeppelin), and the dreams' transferential and object-relational facets contained in one- and two-

DOI: 10.4324/9781032072357-10

person relations in telling of dreams (Psychoanalytic Enunciation Analysis, PEA).

The traumatised mind

The traumatised mind is characterised by disintegrating, dissociative, and potentially rupturing processes that can be released or provoked by stimuli in the present that bear resemblance to aspects of the reminiscences of traumatising events.

Because the integrating functions of the mind are impaired, perceptions of these stimuli activate preconscious or unconscious schemes of danger (Rosenbaum & Varvin, 2007; Varvin & Rosenbaum, 2003b) and often set off cascades of fearful reactions with concomitant neurophysiological patterns of reactions related to the sympathetic nervous system and the hypothalamic-pituitary-adrenal axis. With traumatised individuals one may observe difficulties in organising perceptions of both inner and outer stimuli, of relating perceptions to other perceptions and to earlier experiences in a functioning memory, and, as a result, difficulties in organising experience as a whole, taking different aspects of the situation into consideration. Consequences of traumatisation do not primarily refer to memory traces from the past but more importantly to ongoing problems in regulating negative emotion, a dysfunction that reflects disturbances in symbolising capacity. The symbolising capacity is at the basis of the above-mentioned capacities (that is, integrative and mentalising capacities) and we hold that post-traumatic disturbances basically are a disturbance of this function.

Symbolisation is an ongoing process of binding excitation and re-organising bodily and psychic experience in a way that experience is organised and can acquire meaning. This is in line with Freud's conception of binding as a basic process whereby drive excitation, being a source of (automatic) anxiety, is bound to mental representation so it may be transformed into anxiety that may function as a signal (signal-anxiety (Freud, 1926b)). Lecours and Bouchard (1997) refer to this as mentalisation defined as a linking function "consisting of a connecting of bodily excitations with endopsychic representations" (Lecours & Bouchard, 1997, p. 855), in a process of psychic transformation where "unmentalised" experiences are changed into "mental contents within a human interpersonal and intersubjective matrix". Lecours and Bouchard develop levels of mentalisation and claim that all psychic content may be placed on a continuum of "increasing mental quality between the poles of somatisation and insight" (p. 857). They see this as an ongoing process in which somatic excitation, and thus psychic content, is constantly re-organised on different levels of mentalisation, including bodily excitation, acting, dreaming and higher levels of abstraction.

The symbolising capacity has thus, following Lecours and Bouchard, its origin in the human interpersonal and intersubjective matrix, starting in the early infant-caregiver relation, and is basically an interpersonal process where the other's responses to the signs from the child are transformed into increasingly more meaningful re-presentations, through mother's reverie function (Bion, 1977). Beta-elements are in this process transformed into Alpha-elements that can be "food for thought".

This is an ongoing process in the mind where internal object relations have a basic role in a symbolising, meaning producing process. Dori Laub underline that in traumatising processes the internal bond/link to an empathic other is attacked and sometimes almost destroyed (Laub, 1998). We hold that this traumatising attack on linking is at the core of the deficiencies in the symbolising function we see in severely traumatised people and that this can be observed in traumatic dreams. Annihilation anxieties present in traumatised persons (Hurvich, 2015) are a constant symptom of this failure of binding anxiety through an internal linking process with an "empathic other".

The background for establishing the internal dialogue with the empathic and meaning-giving other is the subject's internalisation of a semiotic universe established in the mother-infant dyad, which lays the ground for the establishment of attachment structures and inner object relations (Muller, 1996). Following Künstlicher we can see dreaming and dream-work as a continuation of the dialogue with this primal object and as an attempt both to create an at-oneness with the primordial mother and to represent and maintain desire, which is the precondition for this dialogue (Künstlicher, 2001). In this way, dreaming is seen as continuous re-working and as symbolisation of impressions and experiences. Dreaming presupposes that this internal dialogue is possible, that is, that faith in the other is preserved.

When the relation to the empathic other is broken or impaired, desire will not have an object or the relation to the object will be impaired. What is left then is the raw, unmediated representation of experience, an experience that is not mediated by symbolic thought.

Our study aims at focusing on processes of failure in the internal dialogues and thus failure in symbolisation. The hypotheses in our work are thus:

1. Traumatic dreams, nightmares with wakening, are results of these failures in otherwise normal symbolising processes in the psyche.
2. Dreams of traumatised persons are attempts to restore this function,
3. Levels of attempts at restorations in traumatic dreams can be observed even if they result in fearful awakening.

Dreaming and nightmares: the traumatic dream

Dreaming serves thus an integrative and adaptive function in which actual problems are connected with previous significant situations and earlier unresolved problems. Clinical experience has shown that even if traumatic dreams relate to, and often appear as, repetition of earlier traumatic experiences, they comprise day residues that have provoked similar feelings and mental experiences as the original traumatic event, for example feelings of shame, humiliation and danger (Lansky & Bley, 1995). The ubiquitous, but often ignored, presence of guilt in trauma survivors is also central.

The study of dreaming of traumatised individuals as the mind's work with unmetabolised, trauma related elements (Bion, 1977; Hartmann, 1984) may thus give a privileged insight into the workings of the mind (Freud, 1900). The traumatised individual tries in his/her dreams to deal with residues of daily emotional experiences that are experienced in terms of earlier traumatic experiences and nightmares and the dreams represent aborted or failed attempts to manage these experiences (Fischmann, 2007). Clinical work with dreams – and nightmares – of traumatised patients is well-known in aiding the traumatised mind to restore its symbolic function (Adams-Silvan & Silvan, 1990; Hartmann, 1984; Pösteny, 1996).

In the dream-generating model of Moser and v. Zeppelin (Moser & v. Zeppelin, 1996) (used in this project), conflictive complexes are differentiated from traumatic complexes. The former revives negative affects together with attempted wish-fulfillment (wish-fulfillment is possible, albeit under restricted conditions), the latter contain episodes in which affective events cannot be integrated into a cognitive structure (traumatic dreams).

In the psychoanalytic enunciation model (the second model used in this research), dreaming is seen as an attempt to achieve containment and integration of unorganised imaginary elements in a symbolic mode of functioning (Rosenbaum & Varvin, 2007). The model describes thus the possible transition from unorganised non-symbolic dream material to more integrated symbolic dream scenes.

In our research we hypothesise that dreaming by traumatised individuals indeed is an attempt to organise experience and turn passivity into activity and that this process can be observed in the person's attempt to organise the traumatising experience in a dream narrative (Fosshage, 1997; Hartmann, 1999). Research on dreaming will, according to this line of thinking, be a kind of laboratory for studying the symbolising process in status nascendi.

Post-traumatic states are, among others, characterised by intrusive phenomena within which dreams referring to original traumatising experiences are frequent. However, what happens during the night for many traumatised individuals may have different qualities and may be a distinct phenomenon on different levels: the phenomenological, structural, dynamic and the neurophysiological level. As it is known from clinical experience, this makes it difficult to distinguish dreams from nightmares, nightmares from hallucinations and hallucinations from vivid imagery (Nightmares are defined by the dreamer's interruption of the dream and awakening due to high anxiety level). In addition, it can be difficult to distinguish so-called night terrors, which are anxiety attacks while asleep with no mental content, from nightmares (Fischmann, 2007). It is therefore of both scientific and clinical interest to study the dream processes of traumatised persons in depth. We will elaborate this in the following using an example from a mixed-method research on persons traumatised in the Balkan wars in the 1990's.

Post-traumatic dreams and symbolisation: context, method and description of the sample

In the last decade of the 20th century there were almost continuous wars throughout the western Balkans in the territory of what has come to be known as "ex-Yugoslavia". Characteristic of these wars was the involvement of huge masses of people and coverage of large multi-ethnic territories. There were diverse ranges of combat activities (frontline to street fighting), but more than anything else it was violence targeting civilians i.e., persecutions, killings, concentration camps, ethnic cleansing and mass murders (Srebrenica not being the only case). Victims and participants of this conflict are the subjects of this study.

At the International Aid Network Centre for Rehabilitation of Torture Victims (IAN) in Belgrade (www.ian.org.rs), help is being provided to thousands of those who were imprisoned and tortured during the war and also to those from eastern Bosnia (including Srebrenica). Torture survivors proved to be the persons with the most complex and long-lasting problems. Torture is in itself inconceivable, as it entails the most monstrous acts of violence against other people without any "understandable" reason.

Years after the war the staff at IAN encountered similar violence in institutions (prisons, psychiatric hospitals and social institutions). Patterns were recognised which were similar into the war-time experiences, namely dehumanisation of others and torture and pain as a vehicle to humiliation. Based on clinical experiences at IAN with war victims and others, this seemed to have its base in a powerful unconscious drive stemming from Oedipal anxieties, where castration fears transformed into humiliation and feminisation of other men (one observation was that sexual acts frequently were present during torture). The so-called "mild" forms of physical abuse (slapping, hitting, spitting, etc.) were regularly followed by humiliating rituals. Breaching of "body barriers" (or "skin barriers") represented the more severe forms of torture: cutting, burning, electrocuting of the skin, inserting objects in body openings.

One line of thinking suggests that traumatic experiences provoke annihilation anxieties that unbinds the death instinct, and that this affects the relation between symbolisation, integration, and development of an interpersonal space as underlying the capacity to relate to others.

Men exposed to war-related stressors were participants in our research. We had two groups: one with current PTSD ("experimental" group, N = 25) and the other without current PTSD, but with previous diagnosis of PTSD ("referential" group, N = 25). Both groups were matched by age, education and by level and type of the traumatising events they survived.[1]

Participants spent two consecutive nights in the sleep laboratory and were interviewed in the mornings by two Serbian psychoanalysts. The interviews comprised narratives of their dreams, which were recorded and translated into English.[2] Subjects from both groups reported a significant number of different war-related experiences. Those in the experimental group (with current PTSD) showed more experiences of being passive victims during the war including being witnesses and not able to act and the non-PTSD group reported more experiences where they were able to be active in war situations. This may indicate that an active role in combat can be a protective factor for development of PTSD, and that a passive role (and helplessness connected with it) could have a specific traumatising effect.

Both groups were mainly refugees settling in Serbia after the war, most of them being unemployed or working in the grey economy, forgotten by everybody in a country that itself is impoverished and drowned in corruption and organised crime. Most of them were ill, suffering not only from psychological disturbances, but also from various psychosomatic disorders.

Interviews

Interviews were carried out by psychoanalysts who had no knowledge of the participants' backgrounds in order to fully concentrate on the dream content and the way the dream was told. Narratives of the participants were abundant with horrible stories, e.g., being witness of another man killing a woman who was holding a child, or of collecting pieces of the friend's body, or how a torturer brought his ten-year-old son to beat the victim making the interviewers deal with undigested non-symbolised introjects or "beta elements", It was often difficult for interviewers to contain feelings that these narratives evoke as is also observed in clinical settings.

Having traumatised individuals in an experimental situation implied a risk for regressive processes for example when interviews were perceived by some participants as an interrogation, as a part of an investigation or judicial procedure. In such situations we observed that elements from the interview situation could appear in dreams dreamt in the laboratory demonstrating how participants tried to cope with this stressful situation. Ambivalence towards the interviewer could be observed in that the interview simultaneously could be characterised by openness and collaboration and causing withdrawal and persecutory anxieties.

Two types of dream narratives were collected during the assessment: dreams dreamt in the laboratory, either recorded during the night upon awakening from sleep (spontaneous or initiated), and dream narratives recorded in the morning immediately after the sleep, when subjects were asked to tell dreams that they dreamt during the last night. In addition, we asked subjects to tell any dream that they had since the war which they considered as important or recurring. We collected 94 dreams from experimental group and 66 dreams from referential group. We did not collect dreams during the night for the referential group, which explains the difference in number (we collected 22 dreams upon awakening in experimental group). Interviewers tried to obtain a spontaneous, uninterrupted dream report and questions were raised by the interviewer after the report. All dreams are analysed. In this chapter we selected one dream typical for the experimental group (with current PTSD).

Post-traumatic dreams and symbolisation. A dream – analysed with the "the Zurich Dream Process Coding System (ZDPCS)" and with the "Psychoanalytic Enunciation Analysis (PEA)"

The dream chosen for this presentation was analysed by two methods for dream analysis: the Zurich Dream Process Coding System (ZDPCS) and the Psychoanalytic Enunciation Analysis (PEA), which shortly will be presented, and we will describe which aspects of the dream material that are possible to focus on with these two methods.

1. *The "Zurich Dream Process Coding System" (ZDPCS) by Moser & v. Zeppelin*

In the dream generating model of Moser and von Zeppelin, dreaming is understood/conceptualised as a simulation-process going on within an inner micro-world that is created at night, an excerpt of the far more complex world of the dreamer in the waking state (Moser & v. Zeppelin, 1996). The simulation processes happening in this micro-world commute between relational activities and safety measures and reveal inner possibilities and constraints as well as individual patterns of both (Moser et al., 1991). Information integration and processing are considered to be actions of cognition as well as of affect-laden thoughts, moderating the dream, giving it its concrete composition. A dream is usually instigated by day residues (experiences, thoughts, wishes, affects), which stimulate a focal conflict and the task of dreaming is to try to find a solution for the activated conflict. For traumatised persons, unsafe areas of the mind related to their traumatic experiences are regularly activated, presented as conflictual areas, e.g., shame vs. pride in relation to others (Hartmann, 1984). Dreaming will then attempt to create situations that are safe, often a wished-for involvement with others, i.e., free of shame. These focal conflicts are embedded in a dream complex, which is conceptualised as a memory model, where affects, self- and object-representations as well as "representations of interactions that have been generalised" ("RIGs", (Stern, 1985)) are included.

Traumatic experiences (with not integrated, free-floating affects) form rigid areas within this otherwise flexible networks. Initially, the dreamer searches for a solution for these traumatic experiences; they are activated in the same form over and over again and are often related to a failure of affect-regulation and in worst case causing fearful awakening.

Interrupting a dream scene for regulating purposes is one of the most effective means to stop affective overflow, e.g., when affects cannot be integrated or become too intensive. Verbalisations of concrete affects emerging in dreams, are considered as an endeavour of the dreamer of distancing from concrete experiencing affects and then to provide the dreamer with more control by transforming the dreamer into an observer commenting on his dream-experience.

The ZDPCS method allows to systematically evaluate a dream by coding three dimensions:

1. a *positioning field* listing all subjects and objects that are used by the dreamer in order to fill the dream scene
2. aspects of *changes, movements* are coded (Loco-Time-Motion), i.e., how the dream develops over time. Here, aspects of "interrupts" are recorded, i.e., moments when actions are stopped, abrupt changes are taking place, or the entire dream is stopped
3. *interactions and moments of relatedness* are registered ("interaction field")

The way a dream-scene is equipped, the types of changes and transformations, as well as the way interactions are developed allow conclusions on *how the dream was dreamt* and on which inner capabilities the dreamer have to regulate affects, to integrate experiences into the inner psychological world and finally to solve current existing psychological conflicts.

2.   *The psychoanalytic enunciation analysis (PEA)*

This method has its roots in psychoanalysis, semiotics and pragmatics. PEA can be defined as a method that combines the phenomenology of the dream with a psychoanalytically informed analysis of the structure and dynamics of the utterances of the dream telling. Similar with the "Zurich Dream Process Coding System" (ZDPCS), interpersonal relations are in focus, and so is the dreamer's attempts to restore internal security by relating to others in the dream in a safer way where traumatic anxieties may be better contained.

The main aim of PEA is to evaluate the levels of symbolisation of the manifest dream, and to evaluate the internal subject-other relations (internal object relations) implicitly present in the dream telling. PEA focuses on the manifest dream-text and on latent emotional content of the dream and, furthermore, it evaluates the transferential relationship implied in the dream as a whole. The core element in the method is the analysis of the structure of the enunciation: how the first person, the "I", in the enunciation relates to the "you" (second person) in the dream and on what is told or referred to. The method operates with levels of symbolisation from fully symbolised – the symbolic mode (thoughts that demonstrate self-reflection and thinking) – to low-level, and sometimes not-symbolised, utterances (like cries, syllables out of context, un-reflected verbal reactions), conceptualised as the mirroring-imaginary mode.

In the symbolic mode, the dream narrative has qualities of mental work where values, attitudes, meaningful and common-sense words are taken in and brought into perspective. In contrast, the mirroring-imaginary mode has characteristics of the concept of projective identification (Bion, 1967; Ogden, 1994). It may consist of an outburst without an understanding of the content of the outburst and without a wish or capacity to relate to it, marked by confusion.

In a dream characterised by integration of difficult mental experiences the two modes are linked. Central in the model is to identify when the bodily expressions of the imaginary mode are transformed or not to more symbolic utterances, very much like identifying the effects of the alpha-function of the mind (Bion, 1967).

The dimensions of symbolisation used in PEA are defined as follows:

Dimension 1 (D1):

The utterances have purely expressive function (e.g., a cry, a sigh, confusion, or elements of disorganised and fragmented speech). The utterance is one-dimensional, i.e., expressed as the subjective 'cry' to the other as an all-containing, all-embracing, holding environment. The expression lacks any kind of metaphorical characteristics; neither does it contain any clear references to space or time

---

Dimension 2 (D2):

The utterance carries spatial and (sometimes) temporal references which are expressed in the I-you relationship. The subject (1 person) is pointing at actions in time and space, but the utterance may lack reference to an explicit symbolic and social context

---

Dimension 4 (D4):

This dimension presents the institutionalised aspects of the subject's utterance, i.e., expressions of information or informative descriptions, teaching, doctrines or moralising clichés. In this mode, the subject adapts itself to rules, laws and norms, is directive, stating facts, gives orders and conveying institutional, moral or social knowledge; "that is how it is"

Dimension 5 (D5):

This represents a dialogical and reciprocal relationship where something is proposed that immediately is taken in and reflected upon (both by the subject and the other). Here mentalising positions in language appear, and the subject is open for reflections. It is dialogic positions where the utterance is presented to the other in a tentative way allowing for other perspectives to appear

---

In short: this dimension presents the subject as self-reflecting and thinking, question-marking thoughts and feelings of self and other, i.e., dialectically constituted and mediated to the other.

Dimension 3 (D3), annotated + or – in the analysis:

This dimension represents the link between the imaginary and the symbolic (therefore placed at the end here). It represents the common-sense function of the mind that integrates the not understandable and disintegrated, that is, the imaginary with symbolic levels of communication and speech, similar to the alpha function of the mind. This has to do with "the we-ness in the enunciation", the socially and culturally-based identification of meaning. This is a necessary structure for establishing common sense, and the possibility for sharing and integrating the meaning of utterances in a group-perspective (versus private talk or solipsistic meaning-making). Talking about common sense requires that a "we", to a certain extent, shares the same foreground-background perspectives (or: the same figure ground configurations) of a scene

---

We will now demonstrate how the two methods of analysing dreams may supplement and complement each other, and then give suggestions on how analyses like these may enrich our understanding of dreaming of traumatised persons. We will then discuss possible clinical implications.

Table 10.1 Sequencing of the dream from the experimental group

S 1	After the "Oluja"[1] I was in prison, I had horrific dreams,
S 2	for example, I dream that they torture me, burn my skin.
S 3	What do I know,
S 4	with hot iron, in different ways.
S 5	Then I had at that time a lot …
S 6	all those things that they capture me, kill me.
S 7	What do I know,
S 8	shoot at me, I see blood.

Note
1 A battle during the war.

Analysis of a dream

The following dream from the experimental group (subjects with current PTSD) was analysed with the two methods. In the Zurich Dream Process Coding System, (ZDPCS) the dream is transcribed into present tense in order to create the impression of the dream as it had been dreamt. PEA on the other side keeps the past tense in the way the dreamer has told it in the morning so it may be possible to get a picture of the transference to the listener/interviewer. This different ways of preparing the dream material for analysis may lead to slightly different versions of their manifest text (Table 10.1).

The dream is put into sequences of different scenes. First, the dream as it was told (analysed by PEA):

Table 10.2 summarises our findings of PEA, including the understanding of the manifest and latent level of the dream. The latent meaning is hypothesised in each utterance or sequence based on the analysis of the whole dream and the sequence seen in context.

Summary of analysis:

The dreamer was overwhelmed by annihilation anxiety, but able to convey his confused emotions. The dream was characterised by a dominance of bodily anchored symbol representation, not-symbolised signifiers and signifiers in the imaginary mode: i.e., blood, destruction, penetration.

Transferential assumptions: the dreamer started with a belief in the interviewer as a "good object" listener. Soon he seemed increasingly overwhelmed by primitive anxieties as if an empathic link was under threat. The relation to an internal emphatic object seemed to fail and fear of body mutilation and fear of death emerged. The interviewer was then not experienced as an empathic container for his anxieties (Table 10.3).

Table 10.2 Summaries of PEA

Sequence/PEA	Manifest level	Latent level
S 1 D3;+D2	My experience of a horrifying event is linked to a horrifying dream	I am filled with feelings of horror. Annihilation anxiety
S 2 D2;+D3	I am imprisoned and brought to pain	Feelings of being mutilated and penetrated. Inability to defend myself
S 3 D1;+	I am not sure of the implication of or of the fact of what I am saying	Feelings of confusion and shaken identity; apprehension of catastrophe
S 4 D2;+	Torturing instruments on my body	Instrumental, impersonal threat: mutilation, penetration
S 5 D2;+	I have many other feelings/visions/ memories of torture that I cannot mention	Wish to escape and fear of being trapped and of bodily mutilation
S 6 D1;+	They kill me	Annihilation anxiety. Anxiety of not getting support for survival
S 7 D1;+	I am not sure about what they exactly are doing	Confusion, no representation
S 8 D1;+	Somebody is shooting, blood is coming	Catastrophic feelings of death, life running out

Table 10.3 Sequencing of dream from the experimental group in present tense

S1	They torture me, burn my skin,
-	Don't know [cognitive process]
S1	With hot iron, in different ways.
-	Then I have a lot; all those things [cognitive process]
S2	They capture me, kill me,
-	I don't know [cognitive process]
S3	(They) shoot at me, I see blood

The dream analysed by the Zurich Dream Process Coding System, ZDPCS

As mentioned above, this dream coding method is an evaluating system based on a model of cognitive-affective regulation. Analysis focuses on formal criteria and structures of a dream: the number of situations contained in a dream; the type of places and social settings named in a dream (descriptions, attributes); objects appearing (and their descriptions, attributes); placements, movements, interactions of objects as well as the question of whether the dreamer himself was involved in interactions or if he remains a spectator; affective reactions;

and finally, the ending and beginning of a situation (how, when interrupts occur).

The dream coding system aims at making these structural aspects of dreaming transparent in order to better understand the affect regulation processes taking place.

Two principles of affect regulation are assumed: (a) a security principle and (b) an involvement principle.

To facilitate transparency of the coding, three columns are being used: (a) the positioning field (PF), (b) the field of trajectories called "loco time motion" (LTM) and (c) the interaction field (IAF). The positioning field contains all objects or rather cognitive elements (CE) as well as their attributes and their positions.

In the field of trajectories, all movements of objects and CEs are coded, and interactions with others are coded in the interaction field column including specifications of changes (Table 10.4).

The coding of this dream reveals the following structure:

The structure of this dream is marked by two interruptions, the C.P. (cognitive process) function, which is to prevent charging the dream with affects. The dreamer remains passive, revealing a helpless self. He fails in creating affective connections. All the objects remain anonymous, "they" are neither concrete as persons nor can one find interactions or mutual involvement in the dream. On the contrary, the threatening element of the underlying dream complex is not transformed but appears undisguised. There is no social setting,

Table 10.4 Coded version of the dream from the experimental group

Situation	Positioning field	LTM	Interaction field
SI	OP$_1$ (they) SP		IR.C kin int[1]
/C.P./ S2	OP$_1$ (they) SP		IR.C kin int
/C.P./ S3	OP$_1$ (they) SP		IR.C kin int DISS IR.S
/C.P./			

Note
1 Interactional relation of kinesthetic intentional quality (moving with an intention).

which would provide many possibilities for involvement; the positioning field is not circumscribed (indicating a total threat, not focused on a specific or circumscribed situation). The only way to handle the underlying affectivity (threat) is to interrupt (C.P.). Even though the dreamer makes three attempts, the situation deteriorates and ends in destruction. No solution can be found for how to integrate and manage the affects connected to the dream complex and thus how to interact, and the security principle cannot develop in an adequate way. In other words: simple interruptions with continuation of the same process again, without transformations. The dreamer has no perspective of a possible solution but can only observe his own disintegration.

Summary of findings of the Zurich Dream Process Coding System, (ZDPCS) and Psychoanalytic Enunciation Analysis, (PEA)

PEA demonstrated how the dream was characterised by an imaginary mode with little access to symbolic transformation of dream elements which stayed quite fragmented. The transference to the listener seemed to deteriorate to more anxiety-laden primitive forms. In the ZDPCS it was maybe more concretely demonstrated how the dream represented a fragmented image of the conflicts evoked in the dream and how the dreamer failed to make connections and relations and was overwhelmed by catastrophic anxiety.

One may say that ZDPCS could specify how lack of symbolic functioning made the dreamer victim of the primitive, overwhelming anxieties relating to memories of traumatic experiences evoked during the day before.

The psychoanalytic enunciation analysis demonstrated the existence and function of both the imaginary mode and the symbolic mode in the dream and in the telling of it to the interviewer/researcher. Both levels of symbolisation and the quality of the relation between them inform about the internal and external relationship between the individual who has had the dream and the listener. Both methods show that the dreamer had high levels of insecurity, low ability to regulate emotions, low capacity to solve problems and few, if any, good interpersonal relations. This is in marked contrast to dreams from the referential group (persons without current PTSD), not presented in this chapter. These persons had also gone through difficult war experiences but had been more able to be active during these, while those with current PTSD had more often been in passive situations (Jovic et al., 2018).

These differences were clear trends in the material presented in other works from this research project (Jovic et al., 2018; Varvin et al., 2012).

Conclusion: clinical significance of empirical results

From what has been demonstrated here, we would like to direct the focus to some aspects that seem to be of special significance in the treatment of patients who have suffered extreme traumatisation.

The analysis of this dream (and other dreams in the project) showed that post-traumatic states and especially post-traumatic dreams represent more or less failed attempts at restoring meaning in the internal world, meaning in relation to others and, maybe most of all, failed attempts to regain a sense of security and safety. A threatening catastrophe is looming everywhere for the traumatised, both from inside and, projected or not, from outside. The traumatised experiences a host of anxieties and fears including fear of loss of object love, fear of loss of the internal good object and castration anxiety. What seems to be at the root of this psychic helplessness characteristic for traumatisation (Freud, 1926a) is the loss of internal protection from an empathic object resulting in predominance of annihilation anxiety (Hurvich, 2003).

Freud distinguished traumatic neuroses from other neuroses in terms of the nature of the conflict in the ego (Freud, 1919b). In ordinary neuroses the "enemy" is the libido, which threatens the ego from within. "In traumatic and war neuroses, the human ego is defending itself from a danger which threatens it from within or which is embodied by a shape assumed by the ego itself" (Freud, 1919a, p. 210). Fixation at the moment of the traumatic experience is the basis of a traumatic neurosis, and such patients regularly repeat the traumatic situation in their dreams (Freud, 1916).

Thus, one may assume that, according to Freud, symptoms of traumatic neuroses represent a regression to a more primitive mode of functioning where a painful traumatic experience that overwhelmed the ego is constantly being repeated in fantasy, thought and dream, as an attempt of the ego to master belatedly the overwhelming influx of stimuli it had failed to handle in the traumatic moment (Freud, 1919a). Furthermore, according to van der Kolk, traumatic memories usually come back as emotional and sensory states without the capacity to represent them verbally (van der Kolk, 1996). He attributes this failure of processing information on a symbolic level to the core of PTSD, as it is this essential ability that is needed to properly categorise and integrate traumatic experience with other experience.

Laub has described the overwhelming experience that hampers the process of construction when attempting to account for traumatic experiences (Laub, 2005b). In order to process information, i.e., to make it our own, the process of symbolisation is necessary. We perceive, grasp, transform and exchange information in order to participate with others in reality.

For this, symbols are needed that will allow us to communicate not only with the outside world, but also to communicate with oneself – i.e., with an empathic object in the internal world – in order to create meaning. This is in line with Freud's conception of the process of symbolisation as an internal psychic event, where a thing-representation, becoming linked to another psychic event, i.e., a psychological word representation, and that this linking of thing- and word-representations creates a symbol. In other words, Freud saw the formation of the symbol as occurring in the context of an internal communicative process, or as Laub puts it: "One comes to know one's story only by telling it to oneself", and "Reality can be grasped only in a condition of affective atunement with oneself" (Laub, 2005, p. 315). In extreme traumatic situations these internal and external dialogic relationships are being subject to deadly assault, in that the empathically, in tune, and responsive other threatens to disappear both in the internal world and also in the external world. This characterises the core of a traumatising assault, which results in the abolishment of the "good object" that enables and safeguards the communicative process of symbolisation.

Traumatic dreams are characterised among others by their repetitiveness. Traumatisation is thus the result of loss of internal protection – primarily the loss of basic trust and mastery, which is experienced as loss of the protective and empathic other, who in other circumstances gives meaning to thoughts and actions. In such traumatic conditions, the process of symbolisation is distorted to the extent that thoughts cannot be given a temporally meaningful place in the emotional autobiographical narrative. As a result, the traumatised person feels dehumanised, frequently accompanied by feelings of shame. In order to regain a humanised state, repetition compulsion comes into play, forcing the traumatised to relive the traumatising experience repeatedly in the attempt to find symbols for opposing forces experienced within to avoid a catastrophic fusion of antagonistic forces and to (re-)gain the ability to distinguish the good from the bad and ultimately avoid psychic death.

Dreaming may be considered as a central part of the mind's work with unmetabolised, trauma-related elements (Bion, 1977; Hartmann, 1984). The study of dreams may thus give a privileged insight into the working of the mind. Working with dreams and especially nightmares of traumatised patients has proved to be of great importance in aiding the traumatised mind to restore its symbolic function (Hartmann, 1984; Adams-Silvan & Silvan, 1990; Pöstenyi, 1996). Furthermore, traumatic dreams seem to be dominated by claustrum-like internal object-relation patterns with little flexibility for change, where narratives of the dream will be more of an imaginary kind and lacking symbolising capacities.

When treating traumatised patients, the quality of the experienced trauma seems to be relevant for enhancing the psychotherapeutic process. Torture survivors in therapy are important here, as the torture itself contains such monstrous acts that make them inconceivable not only to the victim but also to the listener of accounts given by the victim. Both patient and analyst have great difficulty making sense of acts performed by the perpetrator, thus inhibiting the capacity to symbolise these acts in a comprehensible manner. But it is exactly this capacity that will enable the victim to grasp his feelings, emotions, and reactions. It is the dehumanisation that both victims and perpetrators encounter, and the humiliation forced onto the victim that limit the capacity to symbolise, i.e., to put into words what has happened and make sense of it.

This may appear as a defence against anxiety related to connecting current problematic experiences to previous traumatic experiences often frightening, shameful and guilt-laden. One may call this integration anxiety. In a state of non-integration, anxiety threatens from two directions: the past catastrophic experience of loss of the total self and the threat of future integration – a threat because it assumes remembering and thus arouses the fear of renewed anxiety of loss of self and it prevents both integration and the symbolisation process.

Having this in mind and considering the dream process as a special kind of thought process that excludes the common sense reality perception of waking thought will be helpful in understanding the traumatised mind. In this dream-thought process interactions may take place. In contrast to a waking state, subjects and objects in the dream scenario may easily change dimensions which is impossible to conceive in everyday life.

By looking at the dreams of the traumatised through the focal point of the Zurich Dream Process Coding System, (ZDPCS), disturbances of affect-regulation become apparent. Those disturbances reflect the dreamer's inability to get involved with others in the dream scene because of the anxieties, especially annihilation anxiety, evoked by such involvement. In the analysis with ZDPCS we see that the security principle overrules the involvement principle in these dreams. Here the extreme helplessness of the patient becomes evident. From this point of view, a wish is fulfilled, namely the wish to regain a feeling of internal security by avoiding anxiety-provoking situations in the dream scene.

Within the theoretical framework of Moser and von Zeppelin's dream-generating model (Moser & v. Zeppelin, 1996), the dreamer's capacity to get involved is an indicator of his ability to find a solution for an activated conflict, which in the context of trauma is embedded in a rigid traumatic complex. In our study we hypothesised that traumatised dreamers would exhibit a great lack of involvement capacity. This we have demonstrated in the analysed dream from the experimental group. The capacity to get involved – although initially accessible – is consequently disrupted by the dreamer's distancing manoeuvres that are activated in order to avoid upcoming overwhelming emotions of life and death. In contrast, dreams of the referential group (analysis not presented in this chapter) exhibit a higher level of integration, where the involvement principle dominates, and security regulation seems less necessary. This is seen as potentially helping the dreamer towards a resolution of the underlying traumatic complex. This process implies binding free-floating, anxiety laden and incomprehensible emotions to generalised memories of experiences that did make sense earlier in one's own life.

When researching dreams, we have underlined that a dream dreamt in a laboratory setting show differences from one dreamt during a psychoanalytic process. Mainly it is the context that differs, as a dream dreamt within a psychoanalytic process will be determined, to a large extent, by the specific transference situation, which will be quite different from the transferential aspects of dreams dreamt in a laboratory, where the setting will elicit special expectations regarding the researchers.

Nevertheless, changes in transference patterns may be detected by the PEA method, indicating the extent to which the analyst or the interviewer in a laboratory is used as an all-embracing container for anxieties, sadness or fragmented self-experience. The listener of the dream may become a receiver of anxiety and fear of body mutilation, fear of death (Rosenbaum & Varvin, 2007). The dream of the person from the experimental group exhibited bodily anchored symbol presentations, which were mostly not-symbolised signifiers portraying thus the overwhelming annihilation anxiety. Analysing dreams from the referential group (participants without current PTSD but with severe war experiences) showed the dreamer's ability to develop a positive scenario managing to almost create an atmosphere with positive connotations. But often in dreams from this group, the dreamer did not succeed in his integrating endeavours and they seemed to be forced to create a scenario characterised by different forms of defence.

Thus, PEA, by analysing the form and content of the imaginary mode (Lacan, 1977), showed here from the subject from the experimental group, i.e., the mode in which a person presents himself in a monadic and dyadic way, enables a closer analysis of the pain-evacuating, projective, claustrum-like internal object-relation patterns that dominated his dream world and his inner world. PEA thus reflects the influence that trauma has on our psyche: a dominance of the imaginary mode and absence of the symbolic mode of speech. That is, the absence of an other-oriented mode, signifying a mentalising, self-reflective, inter- or trans-subjective internal object-relation pattern.

We do not expect the analyst to apply these methods to dreams presented in the analytic sessions, but we hope to have encouraged analysts to listen to narratives and dreams in a modified way and with a broader perspective on the functions of dreaming. From a clinical perspective the findings presented here call for paying more attention to what degree the dreamer gets involved in his dreams and how this involvement is realised. On the one hand the dreamer may withdraw, for example by interrupting interactions in a scene to fend off unbearable emotions. On the other hand, one may see development of interactions which may imply strengthening of the symbolic mode of functioning.

In summary it can be stated that traumatic dreams are not different from other dreams in that they in fact are dreams containing – like all dreams – thought processes in a dream state with all the mechanisms of dreams at work in a more or less successful search for alleviation of the incomprehensible dehumanising forces at work at the time of the traumatising experience.

Notes

1 They were recruited from a larger group of subjects participating in a "Psychobiology of PTSD" study and assessed by various psychological and neuropsychological instruments, and different biological, endocrinological, and genetic variables where elicited as well (Jovic et al., 2018; Vermetten et al., 2018).

2 Polysomnographic recordings (i.e., comprehensive recording of the biophysiological changes occurring during sleep – like electroencephalography (EEG), eye movements (EOG), muscle activity (EMG), and heart rhythm (ECG), as well as respiratory functions) were elicited for the experimental but not for the referential group.

Chapter 11

"The essay method"

A qualitative method for studying therapeutic dialogues[1,2]

Introduction

The aim of this article is to present and to argue for a psycho-analytically grounded qualitative method for studying therapeutic dialogues. A way of writing up the dialogue inspired by the method of writing an essay, will be demonstrated. The literary essay, a way of disciplined freedom of writing, is used as a model. In the following, the term "The essay method" will be used as a shorthand for this approach. Analysis of dialogues is based in psychoanalytic object relations theory (Sandler & Sandler, 1998) that includes theory of character formation (Killingmo, 2007). This perspective implies focusing both relational aspects as well as formal/non-verbal aspects of dialogues. The method implies a close monitoring of clinical material, guided by an overall theoretical frame, making it particularly suitable for the study of relational qualities of psychotherapeutic dialogues. This will be demonstrated by material from a study of therapeutic competence in a group of student therapists.

This approach is based on general principles of qualitative studies (Frommer, 2007; Kvale, 1999) and by using the essay form, it is in line with recent developments in integration of methods and arts-based qualitative research in psychology (Butler-Kisber, 2018; Chamberlain et al., 2011, 2018). A specific psychoanalytic way of listening to and organising material characterises the method's mode of qualitative research.

In this paper, the origin of the method will be described. Then, its use in practice will be illustrated by material from the study of student therapists. Finally, the background and the context of the

DOI: 10.4324/9781003206057-11

method is outlined. Essential aspects of the implied listening perspective are explained and how the writing of an essay is applied in the research process. The method is then evaluated and compared to other qualitative methods.

The origin of the method

The method was developed as part of a project at the Clinic of Dynamic Psychotherapy, Department of Psychology, University of Oslo. As experienced psychoanalysts the researchers evaluated the competence in psychoanalytic, dynamic psychotherapy of a group of student therapists ($N = 21$) who had completed a three-year training programme. This programme consists of clinical seminars, practice as therapists and supervision of their clinical work (Killingmo et al., 2014).

Based on one audio-recorded session from the end of each therapy session, two researchers recruited for the project (including the author) were instructed to make separate evaluations of the competence of each student according to a set of predefined variables grouped into four main categories:

1. The therapeutic relationship as a whole
2. The analytic attitude
3. Transformation of understanding into concrete interventions
4. Interpersonal interaction skills

Each category had a number of sub-questions. Many of these were adopted from David Tuckett's form for evaluating analytic competence in candidates in psychoanalytic training (Tuckett, 2005). After coding the material according to this manual, the researchers evaluated each therapist and reached a consensus evaluation.

In the course of the coding process, this system of variables proved difficult to apply. It was a top-down approach that necessitated fitting empirical data into a series of predefined variables; thus, it represented a limited way of using the qualitative method. In the process of analysing therapy sessions, it was found that the sub-variables were too distant to match the actual clinical material. Generally, the clinical practice of the student therapists turned out not to fit the theory-driven predefined variables. The therapists appeared to be so "unsophisticated" (inexperienced) that it was impossible to meaningfully code the material, for example in terms of transference dynamics. The theoretical concepts of the registration manual on the one hand and the clinical material on the other were too disparate. The coding process involved further searching for partial elements in the clinical material to fit into separate predefined categories, which led to a fragmentation so that context and wholeness disappeared from the material. The relational atmosphere was lost as well. The researchers saw that a method of analysis was needed that was closer to the distinctive character of the material, implying less predefined theoretical interpretation and, at the same time, being especially directed at global and formal aspects of the session material of psychoanalytic, dynamic psychotherapy. A procedure was needed that was based on a certain preunderstanding but that nevertheless could be free enough to catch the specifics and the wholeness of the material.

This led to a change in the methodological approach in line with qualitative research methodology. Instead of searching for specific, predefined and theoretically based variables (top-down approach), the researchers decided to base the approach on a psychoanalytic way of listening to the material.

The first step was to relax and just listen with an open mind to the audiotape of the session without intermission. Immediately afterwards, the researchers spontaneously wrote down, in their own words, their subjective impression of the totality and relational qualities of the interaction between the two participants in the dialogue. This written impression, based on psychoanalytic listening, was inspired by the "essay" as a literary form in that it was organised and written in order to give expression to thoughts resulting from this way of listening. The essay was estimated to consist of two to three pages of typewritten text for each therapy session. This was followed by a process of hermeneutically going back and forth from the essay to the session material in order to support or disqualify a formulation or an evaluation in the essay. In this way, the researchers reworked the essay several times and identified salient themes, and these themes were seen in the context of the whole session as manifested in the session-based essays. Further, the researchers had no information about the patients or the therapists, and in this way any predisposed perspective of listening based on knowledge of the therapist's competence or the background of the patient were abolished.

The way of listening described here has features in common with the clinical listening of the psychoanalyst. Psychoanalysts endeavour not to listen in prescribed directions, but to "take in" the material without intentional selection and to store it directly in the unconscious. Expressions like listening "with evenly suspended attention" (Freud, 1912) and listening "free of memory and desire" (Bion, 1967) illustrate this aim. These formulations can be viewed as instructions for a way of listening to clinical material which invite an exploration of the subjectivity of listening (Killingmo, 1999). However, the instructions do not by themselves determine the understanding of the material. Understanding the meaning of the material presupposes a theory and is a further step in analysing the material. The theory specifies the content of the listening perspective and it is by way of a theory that the observations of the psychoanalyst will appear as "psychoanalytically" distinguished from any other kind of observations.

The impact of theory is central to this method as well. This concerns how the researcher's preunderstanding influences the way the empirical material is perceived and structured when listening (Kvale, 1999), and as a psychoanalytic theory it acted as a common reference behind the listening perspective of the researchers. Even if they approached the material differently and with an "open mind", on a preconscious level, the same theory influenced the selection of data, how they were organised, and how they were evaluated. In contrast to the analyst at work, the researchers in the present project also had the specific task of evaluating the competence of the students as dynamic therapists. This was the aim of this study and prepared for a certain way of specifying the direction of listening. The method that was developed has, however, a broader perspective in that it can be applied in different research contexts. The main issue is that the method can be used generally in studying dialogues in psychoanalytic therapies.

Why the name "essay" method?

In this study, an "atomistic" method was replaced by a "holistic" one. This does not mean that the holistic approach is always better suited than the atomistic one in studying and evaluating clinical dialogues.

For this procedure to qualify as a method, procedures had to be established. Almost spontaneously, the essay came to the fore as a possible method. An essay is associated with a particular form of written account. Compared to the ordinary scientific treatise, the essay has a short form, and while the former is subordinated to a commonly accepted code of expression, the latter has its own code. The essayist writes on behalf of him-/herself and is free to "play" with the well-known. While the author of a dissertation is expected to follow a disciplined, logical, and coherent style, the essayist can permit him-/herself to employ metaphors and popular phrases.

The essay has a long history as a literary genre. It was developed by Michel Eyquem de Montaigne (1533–92) who thought of it as a short form of prose dealing with even the most serious matters (Montaigne, 1910). This genre could treat every cultural issue in a surprising and unexpected way, often with an element of humour. Even if the essay allows for a more evocative way of expression, it has the hallmark of discussing a topic in a reflective way. Essais, or "attempts", is, in Montaigne's spirit, not a transmission of proven knowledge or of confident opinion, but a project of tentative exploration of topics. Further, it is a remedy against false, unexamined, and externally imposed notions. It is thus a form of inquiry that may be suitable for research. It has developed as a kind of reflective inductive method (Lopate, 1994). As mentioned earlier, this is in line with arts-based qualitative research where art is used in different aspects of the research process (gathering data, presenting results etc).

By launching this procedure as a psychological research method, an established genre of literature has been in the background. As a literary form, the essay involves similar features a clinician's approach to clinical data. These features can be summarised as follows:

1. Compiling a huge amount of data on different levels (emotional, cognitive, relational) (Nielsen, 1995)
2. Relating to different psychological perspectives in a short and consistent form
3. Freedom of observing, as well as reporting the observed
4. Opening for subjectivity in the process of understanding
5. One is not looking for predefined categories
6. Aligned with descriptive aspects of the material, thereby increasing reliable communication

7. Catching predominant relational aspects of the clinical material, such as central points, continuity/fragmentation, level of communication and emotional atmosphere

The starting point was the study of therapeutic competence of students based on pre-defined categories, which then developed into a bottom-up, phenomenological study of therapeutic dialogues that examined the quality of therapy-session dialogues. A basic premise for the essay method is that the researcher has to take a kind of meta-perspective in observing the dialogue. He/she has to be "above" the content of the actual material and instead orient his/her listening-perspective towards the kind of dialogue that is reflected by the material. He/she should ask him-/herself: "What kind of discourse are we listening to here? Who speaks like this to each other"?

The essay method in practice: from an atomistic to a holistic approach

The change in methodological approach also led to a change on the conceptual level from an "atomistic" to a "holistic" conception, in line with the aim of qualitative research to view parts in contexts. Based on work with the first top-down approach, it was considered more relevant to think of dynamic therapeutic competence in terms of global qualities than in terms of separate, distinctive capacities based on summation of predefined categories.

The first step in the method is listening. The listening that is recommended is similar to psychoanalytic listening in that any aspect of the dialogue may be focused. However, the listening will also be shaped by the perspective determined by the aim of the study. Fitting into these frames, there is an emotional listening that uses a psychoanalytic framework. The knowledge required for this type of listening is psychoanalytic theory (here, an object relational perspective that includes theory of character formation), but during the process, this knowledge will be mainly preconscious and not formulated as categories to be sought after. It is thus not free-floating attention, as in the psychoanalytic process, but a special kind of listening that opens up different perspectives and allows the listener to dwell on details and reflect on different meanings throughout the process.

This special form of listening is similar to the way of listening or reading of texts in most qualitative research, but different in that it is a form that involves specific competencies; it presupposes training in psychoanalytic listening through the researcher's background in clinical psychoanalysis. This "deep" listening also facilitates the researcher focusing his/her own state of mind while listening. The researcher may let things open in his/her mind and reflect on what happens in his/her mind while listening. It is a form of free, but disciplined, listening that allows opening up for emotional qualities within the material, the emotional effect it has on the listener, and through that, let patterns and meanings emerge in the mind of the researcher.

What appears in the mind of the listener will thus also be shaped by his/her own psychological preconceptions and states of mind. Using psychoanalytic training, countertransference reactions may be analysed in order to examine the possibility of idiosyncratic aspects of how the material has been perceived and organised in the mind of the researcher. The aim is not to discard preunderstanding and countertransference reactions, but to use them in order to better understand the material. This represents a way of reflecting on the researcher's preunderstanding or pre-judgement in Gadamer's meaning (State, 2000).

The second step is writing the essay. This process will usually have several recursive stages; that is, the writer(s) go back and forth between parts and context and between different parts of the material, doing a hermeneutic reading. The first draft may be an unorganised assembly of impressions and thoughts. In the following rewritings, a more coherent picture may emerge, which then will be the basis of the essay formulated by the researcher. Each aspect, for example a dialogue sequence, has to be evaluated in the context of the whole session, in consonance with the importance of context in qualitative research. In this process, the text will be organised from a point of view which is determined by the aim of the study or the research question(s). In the study where the method was developed, it was an evaluation of therapeutic competence in beginning therapists.

The third step is working toward consensus. The researchers involved shall each write an essay separately, which are then brought to the research group involved in the project (the research group can consist of two or more researchers). Here, it is most fruitful for each researcher's essay to be read out loud. In this way, the essence of each essay, particularly the emotional quality of the text, may be better understood. During the reading, the co-researchers listen in very much the same way as in the previous step: with an open mind, as free as possible and taking their own countertransference into consideration. The ensuing dialogue is an essential part of the process: What stands out in the different essays?

Are there common themes and where are the discrepancies, if any?

What is the meaning embedded in different ways of listening?

Are they incompatible with each other, or are there different aspects that may fit into a common understanding of the material?

This part is the researcher-consensus part of the process (Leuzinger-Bohleber, 2015). The question here is whether it is possible to work towards a consensus on the salient aspects of the material: this involves reflections on the different listening to and understanding the material. If consensus cannot be reached, this is noted, and one should then return to the analysis after working with several cases to see if consensus can be reached or not.

As will be demonstrated in the material from the study of student therapists described in the next part, a specification of what appeared as significant aspects or patterns in the material for each therapist was done. This phase in the research process implies a disciplined re-reading of the material from points of view that had appeared during the initial phases of the research process. Findings can thus be shaped in a bottom-up way based on an intense study of the material. These findings can then be formulated as tentative concepts that in turn can be confronted with the material by a new reading from the conceptual perspectives that had been formulated.

The fourth step is theoretical in that concepts can be formulated and put in relation to present theories that may be modified or changed. In this way, the method can be theory-building as it tests, improves or extends a particular theory in psychoanalysis by systematic confrontation with empirical material, or enriches the theory by giving a deeper understanding of a phenomenon (Stiles, 2015). In the study that will be presented in the following, concepts were specified that can be tested in new research.

Example from research on therapeutic competence of student therapists

The material consists of data from 21 therapies (16 women and 5 men, age 24 to 38) conducted by students in the final year of a six-year professional education programme in psychology. A single session from the last part of each therapy course was selected.

During the last step of the research process, there was a confrontation with the material through several readings/listening and discussion between the researchers, and the following three dimensions of general therapeutic competence were specified: strategic competence, therapeutic attitude and technical competence. On the basis of their essays, the researchers were instructed to return to the material from each therapist and write out their evaluation with these three aspects in mind. Below, examples will be given on how essays were used in this process:

Two research questions were formulated:

1. Did the dialogue pass on meaning from the point of view of psychoanalytic theory?
2. Did the dialogue express emotional coherence on the therapist's side?

These two criteria have in common allusions to intentionality in the therapist. It was assumed that this signified that the clinical practice of the therapist was anchored in psychodynamic or psychoanalytic theory, even if this was not present at the time for the therapist on a conscious level.

All dialogues were re-evaluated from the two research questions mentioned above concerning meaning and coherence. These two criteria were then used to evaluate whether the intentionality (even if not conscious) of the therapist was in accordance with a psychodynamic point of view.

In the first outline of essays, based on a qualitative interview analysis (Kvale, 1999), the three dimensions mentioned above (strategic competence, therapeutic attitude and technical competence) stood out as salient aspects of the therapists' ways of functioning. The sessions were then evaluated again to confirm or disconfirm whether these were meaningful relative to the aim of the study. This process involved clarifications and discussions, and work to reach consensus on these dimensions. The empirical analysis is described in a previous publication (Killingmo et al., 2014).

The three dimensions of therapeutic competence resulting from this approach will be described in the following sections. Examples will be given on how materials from the essays were used to identify and specify the three dimensions. (Material is taken from the previously published research (Killingmo et al., 2014)).

Strategic competence referred to the ability of the therapist to reflect on therapeutic aims and on means to obtain these aims. The researchers found that it supplied the therapeutic dialogue with a quality of meaning and emotional coherence, passing on that the understanding, the attitude, and the interventions of the therapist were informed by dynamic theory.

Session material of a low- and high-level strategic competence will show how this quality was deduced from the material:

1. *Low-level strategic competence:*

> In this session, the therapist demonstrates several good attributes. She listens attentively, and her non-verbal utterances are made in a way that help create the necessary psychological separation between therapist and patient. The therapist's tone of voice is soft and calm, and she is able to contain the patient's grief and sense of loss when such emotions surface during the session. The therapist's most important method of intervention is asking how this or that feels or felt. This is done in a carefully considered manner.
>
> In spite of productive listening and the ability to establish contact, the therapist is unable, at crucial points in the dialogue, to discern key formulations in the material that might have led the process further. An example will demonstrate this: the patient has an on-going conflict with her mother. This is stated openly at the start of the session. The patient expresses a strong yearning for her mother's understanding and acceptance but experiences her only as critical and disapproving. At the same time, she emphasises that she does not dare to "defy" her mother. The mother dominates their relationship. On one occasion during the session, the patient exclaims with intensity in her voice, "There is

a battle between mother and me". This is an example of a key formulation that could have served as an entry point for addressing both the anxiety and the aggression in the patient's conflict with her mother. But the therapist fails to pick up on this formulation and does not pursue the battle scenario further. Thus, the underlying aggression and force (the potential strength) that the patient holds fail to become an open theme. Rather, the patient retains a one-sided perception of herself as the weak and feeble one.

2. *High-level strategic competence:*

The patient begins the session by announcing that she wishes to speak about "the weather". She would rather "dissociate" herself, be rid of the exhausting emotions, "step out" of them and maintain the façade she is so used to. At the same time, she does not know whether she can continue to do so. It is a constant inner battle, and this is what is so exhausting: "I would prefer to push these feelings away, at the same time I don't want to push them away, I don't know where I stand – it's chaos". The patient states this in an emphatic voice, her words running in circles, and she is clearly bothered by uncertainty. But there is also something highly appealing in her voice. The therapist meets this outbreak very calmly. She does not allow herself to be pressured into the role of a "helper" but listens with acceptance and acknowledgement of the fact that the patient does not wish to confront what is uncomfortable. The therapist refrains from asking, reassuring or explaining. Through this attitude, the therapist allows the patient an undisturbed psychological space in which to express herself. After a while, the therapist concludes, "Now you are in the chaos – now you experience it – now you come here and talk about it. To me, it seems as if you are trying to forget what is uncomfortable whilst you are simultaneously facing it". The therapist here displays the ability to provide a summarising formulation of the two opposing attitudes in the patient. On the one hand, the urge to open up to all the feelings of bitterness, vulnerability and anger associated with childhood, and to the role she had to play at the time, the role of being good and "problem free" – the one who sorted things out, that is, the underlying latent or unconscious meaning of her behaviour. And, on the other hand, the urge to leave all the uncomfortable emotions behind, sweep them under the carpet and maintain the "lie of life" (the patient's own expression). The therapist is keenly observant and picks up on the patient's expression in a mirroring comment: "It is precisely this 'lie of life' you have brought up which we can examine here". This shows that the therapist has the ability to bring the dialogue forward, one step at a time. The fact that the therapist uses the word "examine" also demonstrates that she invites the patient to co-operate in finding out. In addition to building a working alliance, this invites the patient to enter into an interpretative mode. The therapist's interpretation also invites the patient to delve more deeply into her emotions. The patient sees more clearly that she has always been aware of her reluctance to acknowledge her true feelings. She has created a dream world for herself since childhood. The therapist listens calmly and intently while the patient reveals her emotions. The patient expresses guilt for shattering the perfect image of childhood. She does not want to disappoint her parents. The therapist interjects, "You were the little grown-up". Here the therapist displays the ability to concentrate a complex situation into a metaphoric formulation that hits home. The last example shows a therapist that creates a productive psychological "space" and who also manages to pick up the emotional subtext, upon which she then invites the patient to reflect.

Cases with a partial strategy were also identified: the therapist could keep the meaning and coherence in his/her way of relating, but then, at crucial moments, slipped out of it and for example gave advice like a friend.

There were also sessions with absence of any strategic thinking: sessions where therapist and patient were talking as friends in a café – or – when the therapist was outmanoeuvred by a demanding, dominating patient; a situation where the therapist was threatened by the underlying aggression and lacked the ability to understand and treat the patient's reaction as an expression of negative transference and was rendered passive and unable to function as a therapist.

A few sessions were labelled as anti-therapeutic as shown in the following example:

> In this session the therapist seemed to have set her mind on freeing the patient from the feelings of inferiority and inadequacy that had been a constant plague to the patient in social contexts.

The therapist seeks to achieve this by taking control of the relationship. Throughout the session, the therapist virtually inundates the patient with "good advice" and points of view, as if she wants to convince the patient that her feeling of defeat is unfounded. The therapist took on a role where her superior vantage point made the patient feel even more inadequate. In other words, the therapist chose a method that directly counteracted her own aim of making the patient feel less inadequate.

Therapeutic attitude refers to the therapist's more stable emotional and cognitive way of being. It came to the fore in the therapist's ability to maintain a relatively sustained quality of presence in the relationship in spite of changing levels of tension. The attitude supplied the relationship with an emotional "atmosphere" which created a frame around the concrete interventions. This professional attitude was found only in those that displayed strategic competence, which is not surprising as the ability to maintain a consistent attitude is one of the clinical characteristics that points in the direction of an underlying strategy. It was of interest to study cases where a professional attitude where not present as is shown in the following two examples:

1. *The optimist ("Things will work out fine")*

The patient has problems with her self-esteem and is involved in a difficult cohabiting relationship. The patient has also been exposed to abuse. The therapist is caring and encourages the patient to take the initiative in different areas. The therapist establishes an optimistic tone that expresses that everything will work out fine. At times, the patient takes the role of the one who ensures the therapist that it will work out fine. On one occasion, the patient talks about her mood swings: she was fine one day but next morning she was at "rock bottom". The therapist asks what she thinks made her feel better. The patient talks about how important it is to reinforce the positive sides of life, but also mentions that she is anxious about delving into the difficult and painful subjects. This last point is not pursued. The positive is reinforced but the negative is played down. A sequence early in the session was typical: the patient talks about preparations for a journey. Therapist: "That's good!" Patient: "Yes, it will work out fine!" The patient's guilt feelings related to this journey, which are clearly present in the material, are not touched upon. It seems as if therapist and patient have entered into a mutual contract to stick to the positive, to what works well. The therapist's need to be positive and optimistic leaves the patient alone with all the doubt and guilt, and all that is "painful and difficult".

2. *The normaliser ("That's perfectly normal")*

The patient is anxiety-ridden and afraid of serious illness but tries to play down her difficult feelings. The therapist is friendly and wants to support her patient and help her calm down. The therapist's most important strategy is to try to neutralise the patient's fears. This becomes particularly obvious in connection with the patient's anxiety about the possibility of having been infected with HIV by a former partner. The therapist addresses this anxiety by referring to her own experiences and that of her social environment and comments that it is quite common to worry about being infected and have oneself tested. In this way, the therapist attempts to shift the patient's attention away from her strong anxiety, and the dynamic importance of this anxiety is not investigated. The patient's anxiety becomes something "perfectly normal". The therapist recognises herself in the patient. The attitude chosen by the therapist thereby acquires a dual function. On a conscious level, it must meet the patient's needs. On an unconscious level, it will meet the therapist's needs.

Technical competence referred to the intentional interventions of the therapist, both verbal and non-verbal. The crucial point was whether the interventions were emotionally relevant to – or able to "grasp" – the material which was actualised in the relationship at every point in time. Three examples will be presented:

1. *Interventions that make the patient safer*

These are interventions that relate to the patient's present concerns and which are formulated so that the patient feels it is safe to continue talking. These may be nonverbal utterances, such as "hmm", said at the proper time and in the appropriate tone of voice. A quiet tone quality from the therapist may often be sufficient. The patient feels the therapist is present and listening, open and interested. Such interventions may help the patient to open up.

2. *Interventions that address latent content*

The therapist introduces into the dialogue feelings, wishes or ideas that have been unconscious for the patient and was mostly seen in cases where strategic competence were present:

> In one session the patient expects to be criticised and considered negatively if she "reveals" herself. She faced a dilemma where, on the one hand, she must not reveal anything, while on the other, she feels she has to "fill the time" and make sure the therapist is satisfied. This pattern emerged with full force in the session. The therapist remained calm and listened with empathy to the patient's "struggle" to fill the session without revealing too much of herself. She is ashamed of her "bad" sides and needs to hide them. The therapist was calm and gradually the patient opened up. The patient felt more understood and revealed that she often had been very frightened when arriving at sessions. She said, "I know no disasters occur here, but even though I see it, it's there all the time – the thought that I might be rejected if I show my bad sides". The therapist takes the initiative to examine what goes on between them in the relationship – here and now. Together they acknowledge that the patient's expectation of criticism is actually her own self-criticism.

Patient: "That's what I always expect". Therapist: "That I should think there's something wrong with you". Patient: "Yes". She adds thoughtfully, "I don't really think so. It has just as much to do with how I view myself". Therapist: "You lend a part of yourself to me". Patient: "Yes, I think I do that a lot".

Here, the therapist expresses, in slightly different words, what the patient is nearly aware of. This is an interpretative intervention, which, so to speak, puts things in place. Self-damnation, which she has been accustomed to projecting onto others, may, after good therapeutic work, be taken back as something she owns herself.

3. *Interventions that are futile*

These are interventions that don't bring the therapeutic dialogue into motion. The interventions don't appear in relation to the patient's material, and dialogue often ends in conventional clichés, unfocused questions meaningless comments and social "small talk". Dialogue stagnates and lacks progress:

In one session a therapist who was friendly and expectant but at the same time appeared insecure. The patient seemed to notice the therapist's insecurity and gradually assumed control of the relationship. She helped the therapist to gradually becomes better able to cope and to show her caring sides. The patient ensures the therapist that things will be fine. This gave the patient control of the situation. The therapist gradually appeared affirmative and listening but takes most of what was said at face value, brings nothing new to the conversation, and was at times strikingly passive. Thus, the rage the patient felt towards her co-habiting partner and her GP – who did not understand her – was not addressed. Rather, it seemed as if the therapist was attempting to be someone who was not like the patient's partner and GP, i.e., someone who was considerate. Nor did the therapist dare address the patient's tendency to take on the role of a victim, the one who always takes the needs of others into account, but whose own needs are not met, and who therefore can be angry at others who "don't understand, don't help". The therapist was satisfied by ensuring the patient that "It's good that you make your own evaluations, that you can be independent".

These dimensions were not sharply separated in the material in the same way as in clinical practice. In clinical practice, they are first and foremost aspects of – and can be seen as – different perspectives on a functional totality. Having all three in mind, the researcher is able to analyse the material in a comprehensive way.

Among these three perspectives, strategy was considered to be paramount: the concept of "strategic competence" (entailing strategic thinking) was the most decisive variable in evaluating dynamic therapy competence. Strategic thinking entailed cognitive mobility and a frame of mind geared towards wholeness and connections between parts and gestalts. It also implied an understanding of the emotional tension actualised in the relationship between patient and therapist as the driving force of the therapeutic dialogue. In the clinical situation, strategic competence mostly took place on an unconscious or a preconscious level. If the dialogue between therapist and patient was actually influenced by underlying strategic competence, it was assumed that this would be marked in the manifest material, signifying that the clinical work of the therapist was based on psychoanalytic theory.

An evaluation of the method

This article's main focus is the research method. To show how the method works, material was presented illustrating how the three main dimensions were identified in the essays. A fuller presentation of the research and results can be seen in the original article (Killingmo et al., 2014). Here, the aim is to discuss how the essay method may function as an instrument in studying and evaluating therapeutic dialogues from different perspectives (and research questions).

As already stated, the main property of the method is that it is geared towards treating the dialogue as a gestalt. All elements of the dialogue (verbal, non-verbal and intonation) that were in the research presented here were considered from the point of view of competence. This implied a metaposition to the clinical material, which means a way of listening that highlighted both the manifest as well as the latent content of the dialogue. With this kind of listening, almost automatically, formal aspects of the dialogue came to the fore, raising questions such as: were we listening to two people that were speaking to each other, or were the two talking at cross purposes? Were they talking about this and that? Did the therapist talk over the patient's head? Could continuity in the discourse be identified, or did it give an all over impression of staccato and fragmentation and, if so, how was the therapist affected by the patient's fragmentation? Was there a moving tension in the interrelation between the two parts, or was it a dry and affectless conversation we are witnessing? These kinds of questions are suited for revealing whether the dialogue is meaningful from a dynamic point of view and if it expresses emotional coherence (on the part of the therapist), the two criteria of the concept of strategic thinking as the main dimension of competence.

It was shown in the analysis that through a holistic approach to the clinical material an underlying strategic competence could be identified in the manifest material. It was argued that this showed how the clinical dialogue was informed by dynamic or psychoanalytic theory. The method here was exemplified by the study of therapeutic competence, but the method can be used and should be tested with other research questions. Further research may also relate the essay method to other measures of therapeutic competence, e.g., the competence framework developed at University College of London (UCL, 2019).

The essay method may be a way of examining the nuances and relational qualities in the clinical work of the therapist. By abstaining from coding therapist behaviour into predetermined categories and instead focusing on simple aspects of the material in a descriptive way, it was possible to demonstrate whether the therapist's understanding and his/her handling of the therapeutic dialogue actually was influenced by dynamic or psychoanalytic theory.

Clinical aspects (a background knowledge based on clinical and supervisory experience and theoretical background (Gullestad & Killingmo, 2013)), that may be visible with this method are:

> The therapist lets the patient express him-/herself at the patient's own pace
> The therapist abstains from steering the course of the dialogue
> The therapist shows tolerance for pauses
> The therapist gives priority to the subjective experience of the patient
> The therapist is attentive to the actualised feeling state of the patient
> The therapist is not driven by an urgent need to help or to do something
> The therapist is not evaluating the actions, feelings or fantasies of the patient
> The therapist maintains a factual, respectful and benevolent attitude towards the patient

These aspects of therapist behaviour reflect a quality of clinical presence. This paves the way for material, which the patient previously has not expressed, to come to the fore and can be verbalised and reflected upon in the therapeutic dialogue. Together they stand for a "silent invitation" to the patient to "let come – what comes". This kind of presence is on par with the baseline in a psychoanalytic listening perspective.

The examples above focus on formal aspects of the discourse, on how the two parts of the dialogue communicate. This is not to say that the essay method is exclusively directed towards structural and relational aspects of personality. Formal aspects may also transmit an underlying content. The use of the simple word "but" may change a discourse from a mutually respectful one, to one of underlying aggressive fantasies, even if no trace of open criticism or scepticism can be identified in the manifest content.

This way of listening and organising material may also be useful in the clinical situation, that is, research using the essay method may be useful for the clinician. Listening to how the patient describes him-/herself or how he/she puts forward his/her points of view can give the sensitive therapist essential information about the internalised world of object relationships of the patient. By asking him-/herself, "to whom does one speak in this way?", the therapist can come closer to an understanding of the underlying scenario that is actualised in the therapeutic relationship, and what object representations that are projected onto him/her in the transference. Is the patient addressing the representation of a critical father, an impatient mother or a competitive brother?

It is argued that the orientation toward descriptive linguistic aspects of the material is a special asset of the essay method. From this linguistic point of view, a fruitful perspective on therapeutic dialogues would be: who is in conversation, in what way, about what, and on what scene?

The essay method in relation to other qualitative methods

The essay method was developed from a study of sessions in psychodynamic psychotherapy with the purpose of evaluating therapeutic competence. In this context, three salient aspects of therapeutic competence were identified (strategic thinking, attitude and therapeutic interventions). Psychoanalytic theory was used as a perspective when approaching the material. This was the researchers' preunderstanding at work when analysing the material. The analysis of the material was phenomenological – taking a critical stance towards the preunderstanding but also reflecting on how the preunderstanding influenced the analysis and understanding of the material. In contrast to the starting point with predefined variables, the essay method was developed as a phenomenological reading of the material, where salient concepts could be developed from the bottom up. This may be seen as a development of Freud's thesis on the inseparable bond between cure and research, the so-called "Junktim" approach.

"In psychoanalysis, there has existed from the very first an inseparable bond between cure and research. Knowledge brought therapeutic success. It was impossible to treat a patient without learning something new; it was impossible to gain fresh insight without perceiving its beneficent results" (Freud, 1926c, p. 255).

The way of reading/listening to research material that is represented in psychoanalysis is in many aspects taken up in modern qualitative research (Kvale, 1999; Varvin, 2011a) even if this has been controversial (Migdley, 2006). Nevertheless, the essay method has similarities with other approaches in qualitative research, which can only be briefly mentioned here. In grounded theory (Glaser & Strauss, 1967), concepts are developed from a thorough and systematic reading of texts by systematising salient aspects that give meaning to the text from a certain perspective (in the research presented here, from the perspective of meaning and coherence). The essay method distinguishes itself from this approach in that it demands a specific way of "listening" to the material based on psychoanalytic competence. The holistic approach implied in the writing of essays is also different from grounded theory.

Interpretative phenomenological analysis (IPA) comes closer to the essay method as it represents a combination of psychological, interpretative, and ideographic components (Smith, 2009). This method has an ideographic focus, which means that it aims to offer insights into how a given person, in a given context, makes sense of a given phenomenon or experience. Usually, these phenomena relate to experiences of some personal significance – such as a major life event, going through a developmental phase, or the development of an important relationship. IPA assumes an epistemological stance with an explicit interpretative methodology whereby it becomes possible to access an individual's cognitive inner world (Biggerstaff & Thompson, 2008). In IPA, salient themes are identified to best capture the essence of the material. In the essay method, salient themes or dimensions are also identified, but the explicit holistic approach of writing the essay produces the basis for identifying and ordering these themes.

The method of psychoanalytic expert "validation" (Leuzinger-Bohleber, 2015; Leuzinger-Bohleber et al., 2002) was developed in the frame of a large retrospective study on long-term outcome of psychoanalytic treatments. Interviews were analysed by an expert group consisting of experienced psychoanalysts and researchers. Through several sessions, psychoanalytic listening was applied to interviews in order to understand the underlying narratives and, in that way, get a deeper understanding of what was transmitted by the interviewee. This was then formulated in salient narratives on the long-term outcomes of psychoanalytic treatments. This method has similarities with the essay method, although developed in another context, in that it uses psychoanalytic listening as a way of understanding the implicit or underlying content of a dialogue or analytic process.

In thematic analysis (Braun & Clarke, 2006), identified themes are also seen in context of the whole material. The essay method does not, however, systematise topics and themes in the same way in the process of analysis of the material as they are not identified in the original material (here the sessions) but extracted as salient aspects of the written essays.

Conclusion

Generally, the essay method can be subsumed under the tradition of ethnographic investigation of narratives derived from observation of events in natural situations (Fangen, 2011). It is an explorative method and not suitable for hypothesis testing. It concerns empirical cases but includes theoretical perspectives to determine how to organise the material in the essays. It is holistic and deals with human experience as a whole within a certain situation. This contrasts with the treatment of the human experience as isolated parts, which was the starting point in the study presented as an example here, and, which implied a study of transference, interpretations etc. isolated from the context.

In the context of psychotherapy research, the essay method as developed delves into the lifeworld of the therapist and patient within a session and aims at giving a salient narrative of what was going on in the session. Psychoanalytic inspired listening will determine how the material is perceived in the first stages of the research process and psychoanalytic theory plays its role when organising the material and in developing theoretical categories.

The epistemology of the method acknowledges that human experience and knowledge in many areas are tacit, not articulated or not reflected upon.

It is argued that the essay method is a way to dig out this unspoken knowledge inherent in therapy sessions, interviews or similar material from real exchanges between human beings. It takes into account that parts, single observations, can only be understood in relation to the context of the wholeness of the encounter.

Notes

1 Published in: The Scandinavian Psychoanalytic Review of psychoanalysis, DOI:10.1080/01062301.2019.1692622. Reprinted here with the kind permission of The Scandinavian Review of Psychoanalysis.
2 This work was developed in collaboration with the late Professor emeritus Bjørn Killingmo. He has been a great inspiration and the article could not have been written without his continuous participation in the process.

Part IV

Psychoanalysis in China
A transformative dialogue

Introduction

I have worked in China for 20 years. In the first phase, from 1999 to 2007, the main focus were dialogues on Human Rights and Patient Rights in psychiatry. This work resulted in fruitful dialogues on the conditions for mentally ill patients in psychiatry, both in hospitals and in outpatient settings, dialogues that continued with my followers up until 2019. In these years, we witnessed profound changes and improvements in the care for mentally ill persons regarding treatment, care and prevention.

From 2001, I developed a collaboration with one of the leading centres for psychiatry in Beijing, and its professor: Anding Hospital and Professor Yang Yunping. Together, we developed the Sino-Norwegian advanced training program for psychoanalytic psychotherapy. This was a success and has been improved and expanded upon. It is a three-year training program on several levels: basic and advanced programs on psychotherapy training, training in psychoanalytic group therapy and training for supervisors in psychoanalytic psychotherapy. Today, the program can be found in Beijing and Qingdao, Shandong province.

Starting from 2007, an IPA-sponsored training programme in psychoanalysis was started. First as a member, and then as chair of the IPA China Committee, I have had the privilege to work with many excellent colleagues from the IPA world to develop a rather successful psychoanalytic training program that now has 8 direct members and more that 40 candidates and which soon will have the status as IPA study group of China.

DOI: 10.4324/9781003206057-104

How is introducing psychoanalysis in a Chinese context possible?

It is our experience that such a process is not possible without learning about ourselves and also risking change. China is in several ways profoundly different from western societies where psychoanalysis developed. Chinese Folk-Psychology with roots in Buddhism, Taoism and Confucianism is characterised by holism, dialecticism, intuitiveness, pragmatism, image-proneness and circular-thinking in contrast to the dominant linear and cause-effect thinking in the western context. In many ways, these principles are compatible with psychoanalytic thinking. What distinguishes and seems contrary to the western mind, is the underlining of the high degree of uncertainty that is inherent in these perspectives. When context is brought as the central way of trying to understand phenomena, a holistic perspective is required. There is a necessity to take into consideration the dynamics between opposing perspectives, or different voices (Bakhtin, 1986), and from this follows adaptation to a pragmatic viewpoint and likely more trust in intuition. Some will recognise these thinking patterns in modern chaos theory where context at different levels determines what characterises a phenomena and also that cause and effect are not in a one-to-one relationship (Moran, 1994; Quinodoz, 1997). We also know these principles from the hermeneutic tradition in qualitative research where the meaning of what is under study only can be derived by taking context into consideration (Varvin, 2011b). This implies understanding that human life and also psychic experience to a large degree is unpredictable (See also the chapter in this section "Western-Eastern differences in habits and ways of thinking: The influence on understanding, and teaching psychoanalytic therapy").

The Chinese conception of the mind is embodied to a much larger extent in folk-psychology than it is in the case of western conceptions. Mind-body is "xin/shenti" (心 /身体) or heart/body, signalling on a semantic level how the mind is a part of the body. This coincides with modern embodied cognitive science and theories of the embodied mind developed in the west (Leuzinger-Bohleber et al., 1998) and goes beyond the view of the body/mind relationship as governed by simple causality.

Some main themes may be considered regarding psychoanalysis in the Chinese context:

1. Generally, we learn about ourselves by seeing ourselves and our ways through another's gaze. Working in China demands self-reflection and reflection on the other's gaze upon you
2. In this context, transcultural encounters must be dialogical and that a monologic psychoanalytic discourse in the Chinese context, "we shall teach them", is mere repetition that kills development and psychoanalysts risk functioning like the Jesuit missionaries some centuries ago, interpreting the thinking and perspectives of the Chinese as not developed enough
3. It is obvious that western thinking, including psychoanalysis, has something to learn from the focus on context. The linear, cause-effect thinking characterising western thought will be more and more outdated in a dynamically changing world, and in relation to recent development in western thinking, including psychiatry and psychoanalysis
4. Trends within psychoanalysis that explicitly take the importance of context for meaning making into consideration can be supported, confirmed and also developed by the encounter with Chinese ways of thinking.

Working in China as a psychoanalyst is thus a dialogical process of reciprocal learning. The two following chapters in this book may give a glimpse into this process. In two books these reflections have been further developed (Gerlach et al., 2013; Scharff & Varvin, 2014), and the newly established Journal: *Psychoanalysis and Psychotherapy in China* (https://firingthemind.com/product-category/journals/ppc/) continues these reflections. There have further been prolific translations of psychoanalytic work to Chinese and a growing number of publications by Chinese colleagues.

There are, however, worries on how psychoanalysis can develop in what many see as an authoritarian context. This is a complicated issue needing deeper reflection, which is outside the scope of this introduction (see the next chapter on the Chinese author Yu Hua). It can be stated, however, that there have been no impingements or hindrances for the development of a growing and creative psycho-analytic community in the years we have worked there.

Chapter 12

"Yu Hua: A narrator of Chinese recent history"

Yu Hua

"When I was writing about the pains of China, I was also writing about my own pain because China's pain is also my personal pain" (Yu, 2010: 105).

These words, from the epilogue of the book "China in 10 words" (published in Taiwan, 2010), depict a way to read Yu Hua's author-ship. He is, through most of his work, intensely occupied with ways to understand the connectedness between different periods of China's recent history and to see how individual destinies are tightly connected with the grand history of society. In his work "To Live (Huózhe)" (Yu, 2003) we can follow the life of Fugui, an overindulged and self-centred son of one of the wealthy, through the upheavals in China from the forties until after the "Cultural revolution". After spoiling the family fortune on gambling, thereby ruining his family life, he struggles through the different changes and upheavals in China as a peddler, a puppeteer and a persecuted peasant experiencing serious losses and misfortunes in post-revolutionary China. The novel starts at the end of his life, where the narrator meets Fugui in the countryside as a man with a sad but satisfied mind who then tells the story of his life. It is a story about life's contingencies and about how the individual's destiny is interwoven in the manifold and often brutal changes in Chinese society. It is a story on how to live on, in spite of the pains and hardships one experiences. He, Fugui, lives but feels in no position to change his destiny. He simply goes on living. One may say this is a story of a specific form of resilience – but it describes a pattern of adapting and maybe resignation.

DOI: 10.4324/9781003206057-12

Yu Hua talks about Fugui: "After going through much pain and hardship, Fugui is inextricably tied to the experience of suffering. So, there is really no place for ideas like 'resistance' in Fugui's mind—he lives simply to live. In this world I have never met anyone who has as much respect for life as Fugui. Although he has more reason to die than most people, he keeps on living" (Yu, 2003 (1993) p. 243).

This capacity to adjust to even the most harmful and difficult circumstances is a theme in several of Yu Hua's books, such as Brothers (Yu, 2005) and Cries in the Drizzle (Yu, 2004) (see later). In the novel Chronicle of a Blood Merchant (Yu, 2003), a more active position is described where the main character struggles to save his family in hard times by selling blood. There was quite a harsh critique of the blood producing system (blood plasma collection stations in public hospitals) in China in the past century.

In many ways, Yu Hua's novels mirror the conditions in a country that has gone through repeated upheavals and atrocities. With the Opium Wars (First Opium War: 1839–42, Second Opium War 1856–60) where the Qing Dynasty tried to stop English opium trade in China, and where foreign forces "easily" defeated Qing troops with modern war technology, as background, the Qing Dynasty came to an end in 1911. After China had transformed into a republic, a power struggle erupted between rival groups which developed into a civil war from 1927 until 1945. This conflict between the Nationalist Kuomintang under Chiang Kaishek ended with the Kuomintang retreat to Taiwan in 1949. The Second Sino-Japanese War, which took place from 1937–1945 (the first Sino-Japanese War had taken place from 1894–1895), overlapped with this. Millions of lives were lost in the civil war and the Japanese invading troops committed atrocities unheard of. The Great Leap Forward from 1958–1962 led to a devastating famine where an estimated 20 to 40,000,000 people died. The "Great Proletarian Revolution" or "Cultural revolution", lasted from 1966–1976. Millions of people were exposed to harsh conditions that could be traumatising. While the number of fatalities is unknown, estimates range from hundreds of thousands to a few million people (Plaenkers, 2014a, 2014b; Wood, 2020).

The Chinese population has thus experienced extreme social traumatisation in recent times. Many families have, as a result, both living and dead members who have been traumatised, killed, suffered starvation and so forth. How this affects family systems and next generations is an understudied theme. We see, however, in the clinic, what may have been the results of traumatisation of parents, grandparents, or any from the extended family, in the form of severe problems of identity development, relational problems, problems in caretaking and protection of children and in open psychic illnesses (personality disorders, posttraumatic conditions and so forth) leading to transmission of problems to the next generations.

These ways of transgenerational transmission are complex and pathways for how parents' and even grandparents' traumatisation may influence coming generations are not entirely clarified (Johansen & Varvin, 2019, 2020). What we hear in the clinic, however, are patients' narratives of how it was to live with parents who, due to earlier hardship (often both due to their own traumatising experiences and those of their parents), may influence their children's development in a negative way.

Upheavals in society has thus affected people in different ways, not only through hardships and traumatisation. Both the "Great leap forward" and the "Cultural Revolution" were mass movements where a majority of people participated. There was an energy in the masses that captured the minds and led people with a fervour and energy that lead to radical changes in society, in spite of how these changes could harm the fabric of society, destroyed relations between people and put productivity to halt.

The later development in China after Deng Xiao Ping came to power, is often described as a radical shift; a U-turn, away from the mass movements of the "Great Leap" and the "Cultural Revolution. Yu Hua's work modifies the view. He argues that the mass-energy and passion released during the cultural revolution has clear parallels in passion characterising modern China's consumerism with hunt for goods and pleasure in what may be called a quite hedonistic culture. He depicts a rather bleak image of social relations in China and his novels demonstrates how individuals to a large degree lack agency. He often describes his characters as mere caricatures in a development where people "follow the stream" rather than decide and form their own destinies, something that in the west often is seen as an ideal – (maybe more illusory than westerners would like to believe).

China, as a society, thus has a past riddled with events that for many, have serious repercussions in the present. Traumatisation hit many during recent history, and it has impacts on following generations in different ways and may become a never-ending story when it is not worked through. Present life in China also has hardships that may lead to societal traumatisation.

Yu Hua tries, as I see it, to address how this happens and his writings may contribute to a working through both on an individual and societal level very much in the way that psychoanalysis teaches us on how hardships and traumatisation may be ameliorated in a "talking cure".

In the view of many, there is an increasing westernisation in Chinese society with more weight on individualism and self-directed goals. It may seem paradoxical that Yu Hua then presents the main characters in his novels as caricatures whose life has little agency and are more determined by circumstances and social forces. His novel "Brothers" has, for example, been criticised for its crudeness and superficialness of the protagonists who seem to lack any psychological depth (see Næser, 2014). It can be argued, however, that this is a way of presenting storylines that reflect, not how history repeats itself when it is not worked through, but rather how the new storylines contain former periods of not worked through features.

I will discuss these themes based on my reading of some of his novels.

The internal world and its relation to external realities in Yu Hua's novels, especially in "Brothers", is described often as flat and inhabited by caricature like characters. This flatness of the characters may be seen as illustrating their lack of agency and that this lack can be understood in the context of insufficient working through of past traumatisation.

The concept of the internal world

The internal world can be conceptualised as a psychic space populated by the self, its objects and the relationships between them. It can be seen, using a theatre metaphor, as a stage where the scenes and dramas of inner life are enacted. As humans basically are related and the inner world is built up in a process of the person's relations to significant others, internal object-relations can be seen as a mental and emotional image of these relations to others; from relations to the primary caregivers in infancy through developmental processes where relations between self and internal others (objects) are built, structured and modified. This developmental process creates internalised images of one's relations to his/her mother, father, primary caregiver, or parts of a person, such as the mother's breast (Freud, 1900, 1916; Gullestad & Killingmo, 2013).

Psychoanalysis tries to understand how individuals and groups develop and interact with the contexts and circumstances they live in; what cultural, social and historical forces shapes the internal world of the individual, of the primary group (e.g., family) and the social larger groups. Psychoanalysis thus gives possibility to explore the conscious and unconscious world at the level of the individual, the family and the group. This, then, includes the upheavals, discontinuities and traumatic breaks in the developmental processes on all these levels.[1]

Working through

Central in any conflictual, deficient or traumatic experience is the need to work through in order to at least be able to live in a better way with past experiences that has influenced a person or the group in a negative way. Working through is central in any psychotherapy and implies a process where memory traces are put in a more meaningful context where emotions connected with the experiences are present and gradually can become more bearable. But working through must rest on cultural processes that can give meaning to experience. This "work of culture" is indispensable for the individual and group in this process (Obeyesekere, 1990).

The mechanisms, structure and dynamics of the mind are in many ways similar between cultures – but the shaping and the meaning is highly influenced by context: historical and social forces impinge on and shape how the mind apprehends and gives meaning to experiences.

In this context, literature plays a significant role in all cultures. The writer and poet are in a privileged position to formulate what is not yet understood or even formulated related to the pain people have suffered and to give word to experiences that have not been articulated, which may exist as open wounds that confuse and haunt individuals and groups and that often are acted out in destructive and/ or self-destructive ways (Varvin & Volkan, 2003).

In this context, Yu Hua's work is important as it helps in understanding the not yet formulated – and thus, not yet understood.

My relation to Yu Hua's writing

Novels and other artforms are essential in any therapist's clinical work. Art gives background, context and metaphors that can work in our mind when listening to our patients. Paradoxically, this context of the mind is a necessity when we try listen freely or to be without desire and knowledge (Symington & Symington, 1996) when listening to a patient as it may give a frame and connectedness to the material in a therapist's mind. As psychotherapists we need to presuppose that we know nothing about the patient in order to be able to take in and gradually understand the meaning inherent in each patient's communication. To understand entails that what we hear can be put in context.

Yu Hua has a rich authorship with many foci. One important aspect for me is how he described the common man's life during the enormous transitions that have happened in recent Chinese history: The Great Leap, The Cultural Revolution, The new era with Deng Xiao Ping and the recent hyper-capitalist development with focus on consumerism, especially in the metropoles, as a supposedly new way to bolster self-identity.

These transitions and developments have affected the Chinese family; how the family functions as a whole and how the functions of being a mother and a father has been impacted as well as relations between siblings.

In clinical practice we see situations where things have gone wrong. I have heard many stories in China regarding the difficulties of being a father: how the father often is absent, feels humiliated, cannot tolerate his wife's and especially his children's developments and relative independence and often becomes angry, violent and even abusive.

In this context it gives insight to read Yu Hua's stories about difficult father-son, father-child, father-mother or couple relationships.

I will in this presentation make short comments on some works of Yu Hua from the perspectives mentioned below:

• How societal transitions in the recent decades have affected the individual and the family: "Their son" (Yu, 1995) and "China in Ten Words" (Yu, 2010)

- Father-son relations ships: "Chronicle of a blood merchant" (Yu, 2003) and "Cries in the Drizzle" (Yu, 2004)
- Reconstruction of childhood traumatisation: "Cries in the Drizzle" (Yu, 2004)
- The reflection of the cultural revolution in today's society: Brothers (Yu, 2005/2006)

Producer-consumer duality in Their Son

Their Son is a short story from 1995 and was first published in the Chinese literary journal Harvest. Yu Hua narrates what happened during one weekend in the life of the middle-aged urban couple, Shi Zhikang (father) and Li Xiulan (mother) and their son who is coming home from university for the weekend. The story is narrated in the third person through the thoughts of the father.

Their Son shows the inherent contradiction but also connectedness of the producer, the worker who delays consuming, and the consumer who may disregard that production is necessary for being able to consume. The characters are built on these dichotomised types; Shi Zhikang and Li Xiulan represent the producers having values much tied to a traditional worker/producer society. The story starts with Shi Zhikang's laborious return from work on public transport. Li Xiulan is likewise travelling via the bus home. Both do physical hard work where people may get physically ill and Shi Zhikang tell us about one colleague who is terminally ill, obviously resulting from the working conditions.

Shi Zhikang and Li Xiulan are thus portrayed as typical factory workers who have learned to save before they spend. They lead modest, hard-working lives. Their orientation and values in life are highly security oriented. Being on fixed salaries they put a strong emphasis on long-term planning demonstrated through their elaborate retirement considerations.

The son's value orientation sharply contrasts that of his parents. He is described as representing the growing consumer society both in his personality and his physical appearance. His taste for fashion and consumer objects is obvious. He has, to his parents' big surprise and almost shock, taken a taxi home from the university. Spending money on a taxi was unthinkable for his parents. He says rather causally that taking a taxi is faster than the bus and in addition, he doesn't like the smell of other people on the bus. He gets nauseous.

Shortly after his arrival, the son takes out his Walkman and listen to music while watching TV portraying, almost as a caricature, the modern consumer identity. The son adds that in the future he will take neither the bus nor a taxi because he plans to buy a car once he graduates and finds a job.

This creates a great and rather surprising shift in the parents' attitude. Gone are their worries on how to spend money and they, without further argument, join in their son's fantasised prosperous future plans. Their son has, in their eyes suddenly become a man (see Næser, 2014).

This rather sudden shift in the parents' attitude, seems to describe how the solid producer identity was conflicted and demonstrated how the frantic ideals of the culture revolution still had a hold on them: everything is possible if only one has "revolutionary will". For the parents, their son has become the fulfilment of a "revolutionary" fantasy that prevailed in society not long ago. At least, this seems like a probable reading of Yu Hua's novel in the context of his other writings, for example "Brothers".

Consumerism

The individual stories about people's lives in China in Ten Words can be seen as symptomatic for the condition of society as a whole. This narrative structure used by Yu can also be applied to the fictional work, "Their Son", in which the individual life trajectories of the characters can be seen in a greater socio-political context. China's pain is reflected through the individual.

> Chinese economic reform, the revolution, has changed dramatically and reappeared in a new form. In other words, inherent to our economic miracle is the revolutionary movement of the Great Leap Forward as well as the violence of the Cultural Revolution (Yu, 2010: 64).

The relationship between the Maoist era, with its fanatical utopianism, and the ensuing Dengist reform period, characterised by more pragmatic high-speed economic expansion, intensified during the 1990s up to present times, is a main point in Yu's analysis.

Even though much has changed since the Maoist era, Yu still sees the same kind of unwavering developmental flurry as before. The current vigour for mass demolitions of entire neighbourhoods and people's private homes mirrors the violence with which the mass energy of the Cultural Revolution destroyed innumerable material possessions in the name of revolution (Yu, 2010: 65–6).

The core idea in Yu Hua's understanding of Chinese history is thus the connectedness of different periods. In China in Ten Words, Yu Hua presents numerous examples of the connection between periods. Yu Hua argues that what both communism and capitalism have in common is the desire to fight for world domination, the struggle for China gaining its central position in the world. "超过英国赶上美国" (Surpass the UK, catch up with the US) (Yu, 2010, p. 64; Næser, 2014). Nothing can stand in the way of development. The utopianism of the Maoist era promised abundance after the period's ascetism. In that way, there is a continuity with the abundance and hedonism of the consumer society. The developmental vigour of today is not a new phenomenon that resembles the energy of the political utopian movements of the Maoist Era, but Yu Hua seems to claim that it is actually the same energy appropriated in a new setting.

"Brothers"

The dualism of ascetism and hedonism is an important aspect in the novel "Brothers" where the connection between the time of the Cultural Revolution and modern China is made explicit. "Brothers" consist of two books: (a) childhood in Cultural Revolution and (b) the new era: Deng Xiao Ping and afterwards. It is a story about two stepbrothers, Li Guangtou and Song Gang, inhabitants of the fictional Liu Town, who are joined by the marriage of their parents during Mao's China.

It is a realistic and painful story about the rise and fall of persons during the cultural revolution. The father of the boys is one day portrayed as a revolutionary hero: "With both hands, Song Fanping lifted the giant red flag above his head. This flag, which was the biggest in our Liu Town, made crackling sounds like firecrackers as it blew in the wind. Then Song Fanping waved the red flag left and right. Li Guangtou and Song Gang watched how the giant flag started flying left, then right, then back again. It flew over the entire bridge. Many people's hairs were blown from the air waves of the flag including the boys'. As Song Fanping waved the flag, the crowd started to roar. Li Guangtou and Song Gang saw waves of fists going up and down and heard their slogans booming like the sounds of canons. (Yu, 2013 [2005], p. 72). The next day Song Fanping is accused as a landowner and arrested and cruelly tortured – and later killed by a band of red guards.

Song Gang and Li Guangtou grew up in poverty. Song Gang is a modest man; always working, very much like the parents in the novel "Their son". He lives off of the land, living an ascetic, frugal life.

Li Guangtou is portrayed as the guy who can adapt, take advantage of opportunities and ends up as extremely rich: as one of the Chinese multi-billionaires. He learned to use opportunities, starting from collecting and selling scrap. He is a man who knows how to utilise the opportunities that the modernisation process gives – with full support of many local party leaders. Song Gang's life ends tragically while his brother Li Guangtou at the end of his life of fortune, ends in extreme existential emptiness.

The two brothers' destinies can be said to exemplify how the ascetism/utopianism of the Mao area connects with the hedonistic but obviously more empty life of the frantic consumerism in late China.

There are, however, serious and tragic accompanying themes that are always connected with recent Chinese history in Yu Hua's writings, and these are prevalent in the novel "Brothers" and also in earlier novels.

Cries in the Drizzle

Yu Hua's first full-length novel, Cries in the Drizzle (在细雨中呼喊), which was completed in 1991, is considered a transitional work bearing traits of both his experimental style of the 1980s and his more realistic narratives of the 1990s. The novel explores the life of a boy, Sun Guanglin, in his childhood and adolescence during the Cultural Revolution.

Cries in the Drizzle is, among others, about how memory works and on how memories of past experiences shape present perceptions and experiences. In Yu Hua's reflections on how the present consumerism is a reflection of the frenzy of the Maoist era, it may also show how past traumatisation set their effects on later generations. The not finished and not worked through past set the stage for later repetitions of the effects on future generations, among others.

Yu Hua:

"After I left Southgate, I never felt any attachment to my childhood home. For a long time, I was convinced that memories of the past or nostalgia for one's birthplace really represent only a contrived effort to restore one's equilibrium and cope better with life's frustrations, and that even if some emotions arise these are simply ornamental. Once when a young woman politely asked about my childhood and hometown, I found myself enraged and retorted: "Why do you want me to accept a reality that I have already left behind me in the past?" (Yu, 2004, p. 21).

Cries in the Drizzle starts with the memory of a "nameless dread". The "I" of the novel remembers how he, as six-year-old child, was in bed when, in the silence of the drizzling rain "there came the sound of a woman's anguished wails". He lay in bed in anguish and waited for another voice, "a voice that would respond to her wails, that could assuage her wails, but it never materialized". Nothing is "more chilling than the sound of inconsolable cries on such a desolate night".

A second memory came "hot in the heels of the first": here three or four lambs are trotting on the grass by the riverside. This memory may be a way of easing the agitation evoked by the first memory.

Several days later, after a storm, "I seem to hear a voice that answered the woman's cries". He sees a man dressed in black approach him. "His clothes waved like a banner under the gloomy sky". The man was staring at him, and suddenly he changed direction and disappeared.

Then he remembers, when he and some village boys were running along the riverside like the lambs, a boy came running, white in face, and said that there was a dead man. The dead man proved to be the one who had approached him, the answer to the woman's cries. He tries to recapture the feelings at the time, but his memory of that incident had "been stripped bare of the reactions I had at the time, and all that is left is the outer shell: the association it now carries simply reflect my current outlook".

The dead man looked as if he was sleeping – and this had the effect that: "After that I dreaded the night. I saw myself standing at the entrance of the village and pictured the gathering darkness surging towards me like floodwater, engulfing me and then swallowing everything else". "I would lie in the dark for ages, not daring to fall asleep, and the silence all around simply intensified my terror" (Yu, 2004, pp. 3–5).

In this connection I hold that this can be seen as memories of events that were traumatising. There are several elements here that point in this direction: the woman's cries in drizzle – the lack of an answer and the terrible silence, nobody is there to comfort or help, and then the possible comforting memories of the lambs, which then turn into the memory where he and the boys are playing like the lambs along the river where they encounter the dark man, a possible father figure – that disappeared and then is found dead. The woman who cries may be a combination of the child and the mother – no supporting figure, no one who can answer. And when the answer comes – it is from a man who is soon to die.

It may seem like a surrealistic start on the novel. A psychoanalytic reading may perhaps shed some light on the important themes in the novel.

Themes of separation, total aloneness, a mother figure in deep desperation, lack of protection and an absent and even dead father who could have protected the mother, is put into this dramatic start of the novel.

The rest of the novel may be read in different ways, but from a psychoanalytic perspective it may be read as a working through of the themes presented in the beginning.

The cultural revolution makes the frame of this boy's life at the time but is scarcely presented in the narrative. What we see is the result of this special societal context. It is as if the I-person in the novel is struggling to put some coherence and meaning into childhood memories that in themselves are stripped of emotional meaning; they had "been stripped bare of the reactions I had" (Yu, 2004, p. 4).

And what is the connection or relation between the crying woman and the dead man? All of this is a prelude to Sun Guanglin's sudden and unprepared loss of his family. Another man in army uniform suddenly arrives. Wang Liqiang is to be his new father and he follows him happily on a boat trip without realising that his parents had given him away.

These memory fragments of situations that are stripped of their emotional meaning and the work to make some coherence in the story – attempts to link memory traces – are similar to what many traumatised people are working with. It may seem that Yu Hua, through this novel, is working on social traumatisation that has affected many people, and which we, even today, see repercussions of in people's experiences in their families: sudden separation, death, inconsolable traumatic anguish, unfinished grief and lack of affirmation and empathy.

Important aspects such as difficult father-son relationships, feelings of homelessness, poverty and struggle for existence, are themes also present in other novels by Yu Hua, for example in "The Chronicle of a Blood Merchant" (Yu, 2003). Central in this novel, which covers Chinese history from the forties until after the cultural revolution, is the story of a father, Xu Sanguan, who sells his blood in order to help his family survive difficult times (the Great Leap, Cultural Revolution). It is a dramatic, harsh but also touching story where Xu Sanguan's relation to his three sons, Yile, Erle and Sanle, plays an important role and is central in Xu Sanguan's insistent and ingenious attempts to help by selling blood.

In "Cries in the Drizzle", "The Chronicle of a Blood Merchant" and in other novels, Yu Hua works with experiences and memories of the individual, which have been traumatic – memories of the repercussion on an individual and family level of the great changes in recent Chinese history.

At one level, Yu Hua deals with changing mindsets, from the "production mindset" of the parents in the short story "Their Son" to the consumerism that dominates their son's mindset. But on a deeper level, as in "Cries in the Drizzle", the raw memory traces of how these societal changes has affected children (and adults) come to the fore – and one can say that Yu Hua's work is a contribution to both an individual and also a societal/cultural working through of these difficult experiences.

Working through and Yu Hua's contribution

One may argue that Yu Hua's writing is filled with pessimism. It seems there is little hope for China: the masses are caught up in consumerism and the main drive now is to achieve goods, to consume, and so on and so forth. Hedonism seems to be the primary mood and to enjoy becomes the prime goal. Relations become unstable: people are using each other, and values are no longer kept. People are portrayed as excessively naïve and self-occupied. A narcissistic culture is described where shame and shaming of others seem pervasive: there seems to be a clear line from shaming during the cultural revolution and the shame in the new area.

Does Yu Hua describe the Zeitgeist (时代精神) in China? Is there a mentality dominating that says we need more and more i.e., more is better? Is this a continuation of the ascetism (禁欲主义) of the cultural revolution: the promise from that time that after suffering and lack, there comes abundance of everything?

This would be a naïve reading of Yu Hua's novels, which are so rich that it is not possible to reduce them to one formula.

I will, however, end by seeing his work from the perspective of working through. As noted earlier, working through implies coming to terms with past difficult experiences in order to be able to go forward, to not being engulfed by unconscious determinations shaped in a difficult or traumatic past. In order to achieve this, the painful past must be described and reflected upon. Most of all, it is necessary to show how the past "works" in the present, among others to show how the other side of ascetism is hedonism 享乐主义. In this way, Yu Hua catches the important aspects, not only of China's development, but also of many western affluent societies' development. Three to four generations before us, many western societies, including Norway, were mostly characterised by hard working industrial workers and rural farming, with a smaller upper class profiting from the masses' hard work. Frugality was the norm and for Northern Europe, a protestant work ethic dominated. A gradual development has secured continuous stability in many countries, but fast changes, as was the case for China, may have the effect that people's mentality does not follow track. In China, the utopianism of the cultural revolution has not been worked through. Utopianism may dominate and take different forms in different contexts (societies, movements, groups), like the idea of a promised future if only what is at present, is torn down.

It is an important task for any society to temper utopianism by giving security and stableness for all. In times of crisis, as we see now with the Covid-19 pandemic, the effort to give security for all may come in sharp conflict with populist interests that seek to appeal to the common man's wish for safety by giving omnipotent, unrealistic solutions and utopian ideations often based on mere denial of reality. The word "denialism" has been used. 100 years ago, the world was struck by a similar pandemic killing millions of people. It came to be called the "Spanish flu" exactly because of the government's denial. In Germany, France and England, there was censorship on the news. Reports on the illness that affected masses of people were suppressed and an extreme denial was organised by the states – with detrimental consequences. In Spain, there was freedom of press at the time, and they reported on the illness – therefore Spain got their name attached to the disease, as if it came from them. The illness probably originated from American military men in Texas, or maybe from some military camp in France.

Societal crisis can bring forth the best in people and governments – as well as the worst. There will always be a conflict between utopian tendencies and the work that benefits all parts of society.

This conflict will be apparent in any society – also in China where consumerism and hedonism, described by Yu Hua, may come in conflict with solidarity and work for the good of common people. During the ongoing pandemic in China there has been an amazingly common and voluntary effort to conquer the outspread of the disease – a contrast to several western societies where laisse-fair and disrespect of ordinary people's lives has led populist leaders to deny the severity of the pandemic and to not recruiting the people for common efforts – with devastating consequences.

What we can learn from Yu Hua's work is not only about Chinese mentality and history, which certainly is an extremely important aspect of his work, but maybe more on the necessity of balancing the producer-consumer duality. Maybe the importance of his work is how it helps us not to just move on and forget – that working through on individual and societal levels is a precondition to live on, develop society and improve mental health of the ordinary man.

Note

1 How the dimensions of the subject's relations on individual, group and societal/ cultural shapes development is discussed in Chapter 8, "The influence of extreme traumatisation on body, mind and social relations".

Chapter 13

Western-Eastern differences in habits and ways of thinking

The influence on understanding and teaching psychoanalytic therapy[1]

Introduction

This chapter builds on the experiences of supervising several hundred case presentations as well as psychoanalytic therapeutic encounters with patients in China in the period of 2002–2012. The challenge for us as teachers and supervisors has been to sense, be informed by and understand the learning process that takes place when a Western approach to the understanding of human beings, partly based on an Aristotelian, self-centred, goal-directed logic, meets the understanding of the human mind largely based on Confucian, family-centred and context-directed ways of relating, mingled with Daoist based preoccupations with practice and form.

Psychoanalysis represents a way of understanding psychic life and its conflictual structure that originates both in a Western Aristotelian tradition and in a Judeo-Christian culture that in certain aspects differs from the linear, goal-directed logic of the Aristotelian tradition and, as we will show, has similarities to Eastern modes of thinking. It is therefore of interest for the psychoanalytic field to highlight the specific features of psychoanalytic thinking and reasoning where a meeting may take place and where obstacles to the meeting occur.

Psychoanalysis is also a way of thinking about the specificity of human suffering and its embeddedness in the culture in which the suffering takes place. As Obeyesekere stresses, individual suffering must meet and be contained by accepted cultural ways of representing mental problems. If these are inadequate, for example in disorganised or traumatised societies, or by lack of public recognition

DOI: 10.4324/9781003206057-13

or appropriate rituals for the persons affected, individual suffering can become private, idiosyncratic and more painful because it is not shared in a common ground (Obeyesekere, 1990). The ground is then prepared for transmission of further suffering to coming generations.

Psychoanalysis had a historical role in giving voice to the private suffering of the neurotics of the late 19th century in Europe. This voice was explained by means of a specific model of the mind and its normal and pathogenetic processes. The model developed further into a more or less coherent theory of psychopathology, personality and mode of treatment. The acceptance of psychoanalysis and of psychoanalytic ways of thinking about and treating patients with mental suffering in China is, as we understand it, based both on a need for help with widespread human suffering, but also on the sense that psychoanalytic understanding represents a way of thinking that in some ways coheres with the Chinese mentality. This concurrence with the "Confucian and Daoist way" may be part of the background for the hope that psychoanalysis can help meet mental ailment in the Chinese context.

As will come through in this chapter, creating and developing the meeting points between psychoanalysis and Chinese culture is a work in progress. It demands change, accommodation and not the least transformations on conceptual and discursive levels both for Western analysts and Chinese colleagues. China has had a dramatic and traumatising history that have affected large parts of the population. There are specific ways of thinking and dealing with mental pain and suffering resulting from these traumatising influences that has its roots in Chinese cultural traditions.

As supervisors and teachers, we have experienced astonishing achievements in the way Chinese therapists deal with these problems. But we have also been surprised by the specific difficulties in listening to and relating to the pains and conflicts of the individual and the group. When we focus on "difficulties" we are not criticising the competence of our Chinese colleagues; the "difficulties" are as much on our side in our efforts to understand.

We base our presentation here on our moments of surprise in listening to both content and form in the presentations of personal histories and material from concrete sessions in which Chinese therapists treat Chinese patients who are not familiar with the psychoanalytic method or thinking. These moments differ from the moments of surprise in our supervisory experiences in Western culture. We have therefore taken some of the moments of surprise as signs of cultural confrontations and/or difficulties on the side of the therapist in his or her understanding of the dynamics of the material or analytic technique. These moments were thus challenges in the psychoanalytic understanding of the case (Nisbett, 2003).

Translating psychoanalysis from one culture and culture of language to another

From its inception, psychoanalysis has been faced with the problems of translation. Firstly, psychoanalysis was born in the Austro-Hungarian monarchy and thus employed not only the German language but also the accumulated European cultural knowledge and worldview of the fin-de-siècle Vienna in the scientific investigation and understanding the function of the psychic apparatus (Bettelheim 1983; Ellenberger 1970; Ticho 1986). In all non-German speaking countries translators struggled with translation of Freud into their respective languages. Best known is of course the English translation of Freud's Gesammelte Werke, the Standard Edition, which in our modern times has been shown to be semantically out of tune with Freud's German, and not catching the content of many concepts of Freud, and thus sometimes leading the psychoanalytic conceptualisation astray. Famous examples are terms in the Standard Edition like "deferred action", "ego", "cathexis" and "instincts". We have no reason to believe that bringing psychoanalysis to China will place the work of translation and thus understanding of psychoanalysis in a different position. We must expect at least a period of change from the first generation of Chinese analysts trained according to IPA-standard to the second generation trained by Chinese analysts. At least one generation of analysts will pass before a Chinese conceptualisation of psychoanalysis will have found a stable ground from which it can develop in its own way.

Secondly, translation has not only to do with the semantic meaning of particular concepts and their denotations. Connotations are just as important in giving the concepts culture-specific nuances and multitudes of significations. Networks of connotations can be seen as an intrinsic structure of cognition that influences perception of reality. From another perspective, connotations are influenced by social conditions and changes in the practice of culture as well as socio-political discourses. Cultural-socio-political structures influence and bring elements into language. Language structures the social reality in which persons and groups live. Chinese understanding of the self for example is: "mostly defined by the utilitarian function and material interest of the individual and the group, instead of by ontological or existential terms" (Yan, 2011, p. 26). "This creates difficulties in apprehending concepts like individual autonomy, individual freedom as it is understood in the West" (ibid), which again makes the Western understanding of how the self is presented in the therapeutic dialogue a challenge for the Western therapist or supervisor. What is connected with individuality has a different cultural contextual background and it requires an effort for the Western supervisor to grasp the full meaning of the patient's utterances and the therapist's way of presenting these. This chapter concerns translation in a wider sense in that the cultural and social context of concepts and meanings need to be taken into consideration.

Undoubtedly conceptualisation plays a role in relation to affective learning and learning from experience (Bion, 1962). Conceptualisation carries the function of alpha-elements that through the alpha-function designates "a symbolic function that is essential for the reception, elaboration and communication of experiences favourable to growth" (Bléandonu, 1994). Learning-from-experience problems are not only matters for the development of the patient but are also applicable to the development of the psychoanalytic psychotherapist and may thus be viewed upon in supervision with psychoanalytic psychotherapists as problems of teaching and transmitting psychoanalysis.

Myths – their roles in the understanding of psychoanalysis, and how to transfer them from one culture to another

When western analysts teach psychoanalytic concepts to others, they do it with a background of metaphors and narratives that illustrate the concepts in a pictorial and process-like way. The understanding of the narcissistic state of mind is linked with the 2500-year-old myth of Narcissus (re-presented in countless stories, paintings and allegories) and linked with the place of narcissism in the developmental process. This is based in an idea of our mental origin, starting in a body-centred view of the world and continuing in a mirroring process of structuring identity. Ordinality – an individual's search for the unconscious truth about himself, or as an individual's attempt to integrate the unconscious symbiotic love for his mother and the unconscious aggression towards and rivalry with his father – is similarly linked with Greek drama and its subsequent representations which appear in all kinds of arts and are repeated again in books and novels. The myths of Narcissus and Oedipus inform the mind of psychoanalysts in several ways. They contribute to determine who are main characters in the dynamics of internal object relations, and determine what the functions of these characters are, designating who is searching for what: pleasure, internal freedom from conflicts, pure conscience, truth, self-knowledge, etc., and in what ways. The complex functions of myths are often tacitly understood within our culture and much of the tacit knowledge cannot be taught directly as such from a Western psychoanalyst to a Chinese colleague. It must be transmitted through a slow experiential process in which the Chinese psychotherapist must internalise it and incorporate it into his therapeutic technique. But it must also resonate with the myths and narratives of China, where the struggle of the human mind in dealing with transitional processes from the primarily non-verbal preoedipal aspects and oedipal language-bound experiences happens in a different context. And this context has different backgrounds in texts, myths, art and literature. For example, for some Chinese, narcissism will be linked to the story of Lin Dai Yu, a heroine in the classic book "A dream of Red Mansions" by Cao Xue Qin (Cao, 1978–1980), or with the intellectual character of scholars since Qin dynasty. The connections with myths and literary figures need, however, to be developed and it is only through such dialectical processes between Western and Chinese pre-conceptualisations that development of psychoanalysis on Chinese grounds may happen (Schlösser, 2009).

Individualism, independence and interdependence

In the Western Greek-inspired world, subjects may be conceived of as independent and independently engaged in verbal contention and debate in an effort to discover for themselves, one by one, what others take to be truth and whether the existential truth of others is one that the subject him/herself finds valid. A subject is thought of as an individual with distinctive properties, as units separated from the others within the society, and to a large extent in control of their own destiny. Die Weltanschauung, even though it is heavily culturally determined, is seen from a perspective that has an anchorage in the individual person and surrounding objects. In this way the individual becomes the unit and the centre of analysis. The individual can be seen as an almost isolated foreground, while the culture (family, school, work, habits, etc.) is seen as a natural background for the individual or as a series of interpersonal objects with whom the individual may, or may not chose to, interact. This is of course a rude caricature since one may counter that the psychic apparatus is in part – through the super-ego for example, made up of identificatory objects with the internalisation of the group (family, peers) and the culture. However, terms like "one-person psychology" and "two-person psychology" in themselves testify to the central role of the individual as a person with distinct characteristics, functioning across many different person-constellations, and less as a person who mainly is determined by the matrix in which he/she lives.

The Chinese language contains many words that qualify the self in different relational ways. Underlying these characteristics, one senses that the culture prefers matrices in which the self is in harmony with a network of supportive social relationships. Breaking away from group, individualising oneself and creating new and more satisfying links has traditionally been less of an option. That is, a greater weight towards interdependence than independence (Nisbett, 2003).

The distinction between relatively independent and relative interdependence plays an important role for the understanding of what analysis may achieve.

The following dimensions are important:

- Insistence on freedom of individual action versus a preference for collective actions. This dimension affects the whole understanding of symbiosis-separation-individuation processes in the development of the individual person
- Desire for individual distinctiveness, the creative apperceptive, versus a preference for blending with the group, the adaptive

work (see Bollas 2013, p. 92). This affects the value of free association and an evenly hovering awareness

- A preference for egalitarian and achieved status versus acceptance of hierarchy and ascribed status. This affects neutrality, transference and countertransference

There are other oppositions of significance. The cultural psychologist and cognition-researcher, Richard Nisbett emphasises that "the Chinese believe in constant change, but with things always moving back to some prior state. They pay attention to a wide range of events; they search for relationships between things; and they think they cannot understand the part without understanding the whole" (Nisbett, 2003, p. 13). In contrast, Westerners have a more linear and more deterministic world perspective. They focus on salient objects and may easily use individual performance as a guideline for their thinking, rather than using small and large group phenomena. Also, Westerners have a firm idea that they can control events and processes because they know the rules that govern the behaviour of objects. Linked to this assumption is the idea that everyone has the same basic cognitive processes, that mental suffering is similar from one culture to another, and finally that reasoning is separate from what is reasoned about (ibid).

Western ways of thinking have a strong emphasis in categorisation and logical reasoning according to rules of logical argumentation. Too many causal, or partly causal, factors spoil reasoning and clarity of thinking, even though the idea of complexity also adheres to logical reasoning. In general, there is a tendency towards having many categories with fewer determining factors defining the content of the category rather than having fewer categories with many determinants. The explosion in numbers of categories in the psychiatric diagnostic system (DSM or ICD) in the last 50 years is a good example.

One may see here principles of thinking that are more in accord with psychoanalysis, with principles of over- or multi-determination, or stress on opposing forces in the mind in dynamic relationship to each other.

It is worth noting that the achievements of Freud's discoveries implied a break with the dominance of the categorical thinking and the logic of strict reference of words. Words could have multiple meanings, not only depending on the culture in which the words were embedded but also dependent on the state of the speaking subject and the condition of the listener. In many ways, psychoanalytic ways of listening and thinking, and psychoanalytic epistemology, is in accordance with principles of non-linearity, multi-causality and over determination, constant change and non-conclusion, polysemy, contradiction and of irrationality underlying rationality.

Even though psychoanalytic understanding of the unconscious broke with some fundamental ideas in Western thinking, it does not automatically make it compatible with Chinese understanding of the mind. This may be illustrated by looking at some principles, e.g., the principle of change, the principles of contradiction, and the principle of relationship or holism (Peng & Nisbett, 1999).

Principle of change (Bian Yi Lu)

This principle holds that reality is a process. It does not stand still but is in constant flux. According to Chinese folk belief, existence is not static but dynamic and changeable. Because reality is dynamic and flexible, the concepts that reflect reality are also active, changeable and subjective rather than being objective, fixed and identifiable entities.

Psychoanalysis also holds to a principle of change and that reality is a process. But at the same time, it underlines the stabilities and fixations of processes in the psychic apparatus. One aim of analysis is, through insight, to free fixated emotionality and lessen anxiety, so that the persons have choices where no choices existed before. The referential anchor points in the Chinese and the psychoanalytic "Weltanschauung" are thus different. The interesting point is how and where do they meet.

Principle of contradiction (Mao Dun Lu)

This principle states that reality is not precise or cut-and-dried but is full of contradictions. Because change is constant, contradiction is constant. Old and new, good and bad, strong and weak, and so on, co-exist in everything. The world is simply a single entity, integrated over opposites. According to the Daoist, the two sides of any contradiction exist in an active harmony, opposed but connected and mutually controlling.

Again, we might find that the principle of contradiction also has a place in psychoanalysis. It is one of the main principles for the working of the Unconscious. As such it should also be seen as a viable principle and guideline for conscious awareness. And so, it is, if the principle of contradiction is equivalent with capacity to integrate opposite feelings and viewpoints. So, for psychoanalysis the principle of integration is rather an endpoint than a statement about the nature of the Universe or of the psychic apparatus. For analysis, the principle of contradiction is disturbed by traumatic events or even by normal development. (The baby cannot take or consider the principle of contradiction as a basis for its existence; it must, so to speak, believe in the good: the good breast, the good enough mother, an environment that is not anxiety-provoking or too frustrating).

Principle of relationship or holism (Zheng He Lu)

This principle probably constitutes the essence of dialectical thinking. It is a consequence of the principles of change and contradiction. It holds that nothing is isolated and independent, but everything is connected. If we really want to know something fully, we must know all of its relations – how it affects and is affected by everything else. Anything regarded in isolation is distorted because the parts are meaningful only in their relations to the whole, like individual musical notes embedded in a melody. The holistic mode of thought rests on the assumption that everything exists in mystical integration of yin and yang, entities that are opposed to one another and yet also are connected in time and space as a whole.

Again, these principles also hold for psychoanalysis, but Yin and Yang are not sufficiently explanatory concepts to satisfy the epistemology of psychoanalysis. They may resemble the dynamic relationship between conscious and unconscious, but that does not differentiate the many processes of psychopathology and so-called normality for which psychoanalysis needs theories and models in order to become a therapeutic discipline and a science.

Observations from case presentations

In the following, we focus some features from a case presentation by a Chinese therapist. (The case is constructed and based on several cases in order to avoid identification and to better underline salient aspects of our discussion).

1. Family constellations, most often encompassing both parents and grandparents, that are unbalanced, take a priority in the presentation. Accordingly, the patient's problems and symptoms are, in part, presented as the problem of how to reinstate balance in the collective family system, and the patient, to a great extent, expects the therapist to come up with good advice on how this is to be done. The therapist is likely, even after having been taught some psychodynamic skills, to be tempted to question and propose advice as how to solve the problems. This tendency to pose questions may, however, also have its background in the need to achieve better understanding of the complex situation (the principle of Zheng He Lu). The abstinent mind-set of the analyst is not so easily reconcilable with the Chinese culture of seeing phenomena in the larger context and seeking and giving advice (which by the way is also the attitude of the patient-doctor relationship in the Western culture).
2. It takes some time for the therapist to learn to shift the focus from advice giving to empathic and open listening, and to let the exploration of feelings, conflicts and intersubjective dynamics have the foreground.

One should also not underestimate the therapist's struggle to find ways of representing individual suffering within a cultural matrix, where the individual's needs and ways of expressing self is to a large degree subordinated to the needs of the family and the group. In addition, we must consider the way traumatising influences undermine the possibility of representation (Rosenbaum & Varvin, 2007).

Case

This case was brought to supervision by a female psychologist working at an outpatient clinic in a large town in China. The therapist had five years of training in psychodynamic psychotherapy.

She presented her patient and the therapy in the following way:

> A woman in her early thirties sought treatment for depression, insomnia and episodes of uncontrolled outbursts of anger, which had caused severe problems in her marriage and also made her relation to her 12-year-old daughter difficult. She had often entertained suicidal thoughts and had once attempted suicide by taking medication. The attempt was considered more as an appeal, although a dangerous one, and she had to be taken to hospital.

The patient described her inner life as chaotic with constant doubt about the right way to see things, what decisions to make and endless arguing with herself about her decision to marry, whether her husband was good enough. She especially had a deeply ambivalent relationship to her daughter. She had a life that alternated between hectic activities where she worked a lot and engaged in social activities, and periods with severe feelings of depression and profound emptiness. She had also engaged in extra-marital affairs several times, which had all ended with her being rejected. Her way of describing her life was fragmented. She had difficulty finding coherence or getting a feeling of meaning in what she told. It was as if things of which she had little control happened to her all the time.

The patient came from a lower middle-class rural family. Her father had worked as teacher and her mother had occasional factory jobs. Being born shortly after the end of the Cultural Revolution, she learned in her teens that both parents had been persecuted without, however, telling their daughter in what way and for what. She knew almost nothing about her grandparents. Her maternal grandfather had lived until she was five years old. She had vague memories of him as a withdrawn old man who mostly sat by himself. At age two she had been sent to a paternal aunt to live for three years when her parents had to work in another part of the country. She remembered this as a good time, but then she was taken home to her parental home without prior notice. She had vague memories of feeling confused and of missing her aunt. She remembered a depressive atmosphere in her family all through her childhood and youth. Father and mother hardly talked with each other. There were severe quarrels when father was drunk in which state he beat her mother. She was criticised by her parents for minor things in a quite unpredictable way and was often called stupid and dumb. She realised that it had to do with the fact that she was a girl. When she became a teenager, especially her father made derogatory remarks about her body and her way of dressing. She did not dare to protest: "Because I feared that he would look at me in contempt. I hate his look. The look hurts me so deeply". She dreamt of being independent from her family as she believed her friends were, but never realised what she could do to make this happen.

A younger sister was born when she was eight years old, just as the one-child policy had started. As a consequence, this child was sent away to live by the aunt. She had little contact with her sister until she came in her early twenties when she moved from her parental home.

When she graduated from high school and went into college in another town, she then moved from her parental home. At first, she experienced this as a relief and engaged in school and social activities. Soon periods of depression came to dominate her life. She managed graduation at bachelor level with great difficulty. She felt she was profoundly entangled in her family: "Whatever I do, I have to report to my family! I know they are concerned about me, but I feel I am chained by them", she said.

About her mother she said: "It's very complicated. I love her, because she is my mother, but I do not like her as a person". Her father she described as a scary and depressive man from whom she tried to keep a distance. This suffering made her think maybe there was something wrong with her. Otherwise, she couldn't explain her parents' behaviours. She was sensitive about small things in daily life. She would pay much attention to others' attitudes towards her. She was passive and often felt ignored by others and she was always afraid that anyone could be angry at her. Accordingly, she sought to please others but felt she could never be close to others or that anyone wanted to be close to her. She often experienced that people she was in contact with changed their attitude to her without her being able to understand why.

The patient met her husband at college. She felt for the first time that anyone wanted to be with her, so she accepted his rough behaviour and heavy drinking habits. They had a child after two years marriage.

At the time of her therapy, she worked as a clerk in a big firm while her husband worked as truck driver. She seldom visited her parents and felt much guilt when her mother called and asked her to come. She had some contact with her younger sister. At the time of the supervision the patient had been in therapy for approximately a half year, with altogether 50 sessions, mostly twice a week. It became increasingly clear during the therapy that both parents struggled with unfinished grief and consequences of traumatic experiences. They had both been treated as class enemies during the Cultural Revolution, had lost their jobs and been sent to labour camps where they lived apart under very hard conditions. Moreover, the parents of the father had suffered similar hardships in the 1950s when the family was categorised as "landowners" and deprived of their property and punished severely. As a consequence of her therapy, the patient had been able to get some of these stories from her parents, but most of it did she had heard from her aunt. The therapist described increasing frustration with a patient who had difficulties talking about her problems, often came late for session and cancelled with short prior notice or no notice at all. The therapist had considered ending treatment several times and felt quite desperate and helpless.

Vignette from 34th session:

P: In fact, I don't like the feeling of being controlled by others. It means others always influence you.

T: Who influences you?

P: My mother, I always want to get rid of the thoughts about her, but I can't.

T: You said last time that you had stopped thinking about her complaints.

P: It's not possible. But why can I not escape from the grip of my mother?

T: How do you think about her so far?

P: It's very complicated. I love her, because she is my mother, but I do not like her as a person.

T: What's her feeling towards you?

P: I don't know. I doubted whether I was born from her. She is my mother, but I felt that she made my life a misery.

T: Do you love her?

P: The truth?

T: (Nod.)

P: She always made me do what I don't like to do. For example, she forced me to be polite to people I didn't know, she made me wear the clothes I didn't like at all. She often lost her temper. I felt depressed.

T: How about father?

P: I was afraid. He was often angry when he drank, and very strange sometimes. He called me things I didn't like. Sometime when he worked in another city, I felt relief, but then mother would criticise me.

P: Now I feel that I'm always carrying a very big burden on my back, whatever I do. It bothers me a lot.(Later in the session)

T: Do you still have thoughts about suicide?

P: (Smile) No, I think there is so much I have not seen yet. Is it the time to end? I'm so hungry. I only ate an orange this morning. I hardly ate anything during last week.

T: Here are some biscuits, do you want some?

P: No, thanks.

T: Why haven't you eaten normally?

P: I have eaten all my special food. The shop has moved faraway place. I asked the aunt downstairs to help me to buy some. She refused and when I went there it proved to be fake products. Why do I always be cheated by the others?

Comments

This vignette shows a complicated relation between the patient and the therapist. The patient brings several themes to treatment. She starts with her feelings of being controlled, which we believe allude to her feeling in the transference and may be a background for her difficulties in attending sessions. "Why can I not escape from the grip of my mother?". A conflict between wish for separation and individuality and for belonging is here represented at regressive level as a feeling of being in mother's "grip".

She goes on with the fantasy that she maybe is not mother's daughter; a kind of negative family romance which probably covers fantasies about being born into another family with good parents and maybe more appreciation and respect.

She then focuses on her difficult relations to father, mentioning the improper and embarrassing behaviour from his side, which seemed to have been of a transgressing nature.

Later in the session the therapist introduces her worries about the actual persistence of suicidal thoughts which the patient has expressed in previous sessions. The patient denies this problem and talks about in an almost manic fashion "all the good things in life" while she at the same time expresses an immense hunger. The therapist, having her mind on problems in the external reality, offers the patient some food, which the patient then rejects. This dynamic probably represents the patient's conflict between wish for distance and closeness in the transference and the therapist's personal countertransference may express itself in her difficulties in relating and understanding external, interpersonal problems and dynamics in the light of inner conflicts. But there may also be a cultural component in the countertransference. The potential inner freedom brought about when problems in external reality is handled on the level of inner psychic life by means of separation-individuation is blocked by an unconscious cultural "reasoning" which blinds both patient and therapist.

We thus get a picture of a therapist who is trying her best but who obviously feel helpless for cultural and personal reasons. The therapist's questioning style reveals her wish to get a fuller picture, see things in context but also her inability to place herself in the third position from where she can reflect and make interventions that brings the here-and-now and the transference into focus. The consequence is that the patient is given the task of bringing more external and interpersonal material (mother, father, food), which may reflect a shared inability to find ways of speaking about the emotional sufferings of the patient and her family. "Now I feel that I'm always carrying a very big burden on my back, whatever I do" has seemingly neither an internal nor an external solution. This may sustain such a strong suicidal despair in the patient that it forces the therapist to overcome her anxiety and make sure that the patient's "impossible" separation from her internal parents is not substituted by fantasies of separation from life. When the therapist at last offers her nourishment, then the offer is rejected. This invitation-rejection pattern was characteristic for this period in therapy and made the therapist feel quite helpless – a projective identification placing the therapist in the same feeling mode as her patient. The impossible development of separation-individuation plays a role in the countertransference and makes it difficult for the therapist to listen with a third ear.

From a technical point of view, this and many other things had to be discussed in this supervision. The therapist felt the patient was quite unpredictable in her responses, often changed in mood, and could easily reject the therapist's efforts. The patient had little capacity to reflect on her behaviour, she demanded that therapist should do this work, and when the therapist attempted to bring her reflection back to her, they were as a rule rejected. At a more profound level, there were difficulties in understanding the patient's inner world, the influence of her background – besides the difficulties related to the separation-individuation process. Also, the influences on the patient's destiny of the parents' and grandparents' previous life with their traumas were such an obvious and recognisable story that it was difficult for the therapist to turn the culture- and family-based narration into an individual internalised object-relational fantasy.

Transgenerational processes

It is to these aspects we now turn our attention to, leaving aside the more technical aspects of how to handle the transference. In this context we will discuss the difficulties of understanding described above in relation to this patient's difficulties with separation-individuation and the transgenerational transmission of the effects of trauma inherent in this story.

The patient was deeply involved with her parents to the extent that she felt controlled. She wanted to get rid of her thoughts about her mother as if trying to expel mother from her mind. The question is, however, what she is trying to get rid of. One may get the impression that mother (with her unconscious ambivalence) had been trying to be something special for her daughter that the patient ambivalently opposed. We know children need parents to have them in their mind in a way that anxieties may be modulated and made more bearable. When the parent is not able to "bear the child in his or her mind" because of own unbearable pain and pain related to their parents' transgenerational transmitted traumatising experiences, then the child often attempts to, or is even assigned the task of, repairing the damage that haunts the minds of the parents and destabilises family coherence. We saw that this patient's family had experienced frequent upheavals and had suffered unbearable painful atrocities and losses – without being able to speak about it. Previous traumatisation had their silent, powerful influence on the succeeding generations. The patient's symptoms and disorganised behaviour seem to be the sign of this, and perhaps also of an attempt to remedy past wounds.

We do not have clinical material here to see how this happened. Our main point here is, however, how the silent force of past traumas is passed onto the next generations and how the lack of words to give the experiences past and present meaning haunts the patient – and in a way also the therapist. Both patient and therapist live in the same context where silencing of past traumas is the rule.

Trauma – in the Chinese context

Trauma can be spoken at different levels. Societal discourse on trauma should be characterised by acknowledgements and inquiry as well as compassion for the victims. At the family or group level of coherent stories, grief and understanding is needed. At the professional psychotherapeutic level, a language of symbolisation, meaning and empathy is needed. It seemed that all this was lacking in this patient's life situation and that the therapist urgently felt the lack of possibility to have the patient in her mind, find words and give meaning to her pains. We see how the separation-individuation process may become hampered when the parents' ability to have their child in their minds in a way that she can develop her own individual self. On the contrary, this patient seemed to have been assigned the task on what to be and do in a way she experienced as alien, strange and intrusive.

We have underlined principles of ways of thinking in Chinese folk-psychology such as the principles of change, contradiction and relationships or holism. The Chinese believe that reality is ever-changing. In order to organise changes in one's mind it is necessary for the Chinese to understand what happens in a complex reality with inherent contradictions that nevertheless can be grasped as whole in a relatively harmonious way. Trauma, especially social trauma is example of an unpredictable change in conditions. Such traumas undoubtedly make extremely difficult grasping and understanding wholeness. In some cases, even impossible as was clear in this patient's story. The not symbolised and not worked through aspects of both parents' and grandparents' experiences seemed to have been acted out in a complicated transgenerational family-dynamic where the girl had been assigned the impossible task of trying to keep the family together. This made the patient with scarce possibilities to separate and individuate and with no other alternative but to act out what had been unconsciously transmitted. The therapist was on her side left helpless in that no coherent story could be achieved from the patient and she was left to further questioning and advice-giving.

What we highlight here is that acquiring psychoanalytic knowledge in a culture distant from the West not only concerns developing concepts and theories in a new societal and cultural context, but also involves working through and acknowledgement of upheavals and traumatising circumstances in the country's history.

Conclusion

We started with assumptions on difficulties in translation of psychoanalytic concepts. We saw that the embeddedness of psychoanalytic concepts and theories in the Western "Aristotelian" culture implied challenges when "translating" these into a "Confucian-Daoist" context. We hold that this implies a collaborative and long work of Western and Chinese analysts before a solid foundation for psychoanalytic theory may be achieved for the Chinese context. What may also be of help for Western analysts working in a Chinese family-oriented culture is to have consciousness of recent historical developments in Western countries. Socially, the development of individualism and freedom of choice on the basis of individual preference relatively independent of the family is a relatively late development in the West. However, it has undoubtedly been part of the Western social unconscious memory and discourse for a longer time. Even though there had been development of individual forms of living and conception of the self as individualised in the modernisation process in the West the last two to three hundred years, this development quite slowly reached many social areas. One finds for example only three to four generations ago, that is the beginning of the twentieth century, in many areas in western societies a strong family orientation and relatively little room for individual development. Especially in rural areas but also in more urban contexts, the family came first when it came to choosing work and education. There were distinct social classes and gender differences that on this level was more similar to the recent Chinese context (for example that boys had easier access to education) even though the understanding of family ties were different (Nielsen & Rudberg, 2004).

New theory implies new perspectives. We have demonstrated how psychoanalytic knowledge on traumatisation and transgenerational transmission of trauma have challenged but also brought to light aspects of the reality of Chinese patients and therapists that may be necessary for the healing process. Our reflections are tentative, but it seems clear how, for example, in supervision, one needs not only to work on technical aspects of the therapy, but also to carry out conceptual integrative work in order for candidates to grasp the complexities that this and similar, case stories represent. This conceptual integrative work has to be done as a joint work between therapists and supervisors.

Epilogue

Homelessness is a central theme in this book. This concerns the house, the village or city but more important, the loss of the feeling of home, about the homeless wanderer, the outsiders, the aliens, enemies of the good order. Culture is also a home. Traditions, folklore, food, colours, smells of the specific place you were born and lived, constitute a wholeness of one's experience of being. The terrors instigated by states, militias and armies, attack homes and the feeling of safety connected with the complex and rich experience of having a home, being at home and feeling at home. Many of those who have lost everything, host horrific experiences in their mind, too much for people to bear and sadly, often too much for those they meet after their flight. Meeting the homeless and traumatised evokes dilemmas. Images of the frightening stranger appear easily in the news alongside with care and sometimes pity. They are not citizens of our country and arrive with few rights and few demands. They have been and are often now shunned.

Psychoanalysis has through its history been bewildered. How can we understand, what can we do? The pioneers relating to the horror of Holocaust (Henry Krystal, Dori Laub, William G. Niederland and others) made seminal contributions that have put us in a better position to take on the task of encountering the horrors in the mind even though ignorance and denial often have been the case. An important way to try catch this ignorance is to see it as countertransference. The development of our understanding of this ubiquitous phenomenon has increased the ability of analysts and other mental health workers to work with the horror of man-made atrocities. Difficulties in listening to and relating to traumatised people have, however, been hindered by the strong countertransference reactions on individual, social and cultural levels. In Norway for example, it took a very long time before our war-sailors were acknowledged for their war-efforts and for their traumatisation – and sadly too late for most (Sem, 2015). Similar patterns have appeared in many countries. In the 1970's and 1980's, the Women's Liberation Movement and Vietnam Veteran's Movement made visible traumatisation both from family violence and wars, and the understanding of post-traumatic conditions came on the agenda. In this book, I try to show my take of this rather newly developed understanding of post-traumatic conditions. The therapeutic help that may be offered to severely traumatised people is developed theoretically and clinically and the need to support the integral capacity for survival and resilience in traumatised persons are underlined. There is an immense potential for survival and resilience that can easily be curbed by neglect and ignorance.

At the core of man-made traumatisation is disturbance of, or often near destruction of, inner links to empathic and comforting objects (Laub, 2005b) resulting in an experience of loss of humanity stemming from being degraded and dehumanised. Psychoanalytic therapy strives to repair inner links. This is an important endeavour because of the lack of care and recognition of traumatised people. This is of central importance as we now have quite solid evidence for that the public acknowledgement of what happens after people have been traumatised is utmost importance for their future life and well-being. War-veterans have been neglected, refugees ignored and left to themselves, victims of child abuse forgotten – the list goes on. When society ignores the sufferers, repetition of traumatisation's terrible experience that nobody cares, is lived again. Psychoanalysis has participated in this neglect and for longer periods largely ignored the real atrocities done against people. This state of affairs has improved – but still the voices of victims and survivors are low-keyed with relatively scarce support from others.

This was evident in my work in China where the suffering over generations of the massive traumatisation in Chinese history has increasingly been put into words and given meaning in the expanding opportunities for entering "talking cures" for second and third generations. The voices of support in the social and political field are still weak but, as my chapter on the writer Yu Hua tries to show, in the field of arts, voices of suffering are given form – and they are increasingly heard.

The main intention with this book has been, and I think this is in line with Freud's work, to expand the use of psychoanalysis into social and cultural fields. This concerns the application of psychoanalytic theory on conflictual social fields like wars, social conflicts, ethnic cleansing, and also the use of psychoanalytic practical knowledge working in conflictual situations. In many ways, psychoanalysis is a contribution to the politics of enlightened understanding, to social responsibility and to the need to curb aggressive and destructive forces.

Positive emotional ties counteract destructive forces – a task extremely difficult also in today's world. It is a Sisyphean task of great dimensions, but nevertheless necessary even if it must be repeated again – and again.

It concerns hope, hope for people who have experienced the worst.

Note

1 Published in: *Psychoanalysis in China* edited by David E. Scharff and Sverre Varvin, pp. 123–36 (2014, Karnac). It is reproduced here by kind permission of Phoenix Publishing House.

References

Adams-Silvan, A., & Silvan, M. (1990). 'A dream is the fulfillment of a wish': Traumatic dream, repetition compulsion, and the pleasure principle. *International Journal of Psychoanalysis, 71*(Pt 3), 513–522. Retrieved from PM:2228449.

Adorno, T. W., Frenkel-Brunswik, E., Levinsin, D. L., & Sanford, R. N. (1982 (1950)). *The authoritarian personality*. New York: Norton & Company.

Akhtar, S. (2003). Dehumanization: Origins, manifestations, and remedies. In S. Varvin & V. D. Volkan (Eds.), *Violence or dialogue. Psychoanalytic insights on terror and terrorism*. London: International Psychoanalytic Association.

Alemi, Q., James, S., Cruz, R., Zepeda, V., & Racadio, M. (2013). Psychological distress in afghan refugees: A mixed-method systematic review. *Journal of Immigrant and Health, 16*, 1247–1251. doi:10.1007/s10903-013-9861-1

Alexander, F. (1963 (1948)). *Fundamentals of psychoanalysis*. The United States of America: The Norton Library.

Allen, J., & Fonagy, P. (2015). Trauma. In P. Luyten, L. Mayes, P. Fonagy, M. Target, & S. Blatt (Eds.), *Handbook of psychodynamic approaches to psychopathology* (pp. 165–198). New York, London: The Guilford Press.

Allen, J., Vaage, A. B., & Hauff, E. (2006). Refugees and asylum seekers in societies. In D. L. Sam & J. W. Berry (Eds.), *The Cambridge handbook of acculturation psychology*. Cambridge, UK: Cambridge University Press.

Amery, J. (1998). *At the mind's limits: Contemplations by a survivor on Auschwitz and its realities*. Bloomington, Indiana, US: Indiana University Press.

APA. (1994). *Diagnostic and statistical manual of mental disorders* (4th ed.). Washington DC: American Psychiatric Association.

Apitzsch, H., Eriksson, N. G., Jakobsson, S. W., Lindgren, L., Lundin, T., Movschenson, P.,... Sundqvist, G (1991). [A study of post-traumatic stress reactions among war refugees based on medical records. A standard model may support the treatment]. *Lakartidningen, 93*(47), 4285–4288.

Appy, J. G. (1993). The meaning of Auschwitz today: Clinical reflections about the depletion of a destructive symbol. In R. Moses (Ed.), *Persistent shadows of the holocaust*. Madison, Connecticut: Int. Univ. Press.

Arendt, H. (2017). *De retsløse og de ydmygede*. København: Information forlag.

Askevold, F. (1980). The war sailor syndrome. *Danish Medical Bulletin, 27*(5), 220–224.

Bakhtin, M. M. (1986). *Speech genres and other late essays*. Austin: University of Texas Press.

Baldwin-Ragaven, L., Bloche, M., Bryant, J., London, L., Orr, W., & Rubenstein, L. (2002). *Dual loyalty & human rights in health professional practice*. USA: Physicians for Hyman Rights and School of Public Health and Primary Health Care, University of Cape Town, Health Sciences Faculty.

Basoglu, M. E. (1992). *Torture and its consequences*. New York, Cambridge: University Press.

Bauman, Z. (1989). *Modernity and holocaust*. Cambridge: Polity Press.

Bernard-Henri Levy, A. F. (Writer). (1994). Bosna! In B.-H. R. Television, Canal+, C. N. d. C. e. d. l. I. Animée, F. Cinéma, & L. F. d. Lendemain (Producer). France: MKL Distribution.

Berry, J. W. (1997). Immigration, acculturation, and adaptation. *Applied Psychology: An International Review, 46*, 5–34.

Berwick, A. (2011). *2083. A European declaration of independence* Retrieved from http://www.fas.org/programs/tap/_docs/2083_-_A_European_Declaration_of_Independence.pdf

Biggerstaff, D., & Thompson, A. R. (2008). Interpretative phenomenological analysis (IPA): A qualitative methodology of choice in healthcare research. *Qualitative Research in Psychology, 5*(3), 214–224. doi:10.1080/14780880802314304

Bion, W. (1952). Group dynamics: A review. *International Journal of Psychoanalysis, 33*, 235–247.

Bion, W. R. (1961). *Experiences in groups*. London: Tavistock Publications.

Bion, W. R. (1962). *Learning from experience*. London: Heinemann.

Bion, W. R. (1967). *Second thoughts. Selected papers on psychoanalysis*. London: Karnac.

Bion, W. R. (1977). *Seven servants*. New York: Jason Aronson.

Blanck-Cereijido, F., & Grynberg Robinson, M. (2010). Prejudice, transgenerational transmission, and neutrality. *International Journal of Psychoanalysis, 91*(5), 1216–1219. doi:10.1111/j.1745-8315.2010.00293.x

Bleger, J. (1967). Psycho-analysis of the psycho-analytic frame. *International Journal of Psychoanalysis, 48*(4), 511–519. Retrieved from PM:5582796.

Block, R. (1994). The tragedy of Rwanda. *The New York Review of Books, XLI*(17).

Boehnke, K. (1998). On the development of xenophobia in Germany: The adolescent years. *Journal of Social Issues, 54*(3), 585–602. https://doi.org/10.1111/0022-4537.841998084

Bohleber, W. (2002). Kollektive Phantasmen, Destruktivität und Terrorismus. *Psyche, 56*(8), 699–720.

Bohleber, W. (2007). Remembrance, trauma and collective memory. The battle for memory in psychoanalysis. *International Journal of Psychoanalysis, 88*, 329–352.

Bohleber, W. (2010). *Destructiveness, intersubjectivity and trauma*. London: Karnac.

Bohleber, w., Fonagy, P., Jiménez, J., Scarfone, D., Varvin, S., & Zysman, S. (2013). Towards a better use of psychoanalytic concepts: A model illustrated using the concept of enactment. *International Journal of Psychoanalysis, 94*(3), 51–530.

Bohleber, W., Jimenez, J., Scarfone, D., Varvin, S., & Zysman, S. (2015). Unconscious phantasy and its conceptualizations: An attempt at conceptual Integration. *International Journal of Psychoanalysis, 96*, 705–730.

Borchrevink, A. S. (2012). *En norsk tragedie. Anders Behring Breivik og veiene til Utøya (A Norwegian tragedy. Anders Behring Breivik and the roads to Utøya).* Oslo: Gyldendal.

Braun, V., & Clarke, V. (2006). Using thematic analysis in psychology. *Qualitative Research in Psychology, 3*, 77–101.

Breuer, J., & Freud, S. (1895). *Studies on hysteria.* London: Penguin Books.

Britannica. (2016). Nansen International Office for Refugees. Retrieved from Britannica http://global.britannica.com/topic/Nansen-International-Office-for-Refugees

Browning, C. R. (1998). *Ordinary men. Reserve Police Battalion 101 and the final solution in Poland.* New York: HarperPerennial.

Bucci, W. (1997). *Psychoanalysis and cognitive science.* New York, London: The Guilford Press.

Bucci, W. (2000). Biological and integrative studies on affect. *International Journal of Psychoanalysis, 81* (Pt 1), 141–144. Retrieved from PM:10816849.

Buruma, I., & Margolit, A. (2004). *Occidentalism. The west in the eyes of its enemies.* New York: The Penguin Press.

Butler-Kisber, L. (2018). *Qualitative inquiry. Thematic, narrative and arts-based perspectives.* McGill University, Canada: Sage.

Cao, X. (1978-1980). *A dream of red mansions.* Beijing: Foreign Language Press.

Chamberlain, K., Cain, T., Sheridan, J., & Dupuis, A. (2011). Pluralisms in qualitative research: From multiple methods to integrated methods. *Qualitative Research in Psychology, 8*, 151–169.

Chamberlain, K., McGuigan, K., Anstiss, D., & Marshall, K. (2018). A change of view: Arts-based research and psychology. *Qualitative Research in Psychology, 15*(2-3), 131–139. doi:10.1080/14730887.2018.1456590

Chasseguet-Smirgel, J. (1990). Reflections of a psychoanalyst upon the Nazi Biocracy and genocide. *International Review of Psychoanalysis, 17*, 167–176.

Chasseguet-Smirgel, J. (1991). De två träden i trädgården (The two trees in the garden). *Svenska föreningen for psykisk hälsovård.* Stockholm: Norstedt.

Chiozza, L. (1999). Body, affect, and language. *Neuro-Psychoanalysis, 1*(1), 111–124.

Classen, C., Pain, C., Field, N. O., Woods, P. (2006). Posttraumatic personality disorder: A reformulation of complex posttraumatic stress disorder and borderline personality disorder. *Psychiatric Clinics of North America, 29*(1), 87–112. http://www.sciencedirect.com/science/journal/0193953X. Retrieved from doi: http://dx.doi.org/10.1016/j.psc.2005.11.001

Clayton, J. (2015). Funding shortage leaves Syrian refugees in danger of missing vital support. UNHCR. http://www.unhcr.org/news/latest/2015/6/558acbbc6/funding-shortage-leaves-syrian-refugees-danger-missing-vital-support.html. (Retrievd 03.05.2017).

Crickley, A., Winkler, B. (2006). The annual report on the situation regarding racism and xenophobia in the member states of the EU. Retrieved from http://fra.europa.eu/fra/material/pub/ar06/AR06-P2-EN.pdf

Crowe, D. M. (2013). *War crimes, genocide, and justice: A global history.*(978-0-230-62224-1). London: Palgrave Macmillan.

Dahl, S., Dahl, C., Sandvik, L., & Hauff, E. (2006). Kronisk smerte hos traumatiserte flyktninger. *Tidskr Nor Lægeforening, 126*, 608–610.

Darré, W. (1930). *La race, nouvelle noblesse du sang et du sol.* Paris: Sorlot.

Daud, A., Skoglund, E., & Rydelius, P. A. (2005). Children in families of torture victims: Transgenerational transmission of parents' traumatic experiences to their children. *International Journal of Social Welfare*, *14*(1), 23–32. Retrieved from http://onlinelibrary.wiley.com/doi/10.1111/j.1468-2397.2005.00336.x/abstract

de Mendelssohn, F. (2008). Transgenerational transmission of trauma: Guilt, shame, and the "Heroic Dilemma". *International Journal of Group Psychotherapy*, *58*(3), 389–401. doi:10.1521/ijgp.2008.58.3.389

Diatkine, G. (1993). La cravatte croate: narcissisme des petits différences et processus de civilisation. *Revue Francaise Psychoanalysis Contenporaine Scientifique*, *4*, 1057–1072.

Drozdek, B., Kamperman, A. M., Tol, W. A., Knipscheer, J. W., & Kleber, R. J. (2013). Seven-year follow-up study of symptoms in asylum seekers and refugees with PTSD treated with trauma-focused groups. *Journal of Clinical Psychology*, *70*(part 4), 376–387. doi: 10.1002/jclp.22035

Eitinger, L. (1973). A follow-up study of the Norwegian concentration camp survivors' mortality and morbidity. *Israel Annals of Psychiatry Related Disciplines*, *11*(3), 199–209. Retrieved from PM:4520331.

Eitinger, L. (1980). Jewish concentration camp survivors in the post-war world. *Danish Medical Bulletin*, *27*(5), 232–235. Retrieved from PM:7449449.

Emde, R. N. (1990). Mobilizing fundamental modes of development: Empathic availability and therapeutic action. *JAPA*, *38*, 881–913.

English, H. B. (1941). Fundamentals and fundamentalism in the preparation of applied psychologists. *Journal of Consulting Psychology*, *5*(1), 1–13.

Enzenberger, H. M. (1994). *Civil war*. London: Granta Books.

Erikson, E. H. (1950). *Childhood and society*. New York: Norton.

Erikson, E. H. (1964). Identity and uprootedness in our time. In E. Erikson (Ed.), *Insight and Responsibility* (pp. 81–107). New York: Norton.

Etchegoyen, H. (2006). *The fundamentals of psychoanalytic technique*. London: Karnac.

Europol. (2016). Europol and Interpol issue comprehensive review of migrant smuggling networks [Press release]. https://www.europol.europa.eu/newsroom/news/europol-and-interpol-issue-comprehensive-review-of-migrant-smuggling-networks. Retrieved: 11.12.2016. Europol.

Fangen, K. (2011). Analyse og organisering av et stort livshistorisk materiale: Komparativt kvalitativt prosjekt (Analysis and organisation of a large material on life history: Comparative qualitative project). In K. Fangen (Ed.), *Mange Ulike Metoder*. Oslo: Gyldendal Akademisk.

Fekete, L. (2009). *A suitable enemy. Racism, migration and Islamophobia in Europe*. London: Pluto Press.

Fischmann, T. (2007). *Einsturz bei Nacht : Verarbeitung traumatischer Erlebnisse im TraumSchlaf und Traum*. Köln: Böhlau.

Fonagy, P. (2001). *Attachment theory and psychoanalysis*. New York: Other Press.

Fonagy, P., & Target, M. (1997). Attachment and reflective function: Their role in self-organization. *Development and Psychopathology*, *9*(4), 679–700. Retrieved from PM:9449001.

Fosshage, J. L. (1997). The organizing functions of dream mentation. *Contemporary Psychoanalysis*, *33*, 429–458.

Freud, A. (1967). Comments on trauma. In S. S. Furst (Ed.), *Psychic Trauma* (pp. 235–245). New York and London: Basic Books.

Freud, S. (1900). *Die Traumdeutung* (Sigmund Freud Studienausgabe. Bd. II ed.). Frankfurt am Main: S. Fischer Verlag.

Freud, S. (1912). Recommendations to physicians practising psycho-analysis. In J. Strachey (Ed.), *The standard edition of the complete psychological works of Sigmund Freud* (Vol. XII, pp. 109–120). London: Hogarth.

Freud, S. (1915a). *Das Unbewusste* (Sigmund Freud Studienausgabe, Band III ed.). Frankfurt am Main: S. Fischer Verlag.

Freud, S. (1915b). *Triebe und Triebschicksale* (Sigmund Freud Studienausgabe, Band III ed.). Frankfurt am Main: S. Fischer Verlag.

Freud, S. (1916). *The complete introductory lectures on psychoanalysis*. London: Georges Allan & Unwin LTD.

Freud, S. (1917). *Trauer und Melancholia*. (Sigmund Freud Studienausgabe. Bd. III ed.). Frankfurt am Main: S. Fischer Verlag.

Freud, S. (1919a). *Das Unheimliche* (Gesammelte Werke Band XII ed.). Frankfurt am Main: Fisher.

Freud, S. (1919b). Einleitung zu: Zur Psychoanalyse der Kriegsneurosen *GW XII*, 321–324.

Freud, S. (1920). *Beyond the pleasure principle. The standard edition of the complete psychological works of Sigmund Freud* (18th ed.). London: The Hogarth Press and The Institute of Psychoanalysis.

Freud, S. (1921). Mass psychology and ego analysis *Standard Edition* (Vol. 18, pp. 69–144). London: Institute of Psychoanalysis.

Freud, S. (1923). *Das Ich und das Es* (Sigmund Freud Studienausgabe, Band III ed.). Frankfurt am Main: S. Fischer Verlag.

Freud, S. (1926a). Hemmung, Symptom und Angst *Sigmund Freud Studienausgabe; Hysterie un Angst, band VI* (pp. 227–310). Frankfurt am Main: S. Fischer Verlag.

Freud, S. (1926b). *Inhibitions, symptoms and anxiety. The standard edition of the complete psychological works of Sigmund Freud* (pp. 179–258). London: The Hogarth Press and The Institute of Psychoanalysis.

Freud, S. (1926c). *The question of lay analysis. The standard edition of the complete psychological works of Sigmund Freud, Volume XX (1925–1926)* (Vol. XX, pp. 177–258). London: Hogarth.

Freud, S. (1927). Nachwort zur Laienanalyse. In S. Freud (Ed.), *Gesammelte Werke* (Vol. 14, p. 293). Nabu Press.

Freud, S. (1930 (1929)). Civilization and its discontents. In J. Strachey (Ed.), *The standard edition of the complete psychological works of Sigmund Freud, Volume XXI*. London: The Hogarth Press and the Institute of Psycho-analysis.

Freud, S. (1933). Why war? (*The standard edition of the complete psychological works of Sigmund Freud* vol XXII ed.). The Hogarth Press and The Institute of Psychoanalysis.

Frommer, J. (2007). Psychoanalytische und qualitative Sozialforschung in Konvergenz: Gibt es Möglichkeiten, voneinander zu lernen? *Psyche, 61*, 781–803.

Gagnon, A. J., & Stewart, D. E. (2013). Resilience in international migrant women following violence associated with pregnancy. *Archives of Women's Mental Health, 17*(4), 303–310. doi:10.1007/s00737-013-0392-5

Galtung, J. (1969). Violence, peace, and peace research. *Journal of Peace Research, 6*(3), 167–191.

Gampel, Y. (1999). Between the background of safety and the background of the Uncanny in the context of social violence. In P. Fonagy, A. Cooper, & R. S. Wallerstein (Eds.). London and New York: Routledge.

Gee, J. P. (1986). Units in the production of narrative discourse. *Discourse Processes*, 9, 391–422.

Geisser, V. (2004). Islamophobia in Europe: From the Christian anti-Muslim prejudice to a modern form of racism. In I. Ramberg (Ed.), *Islamophobia and its consequences on young people*. European. Budapest: Youth Centre Budapest 1–6 June 2004: Council of Europe.

Gerlach, A., Hooke, M. T. S., & Varvin, S. (2013). *Psychoanalysis in Asia*. London: Karnac.

Gerzi, S. (2002). Integrating holes into the whole. To live the absence in the memories of patients who were children during the Holocaust. In S. Varvin & S. Popovic (Eds.), *Upheaval: Psychoanalytic perspectives on trauma* (pp. 101–132). Belgrade: Int. Aid Network.

Glaser, B. G., & Strauss, A. L. (1967). *The discovery of grounded theory*. Chicago: Aldine.

Glenney, M. (1999). *The Balkans. Nationalism, war and the great powers*. London: Granta Books.

Gullestad, S., & Killingmo, B. (2013). *Underteksten. Psykoanalytisk terapi i praksis (The subtext. Psychoanalytic therapy in practice)*. Oslo: Universitetsforlaget.

Hartmann, E. (1984). *The nightmare. The psychology and biology of dreams*. New York: Basic Books.

Hartmann, E. (1999). Träumen kontextualisiert Emotionen. Eine neue Theorie über das Wesen und die Funktionen des Träumens. In H. Bareuther, K. Brede, M. Ebert-Saleh, K. Grünberg, & S. Hau (Eds.), *Traum, Affekt und Selbst* (pp. 115–157). Tübingen: Edition diskord.

Hassan, G., Ventevogel, P., Jefee-Bahloul, H., Barkil-Oteo, A., & Kirmayer, L. J. (2016). Mental health and psychosocial wellbeing of Syrians affected by armed conflict. *Epidemiology and Psychiatric Sciences*, 25(2), 129–141.

Heine, P. (2001). *Terror in Allahs Namen. Extremistische Kräfte im Islam*. Freiburg Basel Wien: Herder.

Heine, P. (2002). In Allahs Namen: Religiös motivierter Extremismus und Terrorismus. In H. Frank & K. Hirschman (Eds.), *Die weltweite Gefahr. Terrorismus als internationale Herausforderung* (pp. 115–168). Berlin: Berlin Verlag Arno Spitz GmbH.

Herald, S. M. (2016). Think Australia's treatment of refugees and asylum seekers is OK? Read this. An open letter from a refugee on Nauru to the leaders of the UN's Summit for Refugees and Migrants. *Sydney Morning Herald*. http://www.smh.com.au/comment/think-australias-treatment-of-refugees-and-asylum-seekers-is-ok-read-this-20160919-grjjz20160912.html

Herman, J. (1992). Complex PTSD: A syndrome in survivors of prolonged and repeated trauma. *Journal of Traumatic Stress*, 5, 377–391.

Herzinger, R., Schuh, H., & Nieuwenhuizen, A. (2002). Der heranwachsende Krieg, Interview mit Gunnar Heinsohn. *Die Zeit*, p. 41. 11 April 2002.

Hilberg, R. (1961). *Die Vernichtung der europ̃ischen Juden. Band I, II, III* (9th ed.). Frankfurt am Main: Fischer Taschenbuch Verlag GmbH.

Hoffman, B. (1998). *Inside terrorism*. New York: Columbia University Press.

Høglend, P. (2014). Exploration of the patient-therapist relationship in psychotherapy. *American Journal of Psychiatry, 171*, 1056–1066.

Høibraaten, H. (1994). Storm over German historians: Claims and backgrounds. In N.J. Lavik, M. Nygård, N. Sveaass, & E. Fannemel (Eds.), *Pain and survival.* Oslo: Universitetsforlaget.

Hoppe, K. D. (1968). Re-somatization of affects in survivors of persecution. *International Journal of Psychoanalysis, 49*(2), 324–326.

Horowitz, M. J. (1986). *The stress response syndrome* (2nd ed.). New York: Jason Aronson.

Hott, L. R. (1974). Individual aggression and a violent society. *American Journal of Psychoanalysis, 34*, 305–310. doi:10.1007/BF01254125

Hübsch, H. (2001). *Fanatische Krieger im Namen Allahs. Die Wurzeln des islamitischen Terrors.* München: Dietrichs.

Hurvich, M. (2003). The place of annihilation anxieties in psychoanalytic theory. *Journal of the American Psychoanalytic Association, 51*, 579–616.

Hurvich, M. (2015). Vernichtungsängste – Traumatische Ängste. *Psyche, 69*(9), 797–825.

ICRC. (1949). Geneva Conventions.

Inamdar, S. C. (2001). *Muhammad and the rise of Islam.* Madison Connecticut: Psychosocial Press.

Jacobs, T. (1986). On countertransference enactments. *Journal of the American Psychoanalytic Association, 34*, 289–307.

Jacobs, T. (2001). On misreading and misleading patients: Some reflections on communications, miscommunications and countertransference enactments. *International Journal of Psychoanalysis, 82*, 653–669.

Johansen, J., & Varvin, S. (2019). I tell my mother that ... sometimes he didn't love us—Young adults' experiences of childhood in refugee families: A qualitative approach. *Childhood, 26*(2), 221–235.

Johansen, J., & Varvin, S. (2020). Negotiating identity at the intersection of family legacy and present time life conditions: A qualitative exploration of central issues connected to identity and belonging in the lives of children of refugees. *Journal of Adolescence, 80*, 1–9.

Jovanović, A., Trivunčić, B., & Đurašinović, V. (2015). *The demographic picture, the assessment of the legal status and needs as well as examination the traumatic experiences of refugees who are in transit through Serbi".* Retrieved from Belgrade Center for Human Rights and UNHCR.

Jovic, V., Varvin, S., Rosenbaum, B., Fischmann, T., Opačić, G., & Hau, S. (2018). Sleep studies in Serbian victims of torture: Analysis of traumatic dreams. In E. Vermetten, A. Germain, & Thomas C. Neylan (Eds.), *Sleep and combat-related post traumatic stress disorder* (pp. 395–410). New York: Springer.

Juergensmeyer, M. (2000). *Terror in the mind of God. Global rise of religious violence.* Berkeley, Los Angeles and London: University of California Press.

Kakar, S. (1996). *The colors of violence.* Chicago & London: The University of Chicago Press.

Keilson, H., & Sarpathie, R. (1979). *Sequentieller Traumatisierung bei Kindern.* Stuttgart: Ferdinand Enke.

Keles, S., Friborg, O., Idsøe, T., Sirin, S., & Oppedal, B. (2016). Depression among unaccompanied minor refugees: The relative contribution of general and acculturation-specific daily hassles. *Ethnicity & Health, 21*(3), 300–317.

Kernberg, O. F. (1992). Psychopathic, paranoid and depressive transferences. *International Journal of Psycho-Analysis, 73* (Pt 1), 13–28. Retrieved from PM:1582756.

Kertesz, I. (1966). *De skebneløse.* Roskilde: Batzer & Co.

Khosrokhavar, F. (2010). The psychology of global Jihadists. In C. Strozier, D. Terman, & J. Jones (Eds.), *The fundamentalist mindset* (pp. 139–155). New York: Oxford University Press.

Killingmo, B. (1995). Affirmation in psychoanalysis. *International Journal of Psychoanalysis, 76*(Pt 3), 503–518. Retrieved from PM:7558609.

Killingmo, B. (1999). A psychoanalytic listening-perspective in a time of pluralism. *Scandinavian Psychoanalytic Review, 22*(2), 151–171.

Killingmo, B. (2007). Relational-oriented character analysis: A position in contemporary psychoanalysis. *Scandinavian Psychoanalytic Review, 30,* 76–83.

Killingmo, B., Varvin, S., & Strømme, H. (2014). What can we expect from beginning therapists? A study of acquisition competence in dynamic psychotherapy training. *Scandinavian Psychoanalytic Review, 37*(1), 24–35. Retrieved from http://tidsskriftet.no/pdf/pdf2013/1469-71.pdf

http://hdl.handle.net/11250/219445

http://www.scandrev.com/

Kingsley, P. (2016). "Prisoners of Europe": The everyday humiliation of refugees stuck in Greece. *The Guardian.* Retrieved from https://www.theguardian.com/world/2016/sep/06/prisoners-of-europe-the-everyday-humiliation-of-refugees-stuck-in-greece-migration

Kirshner, L. (1994). Trauma, the good object, and the symbolic: A theoretical integration. *International Journal of Psycho-Analysis, 75,* 235–242.

Klein, M. (1946). Notes on some schizoid mechanisms. *International Journal of Psychoanalysis, 27,* 99–110.

Kogan, I. (2017). Anti-semitism and xenophobia. *American Journal of Psychoanalysis, 77.* doi:10.1057/s11231-017-9113-6

Krell, R., Suedfeld, P., & Soriano, E. (2011). Child Holocaust survivors as parents: A transgenerational perspective. *American Journal of Orthopsychiatry, 74*(4), 502–508. Retrieved from http://onlinelibrary.wiley.com/doi/10.1037/0002-9432.74.4.502/abstract

Kroll, J., Yusuf, A., & Fujiwara, K. (2011). Psychoses, PTSD, and depression in Somali refugees in Minnesota. *Social Psychiatry and Psychiatric Epidemiology, 46,* 481–493. doi: 10.1007/s00127-010-0216-0

Kruse, J., Jokosimovic, L., Cavka, M., Wöller, W., Schmitz, N. (2009). Effects of trauma-focused psychotherapy upon war refugees. *Journal of Traumatic Stress, 22*(6), 585–592.

Krystal, H. (1978). Trauma and affects. *Psychoanalytic Study of the Child, 33,* 81–116. Retrieved from PM:715118.

Krystal, H. (1988). *Integration and self-healing: Affect-trauma-alexithymia.* Hillsdale, NJ: The Analytic Press.

Kuhn, T. (1962). *The structure of scientific revolutions* (5th ed.). Chicago: University of Chicago Press.

Künstlicher, R. (2001). Human time and dreaming. *Scandinavian Psychoanalytic Review, 24*(2), 75–82.

Kvale, S. (1999). The psychoanalytic interview as qualitative research. *Qualitative Inquiry, 5*(1), 87–113.

Lacan, J. (1977). *Écrits.* Hammondsworth: Penguin Books.

Lacan, J. (2004). *The four fundamental concepts of psycho-analysis*. London: Karnac.

Lansky, M., & Bley, C. R. (1995). *Post traumatic night mares. Psychodynamic explorations*. Hillsdale, NJ & London: The Analytic Press.

Laqueur, W. (2001). *Die globale Bedrohung. Neue Gefahren des Terrorismus*. München: Econ Taschenbuch.

Laub, D. (1998). The empty circle: Children of survivors and the limits of reconstruction. *Journal of the American Psychoanalytic Association, 46*(2), 507–529. Retrieved from PM:9684225.

Laub, D. (2005). Traumatic shutdown of narrative and symbolization: A death instinct derivative? *Contemporary Psychoanalysis, 41*(2), 307–326. Retrieved from http://www.pep-web.org/document.php?id=CPS.041.0307A

Laub, D., & Lee, S. (2003). Thanatos and massive psychic trauma: The impact of the death instinct on knowing, remembering, and forgetting. *Journal of the American Psychoanalytic Association, 51*(2), 433–464. Retrieved from http://apa.sagepub.com/content/51/2/433.short

Laub, D., & Podell, D. (1995). Art and trauma. *International Journal of Psychoanalysis, 76*(5), 991–1005. Retrieved from PM:8926145.

Lavik, N., Christie, H., Solberg, O., & Varvin, S. (1996). A refugee protest action in a host country: Possibilities and limitations of an intervention by a mental health unit. *Journal of Refugee Studies, 9*(1), 73–88.

Lebiger-Vogel, J., Rickmeyer, C., Busse, A., Fritzemeyer, K., Riger, B., & Leuzinger-Bohleber, M. (2015). FIRST STEPS – A randomized controlled trial on the evaluation of the implementation and effectiveness of two early prevention programs for promoting the social integration and a healthy development of children with an immigrant background from 0-3. *BMC Public Health, 3*, 1–11.

Lecours, S., & Bouchard, M. (1997). Dimensions of mentalisation: Outlining levels of psychic transformation. *International Journal of Psychoanalysis, 78*(5), 855–876.

Leirvik, O. (2012). "Islam er i krig med vesten" (Islam Is at War With the West). In S. Indregard, et al. (Eds.), *Motgift. Akademisk respons på den nye høyreekstremismen (Academic Response To The New Right-wing Extremism)*. Oslo: Flamme Forlag og Forlaget Manifest.

Lesley, J., & Varvin, S. (2016). 'Janet vs Freud' on traumatization: A critique of the theory of structural dissociation from an object relations perspective. *British Journal of Psychotherapy, 32*(4), 436–455.

Leuzinger-Bohleber, M. (1996). [Remembering in the transference–On the interdisciplinary dialogue between psychoanalysis and biological memory research]. *Psychotherapie, Psychosomatik, Medizinische Psychologie, 46*(6), 217–227. Retrieved from PM:8767146.

Leuzinger-Bohleber, M. (2012). Changes in dreams—From a psychoanalysis with a traumatised, chronic depressed patient. In H. K. Peter Fonagy, Marianne Leuzinger-Bohleber, and David Taylor (Eds.), *The significance of dreams* (pp. 49–88). London: Karnac.

Leuzinger-Bohleber, M. (2015). *Finding the body in the mind. Embodied memories, trauma and depression*. London: Karnac Books.

Leuzinger-Bohleber, M., Pfeifer, R., & Röckerath, K. (1998). Wo bleibts das Gedächtnis? In M. Koukkou, M. Leuzinger-Bohleber, & W. Mertens (Eds.), *Erinnerung von Wirklichkeiten. Psychoanalyse und Neurowissessnschaften im Dialog. Band I: Bestandsaufnahme* (pp. 517–588). Stuttgart: Verlag Internationale Psychoanalyse.

Leuzinger-Bohleber, M., Rickmeyer, C., Tahiri, M., & Hettich, N. (2016). What can psychoanalysis contribute to the current 1 refugee crisis? Preliminary reports from STEP-BY-STEP: A psychoanalytic pilot project for supporting refugees in a "first reception camp" and crisis interventions with traumatized refugees. *International Journal of Psychoanalysis, 97*(4), 1077–1093.

Leuzinger-Bohleber, M., Rüger, B., Stuhr, U., & Beutel, M. (2002). *"Forschung und Heilen" in der Psychoanalyse. Ergebnisse und Berichte aus Forschung und Praxis.* Stuttgart: Kohlhammer.

Lifton, R. J. (2000). *Destroying the world to save it: Aum Shinrikyo, apocalyptic violence, and the new global terrorism.* New York: Henry Holt and Company.

Lifton, R. J. (2004). Doctors and torture. *New England Journal of Medicine, 351*(5), 415–416.

Loescher, G. (1993). *Beyond charity: International cooperation and the global refugee crisis.* UK: Oxford University press.

Lopate, P. (1994). *The art of the personal essay.* New York: Anchor Books.

Matthis, I. (1997). *Det omedvetandets arkeologi.* Stockholm: Natur och Kultur.

Mc Laughlin, J. T. (1991). Clinical and theoretical aspects of enactment. *Journal of the American Psychoanalytic Association, 39*, 595–614.

McLaughlin, J. T. J. M. (1992). Enactments in psychoanalysis (Panel report). *Journal of the American Psychoanalytic Association, 40*, 827–841.

McLeod, J., & Balamoutsou, S. (1996). Representing narrative process in therapy: Qualitative analysis of a single case. *Counselling Psychology Quarterly, 9*, 61–76.

Meddeb, A. (2003). *The malady of Islam.* New York: Basic Books

Mergemthaler, E. & Stinson, C.H. (1992). Psychotherapy transcript standards. *Psychotherapy Research, 2*, 58–75.

Migdley, N. (2006). Psychoanalysis and qualitative psychology: Complementary or contradictory paradigms? *Qualitative Research in Psychology, 2*, 213–231.

Milgram, S. (1974). *Obedience to authority: An experimental view.* New York: Harper and Row.

Mitscherlich, A., & Mitscherlich, M. (1967). *Die Unfähigkeit zu Trauern: Grundlagen Kollektiven Verhaltens.* Munchen: Piper.

Modell, A. (1990). *Other times other realities-toward a theory of psychoanalytic treatment.* Cambridge: Harvard University Press.

Montaigne, d. M. (1910). *Essays of Montaigne, trans. (New York: 1910). In 10 vols. 8/25/2017.* (r. b. W. C. H. Charles Cotton, Trans.). http://oll.libertyfund.org/titles/168: Edwin C. Hill.

Moran, M. G. (1994). Chaos theory and psychoanalysis: The fluid nature of the soul. *Zeitschrift fur Psychosomatische Medizin und Psychoanalyse, 40*(4), 384–403.

Moser, U., v. Zeppelin, I. (1996). *Der geträumte Traum.* Stuttgart: Kohlhammer.

Moser, U., Zeppelin, I. v., & Schneider, W. (1991). The regulation of cognitive-affective processes. A new psychoanalytic model. In U. Moser & I. v. Zeppelin (Eds.), *Cognitive-affective processes* (pp. 87–134). Berlin: Springer.

Moses, R. e. (1993). *persistent shadows of the holocaust.* Madison, Connecticut: Int. Univ. Press.

Moussaoui, A. S. (2003). *Zacarias, my brother* (S. W. Pleasance, F., Trans.). New York: Seven Stories Press.

Muller, J. (1996). *Beyond the psychoanalytic dyad.* New York & London: Routledge.

Næser, A. (2014). *Consumer society in China: A radical departure from the recent past? – An exploration of the author Yu Hua's brothers and their son* (Master). Århus: Århus University.

Niederland, W. G. (1968). Clinical observations on the "survivor syndrome". *International Journal of Psychoanalysis, 49*(2), 313–315.

Niederland, W. G. (1981). The survivor syndrome: Further observations and dimensions. *Journal of the American Psychoanalytic Association, 29*(2), 413–425. Retrieved from PM:7264182.

Nielsen, H. B. (1995). Seductive texts with serious intentions. *Educational Researcher, 24*(1), 4–12.

Nielsen, H. B., Rudberg M. (2004). Noisy girls. New subjectivities and old gender discourses. *Young. Nordic Journal of Youth Research, 12*(1), 9–30.

Nisbett, R.E. (2003). *The geography of thought. How Asians and Westerners think differently -- and why.* New York, London, Tokyo, Sydney: Free Press.

NRC & Oxfam. (2017). *The reality of the EU-Turkey statement: How Greece has become a testing ground for policies that erode protection for refugees.* Retrieved from http://reliefweb.int/report/greece/reality-eu-turkey-statement-how-greece-has-become-testing-ground-policies-erode

Obeyesekere, G. (1990). *The work of culture.* Chicago and London: The University of Chicago Press.

Ogden, T. H. (1994). The analytic third: Working with intersubjective clinical facts. *International Journal of Psychoanalysis, 75*, 3–19.

Oliner, M. (2014). *Psychic reality in context.* London: Karnac.

Opaas, M., Hartmann, E., Wentzel-Larsen, T., & Varvin, S. (2015). Relationship of pretreatment Rorschach factors to symptoms, quality of life, and real-life functioning in a three-year follow-up of traumatized refugee patients. *Journal of Personality Assessment,* doi:http://dx.doi.org/10.1080/00223891.2015.1089247

Opaas, M., Tore, W. L., & Varvin, S. (2020). The 10-year course of mental health, quality of life, and exile life functioning in traumatized refugees from treatment start. *PLoS One, 15*(2), e0244730. doi: https://doi.org/10.1371/journal.pone.0244730

Opaas, M., & Varvin, S. (2015). Relationships of childhood adverse experiences with mental health and quality of life at treatment start for adult refugees traumatized by pre-flight experiences of war and human rights violations. *The Journal of Nervous and Mental Disease, 203*(9), 684–695. doi:http://dx.doi.org/10.1097/NMD.0000000000000330

Orange, D. (2006). For whom the bell tolls: Context, complexity, and compassion in psychoanalysis. *International Journal of Psychoanalytic Self Psychology, 1*, 5–21.

OUP. (2017). English Oxford living dictionaries. Retrieved from https://en.oxforddictionaries.com/

Packard, P., Rodríguez-Fornells, A., Stein, L., Nicolás, B., & Fuentemilla, L. (2014). Tracking explicit and implicit long-lasting traces of fearful memories in humans. *Neurobiology of Learning and Memory, 116*, 96–104. doi: 10.1016/j.nlm.2014.09.004

Patel, N., & Eikin, D. (2015). Professionalism and conflicting interests: The American Psychological Association's involvement in torture. *AMA Journal of Ethics, 17*(10), 924–930.

Peirce, C. S. (1955). *Philosophical writings of Peirce.* New York: Dover Publ.

Pines, D. (1986). Working with women survivors of the Holocaust: Affective experiences in transference and countertransference. *International Journal of Psychoanalysis, 67*, 295–307.

Plaenkers, T. (2014a). China—A traumatised country? The aftermath of the Chinese Cultural Revolution (1966–1976) for the individual and for society. In D.-E. Scharff & S. Varvin (Eds.), *Psychoanalysis in China* (pp. 33–44). London: Karnac.

Plaenkers, T. (ed.). (2014b). *Landscapes of the Chinese soul: The enduring presence of the cultural revolution (1966–1976)*. London: Karnac.

Pösteny, A. (1996). Hitom lustprincipen. Drom, trauma, dodsdrift., (On this side of the pleasure principle. Dream, trauma, death drive). *Divan, 3,* 4–16.

Purnell, C. (2010). Childhood trauma and adult attachment. *Healthcare Counselling and Psychotherapy Journal, 20*(2), 9–13.

Quinodoz, J.-M. (1997). Transitions in psychic structures in the light of deterministic chaos theory. *International Journal of Psychoanalysis, 78,* 699–718.

Rauschning, H. (1983 (1939)). *Hitler har sagt det. (Hitler said it)*. Oslo: Lanser forlag.

Romer, G. (2012). Transgenerational psychotraumatology. *Praxis der Kinderpsychologie und Kinderpsychiatrie, 61*(8), 559–563. Retrieved from http://sfxeu09.hosted.exlibrisgroup.com/sfx_ubo?sid=Entrez%3APubMed&id=pmid%3A23155783

Rosenbaum, B. (2006). »Das Unheimliche" og muligheden for at integrere det fremmede. *Psyke & Logos, 27,* 967–977.

Rosenbaum, B., & Varvin, S. (2007). The influence of extreme traumatisation on body, mind and social relations. *International Journal of Psychoanalysis, 88,* 1527–1542.

Ruf-Leuschner, M., Roth, M., & Schauer, M. (2014). Traumatized mothers-Traumatized children? Transgenerational trauma exposure and trauma sequelae in refugee families. *Zeitschrift fur Klinische Psychologie und Psychotherapie: Forschung und Praxis, 43*(1), 1–16. doi: 10.1026/1616-3443/a000237

Sackett, D. L., Roseberg, W. M., Muir, J. A., Haynes, R. B., & Richardson, W. S. (1996). Evidence based medicine: What it is and what it isn't. *British Medical Journal, 312,* 333–344.

Salonen, S. (1992). The reconstruction of psychic trauma. *Scandinavian Psychoanalytic Review, 15,* 89–103.

Sandler, J., & Sandler, A. M. (1998). *Internal objects revisited*. London: Karnac Books.

Sas, S. A. (1992). Ambiguity as the route to shame. *International Journal of Psychoanalysis, 73*(Pt 2), 329–341. Retrieved from PM:1512123.

Scarfone, D. (2011). Repetition: Between presence and meaning. *Canadian Journal of Psychoanalysis/Revue canadienne de psychoanalyse, 19*(1), 70–86.

Scharff, D., & Varvin, S. (2014). *Psychoanalysis in China*. London: Karnac.

Schore, A. (2003). *Affect dysregulation & disorders of the self*. New York & London: W.W. Norton & Company.

Schottenbauer, M. A., Glass, C., Arnkoff, D., & Gray, S. (2008). Contributions of psychodynamic approaches to treatment of PTSD and trauma: A review of the empirical treatment and psychopathology literature. *Psychiatry, 71*(1), 13–34.

Schottenbauer, M. A., Glass, C. R., Arnkoff, D. B., Tendick, V., & Gray, S. H. (2008). Nonresponse and dropout rates in outcome studies on PTSD: Review and methodological considerations. *Psychiatry, 71*(2), 134–168.

Sem, I. (2015). *Krigsseilere. Å overleve freden. Etterord ved Sverre Varvin (War sailors. To survive the peace)* (Retrieved from http://hdl.handle.net/10642/3151): Pax Forlag.

Serauky, E. (2000). *Im Namen Allahs. Der Terrorismus in Nahen Osten*. Berlin: Karl Dietz Verlag.

Shahar, G. (2010). Poetics, pragmatics, schematics, and the psychoanalysis-research dialogue. *Psychoanalytic Psychotherapy, 24*(4), 315–328.

Silke, W.-G., & Möller, B. (2012). The transgenerational transmission of traumatic experiences of the Second World War over three generations – A psychoanalytical perspective. *Praxis der Kinderpsychologie und Kinderpsychiatrie, 61*(8), 610–622. Retrieved from http://sfxeu09.hosted.exlibrisgroup.com/sfx_ubo?sid=Entrez%3APubMed&id=pmid%3A23155786

Simich, L., & Andermann, L. (2014). *Refugee and Resilience* (L. Simich & L. Andermann, Eds.). Dordrecht, Heidelberg, New York, London: Springer.

Sironi, F. (1995). *The destinies of the internalised torturer in psychotherapy with torture victims*. Paris: Centre Primc Levi.

Smith, J. (2009). *Interpretative phenomenological analysis*. London: Sage.

Stang, E., & Sveaas, N. (2016). *Hva skal vi med menneskerettigheter? Betydningen av menneskerettigheter i helse-- og sosialfaglig praksis (Why do we need human rigths? The importance of human rigths in health and social work practice)*. Oslo: Gyldendal Akademiske.

State, G. (2000). A new defence of Gadamer's hermeneutics. *Philosophy and Phenomenological Research, LX*(1), 45–65.

Stein, R. (2003a). Evil as love and as liberation: The mind of suicidal terrorist. In D. Moss (Ed.), *Hating in the first person plural: Psychoanalytic essays on racism, homophobia, misogyny, and terror* (pp. 281–310). New York: Other Press.

Stein, R. (2003b). Vertical mystical homoeros: An altered form of desire in fundamentalism. *Studies in Gender and Sexuality, 4*(1), 38–58.

Stensland, S., Zwart, J. A., Wentzel-Larsen, T., & Dyb, G. (2018). The headache of terror: A matched cohort study of adolescents from the Utøya and the HUNT Study. *Neurology, 90*(2), 111–118. doi:10.1212/WNL.0000000000004305

Stern, D. (1985). *The interpersonal world of the infant: A view from psychoanalysis and developmental psychology*. New York: Basic Books.

Stern, M. M. (1968). Fear of death and trauma. *International Journal of Psychoanalysis, 49*, 457–461.

Stiles, W. (2015). Theory-building, enriching, and fact-gathering: Alternative purposes of psychotherapy research. In O. Gelo, A. Pritz, & B. Rieken (Eds.), *Psychotherapy research: Foundations, process, and outcome* (pp. 159–179). New York: Springer-Verlag.

Stora, J. B. (2007). *When the body displaces the mind*. London: Karnac.

Strozier, C., & Boyd, K. (2010). Definitions and dualisms. In C. Strozier, D. Terman, & J. Jones (Eds.), *The fundamentalist mindset*. New York: Oxford University Press.

Strozier, C., Terman, D., & Jones, J. (Eds.). (2010). *The fundamentalist mindset*. New York: Oxford University Press.

Sveaass, N. (2013). Gross human rights violations and reparation under international law: Approaching rehabilitation as a form of reparation. *European Journal of Psychotraumatology, 4*. doi:10.3402/ejpt.v4i0.17191

Symington, J., Symington, N. (1996). *The clinical thinking of Wilfred Bion*. London and New York: Routlegde.

Taft, C., Kaloupek, D., Schumm, J., Marshall, A., Panuzio, J., King, D., & Keane, T. (2007). Posttraumatic stress disorder symptoms, physiological reactivity, alcohol problems, and aggression among military veterans. *Journal of Abnormal Psychology, 116*(3), 498–507.

Teodorescu, D., Heir, T., Hauff, E., Wentzel-Larsen, T., & Lien, L. (2012). Mental health problems and post-migration stress among multi-traumatized refugees attending outpatient clinics upon resettlement to Norway. *Scandinavian Journal of Psychology*, *53*, 316–332.

Tuckett, D. (2005). Does anything go? Towards a framework for the more transparent assessment of psychoanalytic competence. *International Journal of Psychoanalysis*, *86*, 31–49.

Turner, S. (2015). Refugee blues: A UK and European perspective. *European Journal of Psychotraumatology*, *6*. doi:http://dx.doi.org/10.3402/ejpt.v6.293

UCL. (2019). Competence Frameworks Psychoanalytic/Psychodynamic Therapy University College of London Psychology and language Sciences https://www.ucl.ac.uk/pals/research/clinical-educational-and-health-psychology/research-groups/core/competence-frameworks-6.

UN. (1948). The Universal Declaration of Human Rights from United Nations.

UN. (1984). Convention against Torture and Other Cruel, Inhuman or Degrading Treatment or Punishment.

UNCAT. (2012). General comment nr. 3, on article 14 of the Convention against Torture.

Ungar, M. E. (2012). *The social ecology of resilience. A handbook of theory and practice*. New York, Dordrecht, Heidelberg, London: Springer Verlag.

UNHCR. (2016). *UNHCR 2016. Figures at a glance*. Retrieved from http://www.unhcr.org/figures-at-a-glance.html:

UNHCR. (2017). *Refugees and migrants face heightened risks while trying to reach Europe – UNHCR report*. Retrieved from http://www.unhcr.org/news/press/2017/2/58b458654/refugees-migrants-face-heightened-risks-trying-reach-europe-unhcr-report.html

UNHCR. (2020). Operational Portal. Refugee situation. Retrieved 11.02.2020, from UNHCR.

Vaage, A. B., Thomsen, P. H., Silove, D., Wentzel-Larsen, T., Van Ta, T., & Hauff, E. (2010). Long-term mental health of Vietnamese refugees in the aftermath of trauma. *British Journal of Psychiatry*, *196*, 122–125.

van der Hart, O., Nijenhuis, E., & Steele, K. (2006). *The haunted self. Structural dissociation and the treatment of chronic traumatization*. London: W. W. Norton and Company.

van der Kolk, B. (2014). *The body keeps the score. Mind, brain and body in transformation of trauma*. London: Allen Lane, and imprint of Penguin Books.

Van der Kolk, B., McFarlane, A., & Weisæth, L. (1996). *Traumatic stress: The effects of overwhelming experience on mind, body, and society*. New York: Guilford Press.

van der Kolk, B. A. (1994). The body keeps the score: Memory and the evolving psychobiology of posttraumatic stress. *Harvard Review of Psychiatry*, *1*(5), 253–265. Retrieved from PM:9384857.

van der Kolk, B. A. (1996). Trauma and memory. In B. A. van der Kolk, A. C. McFarlane, & L. Weisæth (Eds.), *Traumatic stress* (pp. 279–302). New York London: The Guilford Press.

van der Kolk, B. A., & Fisler, R. (1995). Dissociation and the fragmentary nature of traumatic memories: Overview and exploratory study. *Journal of Traumatic Stress*, *8*(4), 505–525. Retrieved from PM:8564271

van der Kolk, B. A., McFarlane, A. C., & Weisaeth, L. (1996). *Traumatic stress*. New York London: The Guilford Press.

van Ee, E., Kleber, R. J., & Mooren, T. T. (2012). War trauma lingers on: Associations between maternal posttraumatic stress disorder, parent-child interaction, and child development. *Infant Mental Health Journal, 33*(5), 459–468. doi:http://dx.doi.org/10.1002/imhj.21324

Varvin, S. (1995). Genocide and ethnic cleansing: Psychoanalytic and social-psychological viewpoints. *Scandinavian Psychoanalytic Review, 18*(2), 192–210.

Varvin, S. (1998). Psychoanalytic psychotherapy with traumatized refugees: Integration, symbolization, and mourning. *American Journal of Psychotherapy, 52*(1), 64–71. Retrieved from PM:9553641.

Varvin, S. (2001). Genocid i etnicko ciscenje. Psihoanaliticka i socijalno-psiholoska gledista. In Z. Martinovic (Ed.), *Psihoanaliza i rat* (pp. 12–99). Belgrade: Cigoja Stampa.

Varvin, S. (2003a). *Mental Survival Strategies after extreme Traumatisation.* Copenhagen: Multivers.

Varvin, S. (2003b). Terror, terrorism, large-group and societal dynamics. In S. Varvin & V. D. Volkan (Eds.), *Violence or dialogue. Psychoanalytic insights on terror and terrorism.* London: International Psychoanalysis Library.

Varvin, S. (2003c). Terrorist mindsets: Destructive effects of victimisation and humiliation. *Psyke og Logos, 24*(1), 196–208.

Varvin, S. (2011). Phenomena or data? Qualitative and quantitative research strategies in psychoanalysis. *Scandinavian Psychoanalytic Review, 34*, 117–123. Retrieved from http://www.scandrev.com/

Varvin, S. (2013a). Ideologiens galskap eller galskapens ideologi. (The madness of ideology or the ideology of madness). *Matrix, 30*(3), 156–173. Retrieved from http://www.dpf.dk/Default.aspx?Department=23

Varvin, S. (2013b). Trauma als Nonverbaler Kommunikation. *Zeitschrift für psychoanalytische Theorie und Praxis, 28*, 114–130.

Varvin, S. (2015). *Flukt og eksil (Flight and exile).* Oslo: Universitetsforlaget.

Varvin, S. (2016a). Asylsuchende und Geflüchtete: Ihre Situation und ihre Behandlungs bedürfnisse. (Asylum seekers and refugees: Their situation and treatment needs). *Psyche, 70*, 825–854.

Varvin, S. (2016b). Atrocities against mother and child re-presented in the psychoanalytic space. In V. Pender (Ed.), *Status of Women: Violence, identity and activism* (pp. 193–220). London: Karnac.

Varvin, S. (2017). Our relations to refugees: Between compassion and dehumanization. *The American Journal of Psychoanalysis, 77*(4), 1–19.

Varvin, S., & Dahl, C.-I. (2000). Symbolisering og integrering av ekstreme traumer. *Agrippa, 20*(3-4), 131–153.

Varvin, S., Fischmann, T., Jovic, V., Rosenbaum, B., & Hau, S. (2012). Traumatic dreams: Symbolization gone astray. In P. Fonagy, H. Kächele, M. Leuzinger-Bohleber, & D. Taylor (Eds.), *The significance of dreams.* London: Karnac Books.

Varvin, S., & Hauff, E. (1998). Psychoanalytically oriented psychotherapy with torture survivors. In J. M. Jaranson & M. K. Popkin (Eds.), *Caring for victims of torture* (pp. 117–129). Washington DC, & London, England: American Psychiatric Press, Inc.

Varvin, S., & Lægreid, E. (2020). Traumatised women—Organised violence. *Psychoanalysis and Psychotherapy in China, 3*(1). doi: 10.33212/ppc.v3n1.2020.92

Varvin, S., & Rosenbaum, B. (2003). Extreme traumatisation: Strategies for mental survival. *International Forum of Psychoanalysis, 12*(1), 5–16. Retrieved from http://www.tandf.co.uk/journals/titles/0803706x.html

Varvin, S., & Rosenbaum, B. (2011a). Severely traumatized patients' attempt at reorganizing their relations to others in psychotherapy. *Another kind of evidence* (pp. 380). Karnac Books.

Varvin, S., & Rosenbaum, B. (2011b). Severely traumatized patients' attempts at reorganizing their relations to others in psychotherapy: An enunciation analysis In N. Freedman & M. Hurvich, R. Ward (Eds.), *Another kind of evidence. Studies on internalization, annihilation anxiety, and progressive symbolization in the psychoanalytic process* (pp. 226–243). London: Karnac.

Varvin, S., & Stiles, W. B. (1999). Emergence of severe traumatic experiences: An assimilation analysis of psychoanalytic therapy with a political refugee. *Psychotherapy Research, 9*(3), 381–404.

Varvin, S., & Volkan, V. (2003). *Violence or dialogue. Psychoanalytic insights on terror and terrorism.* London: The International Psychoanalytic Association.

Vedantam, S. (2003). When violence masquerades as virtue: A brief history of terrorism. In S. Varvin & V. D. Volkan (Eds.), *Violence or dialogue. Psychoanalytic insights on terror and terrorism.* London: International Psychoanalysis Library.

Vermetten, E., Germain, A., Thomas C. Neylan, & eds. (2018). *Sleep and combat-related post traumatic stress disorder.* New York: Springer.

Vervliet, M., Lammertyn, J., Broekaert, E., & Derluyn, I. (2013). Longitudinal follow-up of the mental health of unaccompanied refugee minors. *European Child & Adolescent Psychiatry, 23*(5), 237–246. doi: 10.1007/s00787-013-0463-1

Viñar, M. N. (2017). The enigma of extreme traumatism: Trauma, exclusion and their impact on subjectivity. *American Journal of Psychoanalysis, 77.* doi: 10.1057/s11231-016-9082-1

Vitriol, V. G., Ballesteros, S. T., Florenzano, R. U., Weil, K. P., & Benadof, D. F. (2009). Evaluation of an outpatient intervention for women with severe depression and a history of childhood trauma. *Psychiatric Services, 60,* 936–942.

Vogt, K. (1993). *Islams hus (The house of Islam).* Oslo: Cappelen.

Volkan, V. (1993). What the holocaust mean to a non-Jewish psychoanalyst. In R. Moses (Ed.), *Persistent shadows of the holocaust.* Madison, Connecticut: Int. Univ. Press.

Volkan, V. (1997). *Bloodlines.* New York: Farrar, Straus and Giroux.

Volkan, V. (1999). The tree model: A comprehensive psychopolitical approach to unofficial diplomacy and the reduction of ethnic tension. *Mind and Human Interaction, 10*(3), 142–210.

Volkan, V. (2004). *Blind trust.* Charlottesville, Virginia: Pitchstone Publishing.

Volkan, V. D. (1996). Bosnia-Herzegovina: Ancient fuel of a modern inferno. *Mind & Human Interaction, 7*(3), 110–127.

Volkan, V. D. (2003). Traumatized societies. In S. Varvin & V. D. Volkan (Eds.), *Violence or dialogue. Psychoanalytic insights on terror and terrorism.* London: International Psychoanalysis Library.

Walther, R. (2003). Die seltsamen Lehren des Doktor Carrel. Wie ein katholischer Arzt aus Frankreich zum Vordenker der radikalen Islamisten wurde. *Die Zeit online.* Retrieved from http://www.zeit.de/2003/32/A-Carrel.

Wiegand-Grefe, S., & Möller, B. (2012). Die transgenerationale Weitergabe von Kriegserfahrungen aus dem Zweiten Weltkrieg über drei Generationen – eine

Betrachtung aus psychoanalytischer Perspektive. *Praxis der Kinderpsychiatrie Kinderpsychiat*, *61*, 610–622.

Winnicott, D. W. (1974). Fear of breakdown. *International Review of Psychoanalysis*, *1*, 103–107.

Winnicott, D. W. (1991). [Fear of breakdown]. *Psyche*, *45*(12), 1116–1126. Retrieved from PM:1775645.

Wood, M. (2020). *The story of China: The epic history of a world power from the middle kingdom to Mao and the China dream*. New York: St. Martin's Press.

Yan, Y. (2011). Introduction: Conflicting images of the individual and contested process of individualization. In M. H. Hasnen & R. Svarverud (Eds.), *iChina* (pp. 1–38). Copenhagen: Nias Press.

Yazda. (2017). «An uncertain future for Yazidis: A report marking three years of an ongoing genocide». *Yazda*. Retrieved from http://www.yazda.org https://www.yazda.org/reports-and-publications (accessed 4 March 2020).

Yu, H. (1995). Their son (他们的儿子). http://book.kanunu.org/book3/7198/159296.html

Yu, H. (2003). *Chronicle of a blood merchant*. New York: Anhor Books.

Yu, H. (2003 (1993)). *To live*. New York: Anchor Books.

Yu, H. (2004). *Cries in the drizzle*. New York: Anchor Books.

Yu, H. (2005). *Brothers*. New York: Pantheon.

Yu, H. (2010). 十个词汇中的中国 *(China in Ten Words)*. Taibei: Ry Field Publishing.

Index

For Product Safety Concerns and Information please contact our EU
representative GPSR@taylorandfrancis.com
Taylor & Francis Verlag GmbH, Kaufingerstraße 24, 80331 München, Germany

www.ingramcontent.com/pod-product-compliance
Lightning Source LLC
Chambersburg PA
CBHW050340270326
41926CB00016B/3540